Gothic Science Fiction 1980–2010

T0385641

Liverpool Science Fiction Texts and Studies, 41

Liverpool Science Fiction Texts and Studies

Editor David Seed, *University of Liverpool*

Gothic Science Fiction
1980–2010

Edited by

SARA WASSON and EMILY ALDER

LIVERPOOL UNIVERSITY PRESS

First published 2011 by
LIVERPOOL UNIVERSITY PRESS
4 Cambridge Street
Liverpool L69 7ZU

This paperback version published 2014.

British Library Cataloguing-in-Publication Data
A British Library CIP record is available.

ISBN 978-1-84631-707-1 hardback
ISBN 978-1-78138-003-1 paperback

Typeset in Meridien by
R. J. Footring Ltd, Derby
Printed and bound in the European Union by
CPI Group (UK) Ltd, Croydon CR0 4YY

For Graham and Rod, with love

Contents

Acknowledgements

We would like to thank DC Comics for granting permission to reproduce two images from *The League of Extraordinary Gentlemen*, © Alan Moore and Kevin O'Neill. Used with Permission of DC Comics.

Illustrations

Foreword

Adam Roberts

The last syllable of 'Gothic' is *thick* – and I'll confess a particular fondness for the archaic eighteenth-century spelling of the word, from that time when the Gothic mode was invented: 'Gothick', with the added kick of that chunky final 'k'. From Walpole's slender *Castle of Otranto,* through its first vogue in the 1790s and early 1800s, via its resurgence at the end of the nineteenth century in the hands of writers as diverse as Stevenson, Stoker, Wells and on into the broad delta of twentieth-century horror, science fiction, fantasy and dark visions, Gothic has strengthened and thickened as it grew. By the time we come to the period covered in this volume, it has become an entire subculture, and its variform manifestations (books, films, comics, musics, clothes, games) have attracted a similarly variform scholarly attention. And what you are holding in your hand right now is the latest addition to the thick body of critical and interpretive work generated by this enduringly popular mode ('another thick, damn, square book', as one celebrated eighteenth-century figure put it. 'Scribble scribble scribble').

This interpretive busyness is one index of the thickness of Gothic as a creative mode: its enduring heft, its richness, its *depth*. It might be thought strange to describe a variety of literature often characterized by melodrama, cliché and gore as 'deep', but it seems to me that the mode endures because its surface effects *do* indeed articulate something buried, something hidden. Perhaps this sounds as if I am advancing a naively Freudian understanding of Gothic's 'uncanny' quality; but I'm not suggesting that contemporary Gothic science fiction can be decoded according to some psychic mapping from the unconscious to conscious mind. I'm not talking about the lucid depths of, as it might be, a lake; I'm talking about the opaque thickness of – for example – a sealed book, or a sarcophagus lid.

These eleven essays provide us with a splendid variety of ways to measure the thickness of Gothic: to unpack some of its semiotic density, to weigh in the hand its heft. Roger Luckhurst moves expertly through the landscape of the New Weird, from the Strugatsky brothers to Harrison, Miéville and Robson; in part to elaborate the sense in which Gothic is a conceptual topography. He argues that the 'Zone', from *Roadside Picnic* (rendered so memorably in the poisoned sublime of Tarkovsky's extraordinary movie *Stalker*), tropes Gothic itself. The earliest examples of the mode were particularly fascinated by the geographies of their fictional realms, or more precisely by the way the geographies of the past interpenetrated the geographies of the present: all those cellars, caverns, secret underground passageways; those venerable castles and forests in which ancient presences uneasily coexist with modern characters. Gothic science fiction constellates precisely this eerie copresence of undead past and contaminated future. Strange weeds and thistles reclaim not only the old medieval castle courtyards, but also the loading bays of factories and the echoing interior spaces of automated storage warehouses. The present-day landscape of Chernobyl and Prypiat are just as eloquent, although perhaps with different intensities, as the old arrangements of ruined Transylvanian castles and creaky New England manor houses. Exhaustion and waste function on the level of relief; the Zone figures by its radical unpredictability. Gothic science fiction is in one sense about the way the dereliction of the past always inflects the shiny new spaces of the present and the future.

In Aeschylus' *Agamemnon*, Cassandra was gifted with prophesy by her rapist, Apollo; and at the same time cursed with the fact that nobody would believe her prophesies. The implication in the play is that people don't believe her prophesies because they don't *understand* them: at the level, that is to say, of simple semantics. I wonder about an alternate spin on this famous myth – that everyone knows Cassandra has been gifted by a god with the power to predict the future; that everybody comprehends her prophesies perfectly well, but that *nevertheless* they do not believe her. They do so not out of any kind of stubbornness of the human spirit, so much as the radical impossibility of the future manifesting itself in the present. Or to put it a little more precisely: the future – what Cassandra prophesies – is, in a word, death; and death is something that haunts us from the past rather than the future. The eerie spaces of Walpole's *Castle of Otranto* (1765), Gothic's ur-text, are the repressed memories of past familial trauma and murder. What gives Gothic science fiction its peculiar, counter-intuitive potency is precisely the way it parses this eerie, spectral pastness as the future.

Scott's *Alien* (1979), a film discussed several times in this collection, has the futuristic technical locale of an interstellar spaceship haunted by an atavistic predatory organic monster. This monster itself is a conceptually dislocating mixture: at once ancient (the mummified remains of another alien spacecraft, encountered by the crew of the *Nostromo* and already overrun with myriad alien eggs, suggest that these monsters have been around for a very long time) and simultaneously more advanced, better adapted, more evolved – stronger, fitter, more durable – than humanity. Humans in the film are preyed upon by a collision of the deep past and the deep future. There's one feature of the imagined world of the various *Alien* films that has always struck me, and it is this: the aliens prey upon humans, ripping and biting them to pieces in frenzied devouring. To them, we are food. But at the same time, they capture us, immobilize us and plant their offspring inside us; for they need us as part of their cycle of reproduction, to incubate their young. Now, on a practical level this is illogical: evolutionarily speaking, it makes no sense to imagine a creature that devours its own means of reproduction. But speaking symbolically, something interesting is going on here, I think. Scott's *Alien* combines death and birth: construes both the process of consigning us into the dead past and the uncanny coming-into-being of new life *as somehow the same thing*.

This is Coleridge's nightmare death-in-life (not, we might note, the other way around; life-in-death would be a banal figure) from his eminently Gothic poem *The Rime of the Ancient Mariner*. The continuing success of the figure of the Zombie – deftly anatomized in Fred Botting's far-reaching essay here – suggests that what is uncanny about death is not the prospect of individual extinction, but on the contrary the hideous intimation that death will *not* snuff out our individual existence. The intimation that the core of death is precisely life. The real terror is not that 'we're here – we're gone'; the real terror is that *we might never go*. When Shelley, in 'Adonais', talks about life 'staining' the white radiance of eternity, I wonder if he means something along these lines. Every washerwoman or washerman knows that there are some stains that you simply can't get rid of, no matter how assiduously you scrub.

As Aris Mousoutzanis comprehensively demonstrates, contemporary recrudesce in Gothic owes a great deal to a widespread fascination with body-horror; as if our apprehension about what is beautiful in our bodies – what is sexy, what is admirable – grounds itself precisely in a discourse of what is disgusting, repellent and appalling in those same bodies. There is, as Mousoutzanis argues, an 'imperial' dimension to this. Partly (as Sara Wasson discusses) this has to do with the way the interpenetration of our bodies by the logic of globalized capital carries with it the uncanny sense of ourselves as a disassemblable collections of organs, each with a certain exchange value in the market.

The other essays collected here analyse this Gothic impulse – the 'gleeful impurity' Laurence Davies finds in the films of del Toro – via specific texts. Gwyneth Peaty's penetrating essay on the recent zombie cinema finds a 'neo-supernaturalism' at work, uncannily pitched between science and magic; itself a reflection of modernity's dependence upon barely understood 'medical magics'. Emily Alder's reading of Donaldson's *Gap* novels connects cultural unease with genetic engineering with a horror at the plasticity of flesh itself – the novel sequence's 'gap' a kind of metaphorical vagina from which emerge strange, disturbing new fleshly possibilities. Mark Williams coordinates a wide-ranging interrogation of the horrific via a reading of David Conway's little-known novella 'Metal Sushi'. Jerrilyn McGregory ingeniously reads Toni Morrison through the lens of Gothic science fiction, to striking effect. Nickianne Moody explores the cultural *stylings* of Gothic science fiction, from the early-century technopunk of *Metropolis* to the late-century card trading game of *Heresy Kingdom Come*. And Laura Hilton persuasively shows the ways in which *The League of Extraordinary Gentlemen* graphic novels feed vampirically upon earlier literatures, transforming them into something rich and strange.

The secret of Gothic's appeal, its ability to trail tendrils of dread across the delicate membrane of our imagination, draws on one really key insight: that pleasure is not a simple or straightforward matter. That the hidden underground spring that is continually replenishing our capacity for pleasure is, precisely, *displeasure*. Simon Schama once summed up the aesthetic revolution of the late eighteenth and early nineteenth centuries in these terms: 'Born from the oxymoron of agreeable horror, Romanticism was nursed on calamity.' This is on the right lines; although it might be closer to the truth to say that 'agreeable horror' (after all, a very ancient human idiom) unveiled for the Romantics a new perspective on subjectivity. To put it another way: Romanticism asks *what part of us finds horror so agreeable?*

And renewal is also part of the mode. Reading these various, fascinating critical interventions into the form makes clear that Gothic is very far from being exhausted. From New Weird to body-horror, from the heterotopic genre-mashups increasingly characteristic of the fantastic today to the subcultural stylings of cosplay, music and fashion: the Gothic is very far from moribund. It is still in motion, on its way somewhere new.

The first syllable of 'Gothic' spells: *go*.

Contributors

The editors

Sara Wasson acquired her doctorate from Cornell University in New York and researches Gothic Studies, literary representations of the city, medical humanities and changing views of community. She is Senior Lecturer in Literature and Culture at Edinburgh Napier University. Her monograph *Urban Gothic of the Second World War: Dark London* (Palgrave, 2010) examines how writing in the Gothic mode subverts the dominant national narrative of the British home front, arguing that Gothic tropes and forms mark moments of fracture in the national mythologies of wartime home, city and fellowship; this book was co-winner of the Allan Lloyd Smith Memorial Prize for Gothic Studies. Her work also appears in *The Journal of Popular Culture*, *Extrapolation*, the *Journal of Stevenson Studies* and in edited collections. Her latest research examines intersections between Gothic science fiction and medical humanities, particularly investigating how horror fiction and science fiction represents organ harvesting, human cloning and genetics in the light of new theory of community.

Emily Alder has a BA (Hons) in English Literature from Newcastle University, and gained her PhD from Edinburgh Napier University in 2009. She continues to work and teach at Edinburgh Napier University and is an Associate Lecturer in Children's Literature for The Open University in Scotland. Emily's doctoral research focused on the weird and science fiction of British Edwardian writer William Hope Hodgson, and she has published on utopia and wilderness in Hodgson and H. G. Wells in *H. G. Wells: Interdisciplinary Essays* (Newcastle: Cambridge Scholars Publishing, 2008). She co-organized *Nature and the Long Nineteenth Century*, a conference held at the University of Edinburgh in 2010. Her research interests include the development of science fiction at the *fin de siècle*, contemporary science fiction and fantasy, and Gothic and the supernatural in Victorian and Edwardian fiction, especially sea fiction. Emily is Scotland Editor for *The OSCHOLARS* and Assistant Editor for *Gothic Studies*.

The contributors

Fred Botting is Professor of English Literature in the School of Humanities, Kingston University, London. His two most recent books are *Limits of Horror* (Manchester: Manchester University Press, 2008) and *Gothic Romanced* (London: Routledge, 2008). He is co-editor (with Scott Wilson) of *Bataille: A Critical Reader* (London: Blackwell, 1998). His research interests include cultural and critical theory (psycho- and schiz-analysis); Bataille and general economy; romanticism and postmodernism; techno-poiesis; uncanny media (Gothic technologies; cybergothic; neuromanticism); smoking, sublimity, consumption and horror.

Laurence Davies is Senior Research Fellow in English Literature at the University of Glasgow. Until recently, he taught for the programme in Comparative Literature at Dartmouth College, USA. While there, he also collaborated with medical researchers, earth scientists and mathematicians on interdisciplinary courses funded by the National Science Foundation, including Life on Mars?, which examined the planet's scientific, cultural and political significance, and Mathematics and Science Fiction, which discussed the literary uses and abuses of n-dimensional geometry. Besides literature and science, Davies's interests include millenarianism, the uncanny, microfictions, relations between 'oral' and 'literary' cultures, and international Modernism. He is co-author of a critical biography of R. B. Cunninghame Graham, the Scottish writer, socialist and anti-imperial campaigner, and general editor of *The Collected Letters of Joseph Conrad*; the ninth and (pending further discoveries) final volume was published by Cambridge University Press in 2007. Currently he is at work on *Old Lamps for New*, a study of creative recycling in the arts and sciences. The essay on Guillermo del Toro has its roots in this project.

Laura Hilton holds a PhD from the University of Birmingham, where she also completed her BA and MA degrees. Her doctoral research investigates representations of the Gothic double in the contemporary graphic novel and focuses on the work of Neil Gaiman, Frank Miller and Alan Moore. She is co-founder and co-editor of the first two issues of *The Birmingham Journal of Literature and Language* (*BJLL*) and has articles forthcoming in *Alan Moore and* *the Gothic Tradition* and *Investigating Heroes: Truth, Justice and Quality TV*. Laura has presented her research at several national and international conferences and her wider research interests include nineteenth-, twentieth- and twenty-first-century literature, comic book and graphic novel studies, and Gothic fiction.

Roger Luckhurst is Professor of Modern and Contemporary Literature at Birkbeck College, University of London. He is the author of books on J. G. Ballard, the history of science fiction and the cultural history of science, including *The Trauma Question* (2008), *Science Fiction* (2005), *The Invention of Telepathy* (2002) and *'The Angle Between Two Walls': The Fiction of J. G. Ballard* (1997). His new book, *The Mummy's Curse*, appears in 2012.

Jerrilyn McGregory is an Associate Professor of Folklore in the English Department at Florida State University. She is the author of *Wiregrass Country* (1997) and *Downhome Gospel: Spiritual Activism in Wiregrass Country* (2010). She is currently conducting ethnographic research and writing a book on Boxing Day in the African Diaspora, including the Bahamas, Belize, Bermuda, St Croix and St Kitts. The Toni Morrison essay draws on another work-in-progress on the dialectics of race and culture in African American literature. She works primarily in folklife, multiculturalism, critical race theory, and Africana Studies. She has published articles on the genre fiction of Nalo Hopkinson and Walter Mosley. She has presented papers at international conferences in Toronto, Canada, Aberystwyth, Wales, and Mainz, Germany. A paper presented in Quebec at the International Council of Onomastic Sciences gained publication in the proceedings of its Conference. At present, she is also working on a book manuscript, 'Aareck to Zsaneka', about African American naming patterns.

Nickianne Moody is a Principal Lecturer in Media and Cultural Studies at Liverpool John Moores University. Her research interests are in popular culture, particularly cultures of reading, popular genres and nineteenth- and twentieth-century fiction; she has published on a range of popular authors, including Marie Corelli and Terry Pratchett. Her publications include *Reading the Popular in Contemporary Spanish Texts* (2004), *Children's Fantasy Fiction: debates for the 21st Century* (2005) and *Judging a Book by its Cover* (2007). Nickianne is convenor for the Association for Research in Popular Fictions.

Aris Mousoutzanis is a Visiting Lecturer in the Department of Media and Cultural Studies at Kingston University. He has researched and published in areas such as psychoanalysis and trauma theory, cybercultures, globalization and postcolonialism, and on popular genres such as the Gothic and science fiction. His PhD thesis, 'Apocalypse, Technoscience, Empire', was an investigation of the function of technological and imperial discourses in the apocalyptic narratives of the last two centuries' ends. He has published on apocalyptic science fiction for the *Routledge Companion to Science Fiction* and has co-edited a collection of essays on *New Media and the Politics of Online Communities*. He is currently co-editing the *Continuum Handbook of Science Fiction*, a collection on *The Apocalypse and its Discontents* and a special journal issue on *Cosmopolitanism, Media and Global Crisis*. He has written on the work of Slavoj Žižek, while he is currently mostly researching on trauma theory, and has written on the significance of technological discourses for theorizations and representations of trauma in official theorizations of the pathology as well as in American narratives from contemporary literature, film and television.

Gwyneth Peaty is a PhD student in English and Cultural Studies at the University of Western Australia. Her research examines the representation of grotesque bodies in popular culture, with an emphasis upon their variable morphology and symbolism. She is particularly interested in how the fears and frictions generated by technological and cultural transformations are expressed through bodies whose forms transgress the perceived borders of human ontology. Peaty's scholarship considers these issues as they relate to a wide spectrum of visual media, including film, television, magazines, comics and video games. Intersecting research interests include science fiction, Gothic, gender and whiteness studies. She has a chapter forthcoming in *Guns, Grenades and Grunts: The First Person Shooter* and has presented papers at a variety of national and international conferences.

Adam Roberts is a science fiction writer and Professor of Nineteenth Century Literature at Royal Holloway, University of London. Adam studied for an MA in English and Classics at Aberdeen University and gained his PhD on Robert Browning from Cambridge University. His critical publications include *Robert Browning Revisited* (1997), *Victorian Culture and Society: the Essential Glossary* (2003) and, more recently, *The History of Science Fiction* (2006). He is the author of a dozen science fiction novels, of which three – *Salt* (2000), *Gradisil* (2006) and *Yellow Blue Tibia* (2009) – have been short-listed for the Arthur C. Clarke award, amongst others.

Mark P. Williams studied literature at the University of Hull and the University of Warwick, and received his doctorate from the University of East Anglia for a thesis entitled 'Radical Fantasy: A Study of Left Radical Politics in the Fantasy Writing of Michael Moorcock, Angela Carter, Alan Moore, Grant Morrison and China Miéville'. His primary interests are in speculative fiction, avant-garde literature and politics. He has published on the fantasy fictions of China Miéville, on Steven Wells' anarchic Attack! Books, and interviewed Michael Moorcock on his interest in William S. Burroughs for RealityStudio.org. Forthcoming projects include an article on avant-garde writing and Dambudzo Marechera for the anthology *Reading Marechera* (ed. Grant Hamilton) and a survey of seventies literary history for *The 1970s: A Decade of Contemporary British Fiction* (ed. Nick Hubble). He recently relocated to Wellington, New Zealand, where he has been working as a tutor at Victoria University of Wellington and publishing regular articles on contemporary literature and politics for the online culture magazine *Werewolf* (http://www.werewolf.co.nz). Future research plans include a study of British alternative fiction since 1980 and a wider project on globalization and contemporary genre fiction; the essay on David Conway is related to these planned projects.

Introduction

Sara Wasson and Emily Alder

This edited collection explores what might be termed 'Gothic' science fiction of the last three decades, 1980–2010. While at first this may seem a curiously contradictory hyphenation, applying such a category to texts of this period permits fresh examination of the ways in which they engage with the dramatic socio-economic changes accompanying these years. The Gothic mode emerges readily in science fiction that explores power, anxiety, resistance and capital. The chapters in this collection reflect the current willingness among researchers to explore anew genre, form and discipline, as well as revealing a buoyant field of research in contemporary Gothic and science fiction studies.

Conjunctions of Gothic and science fiction

The category 'Gothic', like 'science fiction', is notoriously slippery, and the capacity of the Gothic to evolve and diverge has enabled it to become more than a simple category marked by a series of tropes or by a particular form. Its emergence as a literary form in the late eighteenth century was influenced as much, or more, by poetical antecedents, such as the graveyard poetry of Thomas Parnell, as by the rise of the novel. The early texts to bear the Gothic label differed widely, from the ghostly marvels of Horace Walpole's *The Castle of Otranto* (1765) and the demonic dimensions of Matthew Lewis's *The Monk* (1796) to the 'supernatural explained' of Ann Radcliffe's novels. Since then, the Gothic mode has benefited from its hybrid resilience, its capacity to adapt to new historical moments.

Gothic tropes have sprung up in other nineteenth-century literary forms and modes: stage plays and Romantic poetry, the sensation fiction of Wilkie Collins and the urban London of Charles Dickens and G. W. M. Reynolds all feature an uncanny ambience, revelations of family secrets and nested narratives, along with associated stock characters of Gothic. This profusion of texts began to blur any perceived dividing line circumscribing the Gothic as a genre. Increasingly, scholars identify the Gothic as a mode or a 'tone' of writing (Wilt 619). As such, the Gothic lends itself more readily to a set, or choice, of defining concepts than to definition by a list of characteristic images or narrative forms. The essays in this collection reflect a consensus of recent scholarship about the key characteristics of the Gothic. The first defining element may be described as a disturbing affective lens, one which overlays the narrative either with profound emotional distress or with an unnatural emotional void (Punter, *Terror* 2: 184; Botting, *Gothic* 3). The second defining element of Gothic is arguably spatial: distressing emotions play out within a confined or claustrophobic environment (Baldick xix; Botting, *Gothic* 2; Wasson, *Urban Gothic* 2), be that a castle dungeon, a labyrinthine city … or a stifling spaceship designed by H. R. Giger, in the case of *Alien*.

'Gothic science fiction' is arguably an oxymoron. The two categories are potentially incompatible, for two reasons. Firstly, the Gothic often seems to be about inexplicable phenomena, often featuring the supernatural, dark magic and fantastical strangeness, while science fiction tends to depict a rational world which obeys natural laws even if that world's technology is substantially ahead of our own. This idea of Gothic as fantastical while science fiction is rational is at the heart of Darko Suvin's famous definition of science fiction: he argues that science fiction is 'the *literature of cognitive estrangement*'; in other words, it 'takes off from a fictional … hypothesis and develops it with … scientific rigour' (24–25, emphasis in original). In Suvin's view, science fiction is set in an unfamiliar world, but one in which empirical laws hold sway just as in our own and in which phenomena can be explained by recourse to the rational discourse of science rather than supernatural forces. Suvin argues that, by contrast, 'fantasy (ghost, horror, Gothic, [the] weird)' are 'committed to the interposition of anti-cognitive laws into the empirical environment' (27). Suvin draws this distinction between the fantastic and science fiction in order to argue for the political irrelevance of the former. More recently, while differing from Suvin in key points, Fredric Jameson maintains a distinction between the two categories, arguing that fantastic literature tends to be politically reactionary by comparison with much science fiction, often in thrall to a romanticized concept of the 'medieval' (63).

Despite such critical distinctions, however, other literary criticism has seen science fiction and Gothic as firmly yoked. Mary Shelley's *Frankenstein* (1818) is an iconic text for critical studies of such conjunctions: her darkly fantastical vision of transgressive medical science has inspired many to contemplate the connections between the two categories. Brian Aldiss and David Wingrove, for example, define science fiction as 'the search for a definition of mankind and his status in the universe which will stand in our advanced but confused state of knowledge (science), and is characteristically cast in the Gothic or post-Gothic mode' (164), and hail *Frankenstein* as early science fiction. Marjean Purinton, Theodora Goss and John Paul Riquelme argue that science fiction emerges directly from the Gothic tradition, and locate *Frankenstein* as the point of emergence. Purinton contends that Gothic and science fiction have been entangled since the nineteenth century, when 'techno-Gothic' drama combined science and the supernatural, while Goss and Riquelme argue that in science fiction, the diabolic villain of Gothic is replaced by scientists determined to 'dominate and manipulate nature' (435). Judith Wilt locates the blend of the two as occurring later, arguing that 'science fiction Gothic' was inaugurated by H. G. Wells's *War of the Worlds* (1898), which, taking 'pains to emphasize the un-humanness of the encountered monster, is the truest of all Victorian gothic forms, that is Victorian, or classic, science fiction' (621). Despite differences, these critics agree that the Gothic tradition was an influential part of the complex mesh of forms and cultural developments that saw the emergence of what we now call science fiction.

Furthermore, Suvin's distinction has grown far less relevant in recent decades as the Gothic has increasingly become associated with a non-supernatural world. Gothic can now be primarily a function of a particular kind of dreadful narrative voice bespeaking either overwrought affect, paranoiac sensibility or perverse emotional deadness. As Botting notes, the Gothic increasingly exists 'in excess of, and often within, realist forms, both inhabiting and excluded from its homogenizing representations of the world' (*Gothic* 12). As such, the Gothic mode can readily be deployed in representations of believable worlds following natural laws. Suvin's argument that the two modes are mutually exclusive is no longer tenable, and the contributors in this volume nuance Suvin's theory in the light of more recent critical developments. Jerrilyn McGregory's chapter on Toni Morrison, for example, explores 'enchantment' as a variation of Suvin's cognitive estrangement. In McGregory's discussion, 'enchantment' occurs when fantastical devices are used to express the cruel truths of a reality. Roger Luckhurst critiques the narrowness of Suvin's genre categories and his view that science fiction verging on Gothic is inevitably degenerate and reactionary, while Laurence Davies suggests that Suvin's fictional 'novum' may be identified in narratives that begin at a branching of past history.

The second reason science fiction and Gothic may seem mutually exclusive is their contrary relationships to time. Chris Baldick argues that the Gothic, by definition, refers to texts preoccupied with the menace of past ages, threatened by 'an age-old regime of oppression and persecution which threatens still to fix its dead hand upon us' (xxi). As Fred Botting notes, unlike Gothic, science fiction usually projects its contemporary anxieties onto the future rather than the past (*Gothic Romanced* 131).

Yet here, too, recent decades have seen complications of such neat differentiation. Alternative history 'steampunk' science fiction, for example, unsettles the notion that science fiction always occurs in a future world. Steampunk is a mutation of science fiction informed by and concerned with aspects of Victoriana and/or the medieval, integrating these details into narratives of speculative fiction. The form came into being during the 1980s and is often connected with cyberpunk. As the name suggests, the narratives are often set in the era in which steam power was prominent, but often depict a less dystopian environment than cyberpunk. Part IV of this critical collection – 'Strange Cities, Strange Temporalities' – explores Gothic science fiction's complex engagement with time. Laura Hilton analyses the steampunk visions of Alan Moore, acknowledging the complex nostalgia and melancholia underlying the steampunk graphic novel series *The League of Extraordinary Gentlemen* (2000; 2003). Science fiction temporality becomes similarly complex in cyberpunk, that paradigmatic form of Gothic science fiction in which all technology is in constant disintegration. Although cyberpunk, as Roberts points out, 'prioritizes the technological over the psychological' (168), it is arguably here that strands of Gothic science fiction best flourish, probing the darker functions of technology and urban environments in modern life. In this vein, Nickianne Moody's chapter examines late 1990s cyberpunk, where the city is a wilderness of decay. In these texts, technological artefacts themselves have history and experience entropy.

A further similarity is that both Gothic and science fiction have been hybrid creatures from their inception. Even in the late eighteenth century, at the height of the Gothic novel, the form was 'hybrid ... incorporating and transforming other literary forms as well as developing and changing its own conventions in relation to newer modes of writing' (Botting, *Gothic* 14). If, since the early nineteenth century the Gothic has increasingly come to be less a clear genre than a 'mode', a quality of narrative voice, then similarly, the genre of science fiction is hybrid, invoking characteristics from pulp fiction, detective fiction and urban fantasy. Adam Roberts's definition of science fiction emphasizes this hybridity, suggesting that 'the term "science fiction" resists easy definition ... science fiction as a genre or division of literature distinguishes its fictional worlds to one degree or another from the world in which we actually live: a fiction of the imagination rather than an observed reality, a fantastic literature' (1). Botting interprets both modes as fused by their preoccupation with monstrosity; in their 'long and interwoven association in the realms of modern popular literature and culture, both genres give form to a sense of otherness, a strangeness which is difficult to locate: monstrosity appears in the future and the past, in the mind and in culture at large, taking form in individual, social and textual bodies' (*Gothic Romanced* 131). Otherness and monstrosity, then, in their literal and symbolic forms, conjoin Gothic and science fiction.

During these three decades, certain monstrous figures originally associated with the Gothic populate science fiction in new shapes and bearing new meaning – notably Frankenstein's monster and the figures of the zombie and vampire. From its pioneering blend of scientific rationalism and the supernatural in Shelley's original novel, the *Frankenstein* myth is repeatedly invoked in narratives of artificial life, hybrid amalgamation and technological ambition. Frankenstein's monster is organically revisited as mutant or genetically engineered organism, reworked as artificial intelligence or mechanical construction. Frankenstein himself becomes a symbol of overreaching science, of the desire to transcend the boundary between life and death; he stands for the hope that science, technology and human endeavour can find answers to mortality. In Shelley's *Frankenstein*, the scientist's utopian vision shades into horror as his actions inflict torment on himself, his family and his creation. Gothic science fiction, too, generates narratives of human-created horror through unbridled science and technology; these operate at the level of institution and state as much as the individual, as explored in this collection's chapters by Wasson and Mousoutzanis.

Frankenstein influences, too, the figure of the zombie, first growing in prevalence in twentieth century texts. Deriving also from traditional Caribbean voodoo legend, the zombie draws on the patchwork unnaturalness of Frankenstein's creation, its liminal position between living and dead, its association with a horror produced by humans. As Botting notes in this collection, characteristically, zombies inspire repulsion without the capacity for identification central to Frankenstein's monster; they form an abjected underclass of modern capitalism. In Peaty's essay, the ultimate curability of the undead condition suggests a desire to retreat from a posthuman state to a state of 'normal' humanity. Embodying the tension between humanity's forward- and backward-looking urges, the zombie becomes an emblematic figure of Gothic science fiction.

In science fiction, vampires and their long-standing Gothic associations with invasion, retrogression and infection are revived in new and varied forms through their relationship with capital and technology. From individual haemophagy, vampirism is displaced into the consuming networks of corporations or the viral spread of disease; instead of supernatural explanations vampirism is explained as a result of genetic change or alien evolution. Vampires' capacity for mutation in response to cultural desires and anxieties makes them a rich source of Gothic literary innovation.

Often, the three Gothic emblems described here combine in new forms within science fiction. *Star Trek*'s Borg, for example, are cyborg creatures bent on universal species assimilation, and thus contain traces of all three monsters – the composite artificiality of Frankenstein's creation, the liminal vitality of the zombie and the distributed voraciousness of the vampire. Judith Halberstam notes the capacity of vampires to employ a 'Gothic economy in their ability to condense many monstrous traits in one body' (88). As the texts examined in this collection show, together vampires, zombies and Frankenstein's monster can be seen as Gothic palimpsests, overwritten by modern narratives of science fiction.

Science fiction and Gothic have become even more closely entangled in niche genre innovations of the last fifteen years. In addition to steampunk and cyberpunk, chapters in this collection analyse other types of genre fluidity possible between Gothic and science fiction. The 'New Weird', for example, which flourished from the 1990s to 2005, has been defined as 'a type of urban, secondary-world fiction that subverts the romanticized ideas about place found in traditional fantasy, largely by choosing realistic, complex real-world models as the jumping off point for creation of settings that may combine elements of both science fiction and fantasy' (VanderMeer and VanderMeer xvi). In this collection, Mark Williams examines the subversion of genre in the New Weird, understanding it as an enabling force for the revision of established gender models in the prose of David Conway. For Luckhurst, 'weird' itself encapsulates the generic entanglement of science fiction and Gothic; in this collection, he identifies 'Zones' as regions of generic potential and hybridization, and invites new ways of thinking about genre to account, for example, for the gleeful polytemporality that marks the 'post-genre' situation of the fantastic.

Changes in generic form can also respond to changing socio-economic realities. Laurence Davies, for example, suggests in this collection that the 'generic impurity' of Guillermo del Toro's film *Cronos* (1993) invites comparison with the changing socio-economic context of Mexico in the early to mid-1990s, and Aris Mousoutzanis suggests that the genres of Gothic and science fiction typically become increasingly interwoven during periods when imperial powers seek to control and exploit 'biopower', the tissues of human life in service of complex networks of global control. In addition, generic transformations can be figured in spatial terms, and the chapters by Luckhurst, Mousoutzanis and McGregory consider generic transformations alongside literary representations of liminal, hybrid spaces in which ambiguous terrains can represent hybrid literary forms, and vice versa.

In addition to complicating stable definitions of literary genres, the 1980s, 1990s and 2000s saw the emergence of new platforms for narrative: hybrid platforms combining visuals, text and audience interactivity. Graphic novels and trading card games, for example, reached unprecedented sales in the 1990s through the upsurge in popularity of such games as Wizards of the Coast's *Magic: The Gathering* (Garfield) and Neil Gaiman's *Sandman* series of graphic novels. Roleplaying games, too, have become increasingly widespread, with cyberpunk *Shadowrun* (Fasa Corporation) and the popular *Vampire: The Masquerade* 'story-telling' system from White Wolf Studios (Rein-Hagen). These hybrid media have become increasingly more celebrated, abundant and varied. Two of the essays in this collection explore these hybrid visual/textual worlds: Nickianne Moody discusses *Heresy: Kingdom Come*, a cyberpunk trading card game from the late 1990s, and Hilton examines Moore's graphic novel *League of Gentlemen*.

The value of historicized Gothic studies

This project is another instance of the 'hyphenated' Gothics that have abounded in recent years. In order to distinguish between textual forms or historical periods, or to acknowledge the imaginative diversity within the broader Gothic mode, scholars have identified Victorian Gothic (Robbins and Wolfreys), urban Gothic (Kathleen Spencer; Pritchard; Ehrlich; Rzepcka; Wasson), postmodern Gothic (Hantke; Punter, 'Postmodern Gothic'; Helyer; Nash) and European Gothic (Horner; Horner and Zlosnik), to list just a few. Such hyphenations have enabled critics to view well-studied texts or historical periods anew through a Gothic filter, yielding a rich diversity of critical interpretation. Recent criticism has embraced scholarship combining 'the rediscovery of literature and art that have largely unnoticed Gothic dimensions with revelations about the broader cultural context(s)' to which they belong (Hogle 6).

While such a historically inflected approach to the diversity of 'Gothics' is fruitful and productive, it is important that the nuances of the Gothic label itself are carefully considered. The impact on literary studies of Derridan metaphors of spectrality creates an interesting case in point. Derrida's *Specters of Marx* (1993) ushered a new discourse into Gothic studies of a modernity haunted by uncanny traces of cultural past. However, the complexity of Derrida's ideas requires cautious handling. Alexandra Warwick, for example, warns against the dangers of applying Derridean metaphors of haunting too literally, arguing that 'Gothic is being used to explain itself' and 'actual, as far as we can call them actual, ghosts, burials, deaths and undead are confused with the metaphors of textuality, trace, echo, spectre' (7, 8). For the Gothic to form a lens through which valuable insights into a text can be made, we must recognize that the simple use of 'uncanny' occurrences or the appearance of phantoms do not necessarily signal a Gothic text. Otherwise, as Luckhurst points out, spectrality risks becoming 'a generalized deconstructive lever discernible everywhere' ('Contemporary London Gothic' 535). Such a generalized analytical tool risks the creation of generalized conclusions, and thus, for example, Link, Punter, Warwick and others criticize broad arguments that Gothic forms signify a fraught subjectivity that is universally typical of late capitalism.

As we have noted, therefore, 'Gothic' labels an elusive and diverse cultural corpus, and the term should be used with care to avoid generalizing about the human condition and subjectivity over a variety of different historical periods or across different cultures. In such a cultural climate, the value of localized, historicized studies of the Gothic emerges even more clearly; literary criticism examining how Gothic tropes and forms are inflected for particular times and places has become increasingly important and welcomed by Gothic critics. In this spirit, *Gothic Science Fiction* combines Gothic criticism with awareness of social history and local specificity.

This collection identifies four preoccupations dominating science fiction in the Gothic mode since 1980: anxieties and taboo pleasures around the rise of global capitalism and national identity in a post-imperial world; the profusion of technology; the sanctity of body boundaries and the place of the human subject within the grip of the abstractions of law; and the threat of apocalyptic destruction of the human race. We will briefly state how the collection examines each of these issues.

Late capitalism and its discontents

The 1980s saw an economic transformation in the West. Supported by the laissez-faire financial regulation policies of Ronald Reagan and Margaret Thatcher, capitalism reached a new aporia in the form of multinational companies freed of many government constraints. The consequence was rapid globalization. In the 1990s, multinational corporations became even more vast and opaque, with the internet intensifying the network of global capital worldwide (Luckhurst, *Science Fiction* 220–221); the resulting con- temporary networks of global capital are so complex that they resist human comprehension. The story of capital in the last three decades also involves dramatic stories of national transformation. In the 1980s, for example, cyberpunk fetishized Japanese culture, structuring it as edgy and desirable, but at the same time these texts bespeak Western anxiety about Japan emerging as a serious player in the global marketplace.

Just as global capitalism proliferated and transformed in these decades, so to did nations convulse and change. The 1990s, in particular, saw many national transformations, not least the breakup of the USSR, the reunifica- tion of Germany and the disaggregation of Yugoslavia and Czechoslovakia. In the early years of the twenty-first century, the impact of 9/11 and the US backlash against terrorism have affected the ways in which we understand nationhood and citizenship in a global context. In her recent essay 'Sexual Politics, Torture, and Secular Time', Judith Butler challenges us to rethink the workings of state power and freedom, identity, citizenship and community. If, as she suggests, new sexual freedoms can be rhetorically recruited to a notion of progress that serves the coercive instruments of a state, where, we ask, does that leave our interpretation of sexually marginalized figures in science fiction? In a modern globalized world, Butler argues, new frameworks are required to restore freedom to its stated function. She notes how easily 'freedom can become deployed in the name of a state self-legitimation whose coercive force gives the lie to its claim to safeguard humanity' (Butler 21). Science fiction scholarship may need to revisit the political dynamics at play in texts engaging with civil liberties or the terrors of state control, and explore new constructions of global citizenship and human freedom.

Several chapters in this collection engage with the vagaries of capital in the last three decades. Karl Marx was the first to compare capitalism to vampirism, and Laurence Davies updates this symbol in his analysis of Guillermo del Toro's film *Cronos* (1992), which weaves a vampire plot alongside the capitalist threat of NAFTA seeking to transform Mexico's socio-economy in the early to mid-1990s. In Fred Botting's chapter, the figure of the zombie is seen to function in a science fictional mode as a manifestation of potentially destructive aspects of capitalist society. Botting suggests that these zombies belong to a science fiction 'that is less about iconic images of an expansive utopia and more concerned with the imploding biotechnological dystopia of cyberpunk' (this collection, p. 51). As such, they are seen to represent unproductive capital, exposing the underside of modern urban life.

Sara Wasson's chapter examines a different form of global capital: the traffic in human organs, a trade that has proliferated since the 1990s discovery of immunosuppressant drugs. Analysing three science fictions of human cloning for organ harvesting, Wasson updates the traditional Gothic trope of the grotesque double, arguing that these texts' harrowing juxtapositions of 'self' versus harvested 'other' echo a very real contemporary colonizing binary. China Miéville notes that the modern Gothic is often gripped by anxiety that humans are dominated, shaped and devoured by the built structures of late capitalism (10). These science fiction texts depicting circulations of human flesh illuminate additional rapacious architectures.

Technology's terrors and biopower

Technology of course helps make possible capitalism's global transformations. Just as nineteenth-century capitalism saw technology enabling the exploitation of human bodies in brutal labour, so too do the late twentieth and twenty-first centuries' forms of capitalism see technological innovations deployed to disturbing ends. The Gothic mode is often deployed in science fiction preoccupied with the threatening nature of technology. Admittedly, cyberpunk depicts technology as time-limited artefacts condemned to age and obsolescence, and as such destabilizes triumphant narratives of capitalism's technological progress in two ways: first, by showing that technology is itself fragile and doomed to decay, and second, by showing that as technologies age and are discarded they can be retooled to new, subversive purposes. Yet technology evokes dread too, and Luckhurst notes that 'there is a significant strand of science fiction writing that regards the impacts of Mechanism as profoundly traumatic, and can produce accounts in which the human subject is pierced or wounded by invasive technologies that subvert, enslave or ultimately destroy. In this version, science fiction shades into horror or Gothic writing' (*Science Fiction* 5).

Cathy Caruth defines trauma as the constellation of psychological agony that ensues from 'the inability fully to witness the event as it occurs, or the ability to witness the *event* fully only at the cost of witnessing oneself' (7, emphasis in original). In other words, the horror of the experience is so vast that at that moment of witnessing the subject cannot make sense of the scene or, crucially, process his or her own emotional response. For this reason, Dori Laub describes a trauma as 'a record that has yet to be made':

> While historical evidence to the event which constitutes the trauma may be abundant and documents in vast supply, the trauma – as a known event and not simply as an overwhelming shock – has not been fully witnessed yet, not been taken cognizance of. (57)

To say that technology can be traumatic is to say that, in certain cases, an encounter with a machine can be experienced as a profound violence to either human body or mind. Many of the chapters in this collection explore this menacing conjunction and the trauma it generates, exemplified by Kazuhiko Nakamura's disturbing image adorning our cover.

The relationship between humans and technology has become increasingly important for cultural scholars. In the last few decades, advances in medical and information technology in particular have required new ways of thinking about what it means to be human in a modern, technoscientific world. The essays in the 'Biopower and Capital' section of this collection examine some of the ways in which Gothic science fictions can negotiate the ethical and political questions generated by new technologies such as cloning, genetic engineering and cybernetics. Many of the aspects of these technologies that most fascinate the public (such as the elimination of genetically inherited disease, human cloning and 'designer' babies) are not yet fully realized scientific or social possibilities, and it falls to science fiction to extrapolate their potential impact on human communities and ontology. In particular, bio- and information technologies call into question the status of the body, and Gothic representations proliferate when depicting bodies being controlled, manipulated and dissolved.

Michel Foucault's concept of 'biopower' is often used to analyse the power mechanisms that operate in the relations between individuals and social, scientific and medical establishments, relations that saturate health and social management with 'numerous and diverse techniques for achieving the subjugation of bodies and the control of populations' (*History of Sexuality* 140). Biopower understands the position of human health and living in established Western social and political structures as part of a web of knowledge and power around technology, especially medical technology and its capacity to transform, direct, and control lived experience. Elaine Graham, for example, examines the ambiguous ethics of new reproductive technologies, arguing that, despite the appearance of greater freedom of choice for women, they represent 'an intensification of medical selectivity and control over those deemed *socially* suitable.... Far from guaranteeing reproductive choice, therefore, technoscientific intervention represents an intrusive intervention, which is the very paradox at the heart of Foucault's concept of bio-power' (115, emphasis in original). For Graham, then, biopower means intrusion on, or limitation of, individual liberties on the part of institutions, in the name of freedom of choice.

While some commentators see biopower as enshrined in the state, Rabinow and Rose argue that the future operations of biopower will, rather, be shaped by the urges of biosocial communities, for example to control inherited disease through genomic management (211). The essays in this collection employ both perspectives. Aris Mousoutzanis, for example, explores the biopolitics of bodies and technology in science fiction texts, reading the role of biopower in the production of models of global sovereignty through the cybernetic empire of the Borg, while Wasson critiques the complicity of recipients of organ harvesting in the treatment of tissue 'donors'. Indeed, the very apparatus of medical process and law itself can globally construct vulnerable populations as a ripe field for harvest.

Boundaries of the body in flesh and law: the post/human

Particular uses of technology, then, can see human agency annihilated or subsumed. Yet, for some readers (notably none in this collection), advanced technologies have also been held as potentially liberating, even perhaps offering opportunities to fulfil humanity's most magnificent potentials.

'Transhumanist' discourse sees history as a confident progress narrative, recruiting technology to an uncomplicated story of evolutionary ascension: as Graham says, such writing idealizes a 'postbiological *Homo cyberneticus*' (9). Graham questions such a neat narrative, representing her doubts typographically in her term 'post/human', in which the dividing slash mark challenges the idea of transhumanist evolutionary progress, as well as raising doubt about the ultimate impact of advanced technologies on the future lived experience of people (11). The term 'posthuman' emerged to describe a humanity taken beyond its original form and subjectivity by the technologies of the post-industrial West.

Less naively idealistic than transhumanism and more materially grounded, Donna Haraway's influential 'A Cyborg Manifesto' (1985) posits that the ubiquity of technology in Western culture meant we have all become cyborgs, 'chimeras, theorized and fabricated hybrids of machine and organism' (150). Haraway sees this 'cyborg' subjectivity as holding the potential to subvert dominant Western ideologies and move beyond familiar binaries of gender, race and class, enabling people to connect in new ways. The capacity of technological augmentation to help people *connect* is another key dimension of Kazuhiko Nakamura's image on the cover of this collection: the two cybernetically enhanced figures face each other, ready for dialogue, for communication.

Haraway's argument paved the way for other theorists to explore the politics of embodied identity. New ways of understanding the self have germinated in response to the range of new technologies that influence the way we live. Most of all, as N. Katherine Hayles points out, discussion of the posthuman is 'deeply influenced by thinking of the human mind/body as information' (241). Posthuman theory considers human identity in terms of information, whether in biological or digital form. The risk, as Hayles sees it, is that the significance of material, embodied identity could be lost amid too much emphasis on the capacity of human personality to be digitally translated and reproduced. Instead, Hayles endorses a dynamic, embodied progressive posthumanity that can adjust to inevitable technological and biological change without subverting it in the service of power and control.

This posthuman is a hybrid: 'an amalgam, a collection of hetereogenous components, a material-informational entity whose boundaries undergo continuous construction and reconstruction' (Hayles 3). In these terms, the posthuman can become monstrous, exceeding and redefining its own boundaries and resisting a single classification. Judith Halberstam and Ira Livingston see this monstrosity as the most politically valuable aspect of the posthuman. Rather than read the prefix 'post' as a marker of evolutionary ascension, Halberstam and Livingston see that prefix as recalling prefix of lack, of wounding, of inferiority: '*sub-, inter-, infra-, trans-, pre-, anti-*' (viii).

Like Haraway, they see the political value of the posthuman in the degree to which it resists stable identity categories. They read posthuman studies as fundamentally about resisting essentialisms and confronting 'the emergence of "the body" in history' (2).

When the posthuman subject is considered in terms of its biological information, a tangled relationship with embodiment is revealed, molecular biology in particular rendering the boundary between body and technology increasingly unstable. As Haraway notes, progress in biotechnology is accompanied by reconfigurations of the boundaries of the human body; we have been transformed at a cellular level by vaccines, for example, troubling our understanding of bodily integrity. Edge technologies like nanotech blur this boundary even more radically, and Gothic science fiction often features horror at the prospect that technology might annihilate, liquefy or collapse the human corporeal presence into mutant, grotesque forms. 'Bodies', Botting writes, 'are repeatedly invaded, penetrated, slashed, possessed, snatched, manipulated and controlled in the horrors that link gothic and science fictions' (*Gothic Romanced* 145). The human body becomes a focus for ambivalent transformative possibility, dissolution, agency and the struggle between otherness and self.

In this regard, Julia Kristeva's concept of abjection is pivotal: the 'abject' is that which simultaneously revolts and fascinates us by triggering the fantasy that we might be violated and consumed, a horror which we repudiate by constructing the abject catalyst as obscene, filthy and grotesque (4, 10, 13). Kelly Hurley deploys the Kristevan abject in her analysis of the repulsive 'abhuman', the horrifying, liminal, disintegrating or metamorphosing body that expresses *fin-de-siècle* anxieties over evolution and degeneration. The term 'abhuman' derives from William Hope Hodgson's *The Night Land* (1912), itself a Gothic science fiction novel in the wake of H. G. Wells's scientific romances, and here used by Hurley to encapsulate the 'not-quite-human subject, characterized by its morphic variability, continually in danger of becoming not-itself, becoming other' (4). Kristeva tends to approach literary representations of abjection as exemplifying revulsion at (and longing for) the maternal body, but more recently other critics have applied her concepts to social contexts as well as psychoanalytic (e.g. Hogle; Miles; Wasson, *Urban Gothic*). As Luckhurst notes, 'Anxieties about border violations in the 1980s could be ascribed not only to transformed geopolitics, newly invasive markets and disorienting kinds of technological embodiment but also, most obviously, to panics about bodily purity and contamination in the wake of "new" immune-system illnesses such as AIDS' (*Science Fiction* 216). As a result, a contemporary discourse around bodies and medicalized conditions has arisen in recent decades which offers new ways of understanding the human subject in Gothic science fiction.

In this collection, the non-humans of Wasson's chapter exemplify the abject and the abhuman, inviting us to analyse this established Gothic trope in terms of the subjections inherent within global capitalism and contemporary pharmaco-medical industries. In Alder's chapter, the metamorphosing body offered up by late twentieth-century molecular biology draws established constructions of human identity into question; the abhumanity of interstitial alien/human bodies assails normative cognitions of human shape. Botting notes the abject position of zombies in modern texts, seeing them as an outcast and overlooked cultural underclass, and similarly, as Wasson points out, organ tissue harvestees are constructed as 'nonpersons', abjected and unrecognized through their very centrality to the transaction of organ transfer. In Mark Williams's chapter, however, abjection becomes an interstitial position, expectant with subversive possibility and the potential to overturn polarized categories of genre and gender.

The network of legal discourse around human bodies also inspires Gothic science fiction, since Gothic tropes and narrative trajectories are frequently invoked in depictions of the human subject's erasure within the grip of the law. David Punter notes that the law (both civil and criminal) is an abstraction exiling the body: 'The law is a purified abstract whole, perfected according to the processes of taboo' (*Gothic Pathologies* 2–3). Wasson's chapter examines some of the processes by which law achieves this relentless reification, and Nickianne Moody's chapter examines texts which challenge corporate control and surveillance.

Apocalypse and erasure: millennarial anxieties

As the human subject becomes increasingly biologized, the ideological hold of liberal humanism over the foundations of identity is destabilized, leading critics to question humanity's ultimate future. In a similar vein, the 1990s saw millennarial anxieties peak, and science fiction echoed these anxieties in multiple apocalyptic fictions. Peaty's chapter explores a strand of this apocalyptic discourse in its discussion of zombie films. In these films, zombies are reimagined as figures generated by science, existing in a diseased condition that 'speaks of human technologies spun out of control, generating the very pandemic horrors they are intended to eradicate' (this collection, p. 102). Within the medical discourse of recent decades, zombies newly embody the apocalyptic potential of technology rather than of superstition.

Gothic criticism can be repetitive; as Botting says: 'if Gothic works tend to repeat a number of stock formulas, so does its criticism' (*Essays and Studies: The Gothic*, 5). The most common of these stock critical approaches is to approach Gothic texts as representing hidden longings and dreads, reading the material as product of a kind of Freudian dream-logic that converts inadmissible fantasy into fantastic symbols that disguise taboo longings. With such processes in mind, Gothic criticism has often tried to identify what symbolic equivalences might underlie its fantastic figures, and as the twentieth century progressed Freud's analytic machinery was fruitfully augmented with other discourses of the hidden, like trauma theory (e.g. Caruth, Laub) and Kristeva's theories of abjection. Several of the papers in this collection, however, seek to move beyond the work of unearthing the hidden, be it repressed desire or secret anxiety: some of the following chapters recognize the Gothic as not only revealing hidden desires or anxieties, but also as *itself* a thing of desire. The Gothic mode can render visible as well as disguise, and as such it can be deployed in pragmatic ways: Nickianne Moody's chapter, for example, examines how a cyberpunk trading card game depicts youth resistance to external control and surveillance, the narratives played out in the course of the game providing a platform for imagining overcoming authoritarian pressures. The Gothic mode is not inevitably a disguised rendering of repressed fantasy; on the contrary, it can accompany attempts to resist dominant narratives of normative obedience and constraint. Similarly, Davies argues that the Gothic tropes of del Toro's film *Cronos* cannot readily be seen in terms of the current association in the Anglophone world of Gothicism with anxiety: instead, Davies argues, the film stages Gothic as resistance. Davies's chapter presents the Gothic mode as seeking to recognize, control or manage that which it represents.

Neither Gothic nor science fiction is inevitably subversive (Punter and Bronfen 7); both can also do reactionary ideological work. The eighteenth-century novels labelled 'Gothic' often domesticate their taboo horrors and transgressive delights, ending by neatly rounding off the adventures with rational explanations, reassuring marriages and reaffirmed faith in Enlightenment modernity. It thus behooves critics to be cautious in reading Gothic as fundamentally politically progressive. The same caution is necessary in reading science fiction. Partly as a result of the work of Darko Suvin, Carl Freedman and others who venerate attempts to shock audiences into awareness of capitalist oppression, science fiction criticism has tended to pay most attention to texts that challenge capitalism. Rob Latham argues that we also need to acknowledge and analyse the conservative political work that can be done by science fiction fantasies (par. 2, 10–11). In each of the decades under consideration, science fiction texts do not always neatly echo anti-capitalist values, but rather occupy a wide range of ideological positions. The 1980s, for example, saw a profusion of science fiction texts which exemplify what Luckhurst calls the 'New Right' (*Science Fiction* 199–202), a combination of an array of right-wing and libertarian ideologies in the service of a narrative of a certain kind of strong America, magnificent in military-industrial supremacy, and this rhetoric intensified through the 1990s. The texts in this critical collection recognize that conjunctions of the Gothic and science fiction are not inherently liberatory. Rather than imagining escape from hegemony, Gothic science fictions can also readily be pressed into the service of reactionary ideologies, particularly when xeno-phobically depicting 'others' as threatening aliens, yearning nostalgically for an (imaginary) era of wholly 'intact' human bodies, romanticizing a pre-industrial age or depicting humanity as under threat from malign forces that justify forceful state intervention.

In closing, then, Gothic science fiction is a hybrid category that can be deployed in the service of a wide range of ideologies, world-views and stra-tegic investments. This collection explores a sampling of some of the ways in which this category has been used over the past thirty years, approaching the literary texts as not merely symptoms of, but also commentaries on, their socio-historical contexts. Samuel Delany argues that science fiction is 'not "about the future" … [but] in dialogue with the present' (176). The texts explored in this collection describe dark futures … but their greatest value may lie in what they have to say about our dark present.

Works cited

Aldiss, Brian and David Wingrove. *Trillion Year Spree*. London: Gollancz, 1986. Print.
Alien. Dir. Ridley Scott. Brandywine Productions and Twentieth Century Fox. 1979. Film.
Baldick, Chris, ed. 'Introduction.' *The Oxford Book of Gothic Tales*. Oxford: Oxford UP, 1992. xi–xxiii. Print.
Botting, Fred, ed. *Essays and Studies: The Gothic*. English Association. Cambridge: Boydell and Brewer, 2001. Print.
—. *Gothic*. London: Routledge, 1996. Print.
—. *Gothic Romanced: Consumption, Gender and Technology in Contemporary Fictions*. London: Routledge, 2008. Print.
Butler, Judith. 'Sexual Politics, Torture, and Secular Time.' *British Journal of Sociology* 59.1 (2008): 1–23. *Wiley Online Library*. Web. 15 October 2010.
Caruth, Cathy. 'Trauma and Experience.' *Trauma*. Ed. Cathy Caruth. Baltimore: Johns Hopkins UP, 1995. 3–12. Print.
Cronos. Dir. Guillermo del Toro. October Films, 1993. Film.
Delany, Samuel R. *Starboard Wine: More Notes on the Language of Science Fiction*. Elizabeth Town, NY: Dragon, 1984. Print.
Derrida, Jaques. *Specters of Marx: The State of the Debt, the Work of Mourning, and the New International*. Trans. P. Kamuf. New York: Routledge, 1994. Print.
Ehrlich, Heyward. 'The "Mysteries" of Philadelphia: Lippard's Quaker City and "Urban" Gothic.' *ESQ: A Journal of the American Renaissance* 66 (1972): 50–65. Print.
Fasa Corporation. *Shadowrun: Where Man Meets Magic and Machine*. 1st ed. Seattle: FASA Corporation, 1989. Print.

Foucault, Michel. *The History of Sexuality: Volume I: An Introduction*. Trans. R. Hurley. Harmondsworth: Penguin, 1978. Print.

Gaiman, Neil. *The Sandman*. London: Titan, 1990. Print.

Garfield, Richard. *Magic: The Gathering*. Seattle: Wizard of the Coast, 1993. Card game.

Goss, Theodora and John Paul Riquelme. 'From Superhuman to Posthuman: The Gothic Technological Imaginary in Mary Shelley's *Frankenstein* and Octavia Butler's *Xenogenesis*.' *Modern Fiction Studies* 53.3 (2007): 434–59. *Literature Online*. Web. 15 October 2010.

Graham, Elaine L. *Representations of the Post/Human: Monsters, Aliens, and Others in Popular Culture*. New Brunswick, NJ: Rutgers UP, 2002. Print.

Halberstam, Judith. *Skin Shows: Gothic Horror and the Technology of Monsters*. Durham, NC: Duke UP, 1995. Print.

Halberstam, Judith and Ira Livingston (eds). *Posthuman Bodies*. Indiana: Indiana UP, 1995. Print.

Hantke, Steffen. 'Dead Center: Berlin, the Postmodern Gothic, and Norman Ohler's *Mitte*.' *Studies in Twentieth and Twenty-First Century Literature* 30.2 (Summer 2006): 305–32. Print.

Haraway, Donna J. 'A Cyborg Manifesto: Science, Technology, and Socialist-Feminism in the Late Twentieth Century.' 1985. *Simians, Cyborgs, and Women: The Reinvention of Nature*. London: Routledge, 1991. 203–230. Print.

Hayles, N. Katherine. *How We Became Posthuman: Virtual Bodies in Cybernetics, Literature, and Informatics*. London: U of Chicago P, 1999. Print.

Helyer, Ruth. 'Parodied to Death: The Postmodern Gothic of American Psycho.' *Modern Fiction Studies* 46.3 (Fall 2000): 725–46. Print.

Hodgson, William Hope. *The Night Land*. 1912. *The House on the Borderland and Other Novels*. London: Gollancz, 2002. Print.

Hogle, Jerrold. 'The Gothic Ghost of the Counterfeit and the Progress of Abjection.' *A Companion to the Gothic*. Ed. David Punter. Oxford: Blackwell, 2001. 293–304. Print.

Horner, Avril (ed). *European Gothic: A Spirited Exchange, 1760–1960*. Manchester: Manchester UP; 2002. Print.

Horner, Avril and Sue Zlosnik (eds). *Le Gothic: Influences and Appropriations in Europe and America*. Basingstoke: Palgrave, 2008. Print.

Hurley, Kelly. *The Gothic Body: Sexuality, Materialism, and Degeneration at the Fin de Siècle*. Cambridge: Cambridge UP, 1996. Print.

Jameson, Fredric. *Archaeologies of the Future: the Desire Called Utopia and Other Science Fictions*. London: Verso, 2005. Print.

Kristeva, Julia. *Powers of Horror: An Essay on Abjection*. 1980. Trans. Leon S. Roudiez. New York: Columbia UP, 1982. Print.

Latham, Rob. 'A Tendentious Tendency in Science Fiction Criticism.' *Science Fiction Studies* 29.1 (March 2002): 100–110. Web. 23 October 2010.

Laub, Dori. 'Bearing Witness, or the Vicissitudes of Listening.' *Testimony: Crises of Witnessing in Literature, Psychoanalysis, and History*. Eds. Shoshana Felman and Dori Laub. New York: Routledge, 1992. 57–74. Print.

Lewis, Matthew G. *The Monk: A Romance*. 1796. Ed. D. L. Macdonald and Kathleen Scherf. Playmouth: Broadview, 2003. Print.

Link, Alex. '"The Capitol of Darknesse": Gothic Spatialities in the London of Peter Ackroyd's *Hawksmoor*.' *Contemporary Literature* 45.3 (Fall 2004): 516–537. Print.

Luckhurst, Roger. 'The Contemporary London Gothic and the Limits of the "Spectral Turn."' *Textual Practice* 16.3 (Winter 2002): 527–46. Print.

—. *Science Fiction*. Cambridge: Polity, 2005. Print.

Miéville, China. 'The Conspiracy of Architecture: Notes on a Modern Anxiety.' *Historical Materialism* 2.1 (1998): 1–32. Print.

Miles, Robert. 'Abjection, Nationalism and the Gothic.' *The Gothic*. Ed. Fred Botting. Cambridge: Brewer, 2001. 47–70. Print.

Moore, Alan and Kevin O'Neill. *The League of Extraordinary Gentlemen: Volume I*. London: Titan, 2000. Print.

Nash, Jesse W. 'Postmodern Gothic: Stephen King's *Pet Sematary*.' *Journal of Popular Culture* 30.4 (1997): 151–60. Print.

Pritchard, Allan. 'The Urban Gothic of Bleak House.' *Nineteenth Century Literature* 45.4 (March 1991): 432–52. Print.

Punter, David. *Gothic Pathologies: The Text, the Body, and the Law*. Basingstoke: Macmillan, 1998. Print.

—. *The Literature of Terror*. 2nd ed. 2 vols. Edinburgh: Pearson Education, 1996. Print.

—. 'Postmodern Gothic: The Moment beneath the Moment.' *Etudes Britanniques Contemporaines* 22 (June 2002): 1–17, 167. Print.

Punter, David and Elisabeth Bronfen. 'Gothic: Violence, Trauma and the Ethical.' *The Gothic*. Ed. Fred Botting. Cambridge: Brewer, 2001. 7–22. Print.

Purinton, Marjean D. 'Science Fiction and Techno-Gothic Drama: Romantic Playwrights Joanna Baillie and Jane Scott.' *Romanticism on the Net* 21 (February 2001). Web. 23 September 2009.

Rabinow, Paul and Nikolas Rose. 'Biopower Today.' *BioSocieties* 1.2 (2006): 195–217. *Cambridge Journals Online*. Web. 15 October 2010.

Rein-Hagen, Mark. *Vampire the Masquerade*. 3rd rev. ed. Stone Mountain, GA: White Wolf Publishing, 1998. Print.

Roberts, Adam. *Science Fiction*. London: Routledge, 2000. Print.

Rzepka, Charles J. 'Slavery, Sodomy, and De Quincey's "Savannah-La-Mar": Surplus Labor Value in Urban Gothic.' *The Wordsworth Circle* 27.1 (Winter 1996): 33–37. Print.

Shelley, Mary. *Frankenstein*. 1818. New York and London: Norton, 1996. Print.

Spencer, Kathleen L. 'Purity and Danger: *Dracula*, the Urban Gothic, and the Late Victorian Degeneracy Crisis.' *ELH* 59.1 (Spring 1992): 197–225. Print.

Suvin, Darko. 'Estrangement and Cognition.' 1979. *Speculations on Speculation: Theories of Science Fiction*. Ed. James Gunn and Mathew Candelaria. Lanham, MD: Scarecrow Press, 2005. 23–35. Print.

VanderMeer, Jeff and Ann VanderMeer. *The New Weird*. San Francisco, CA: Tachyon, 2008. Print.

Walpole, Horace. *The Castle of Otranto*. 1765. London: Penguin. 2010. Print.

Warwick, Alexandra. 'Feeling Gothicky?' *Gothic Studies* 9.1 (2007): 5–19. Print.

Wasson, Sara. *Urban Gothic of the Second World War: Dark London*. Basingstoke: Palgrave, 2010. Print.

Wells, H. G. *The War of the Worlds*. 1898. London: Penguin, 2006. Print.

Wilt, Judith. 'The Imperial Mouth: Imperialism, the Gothic and Science Fiction.' *Journal of Popular Culture* 14.4 (1981): 618–628. *Periodicals Archive Online*. Web. 15 October 2010.

Wolfreys, Julian and Ruth Robbins (eds). *Victorian Gothic: Literary and Cultural Manifestations in the Nineteenth Century*. Basingstoke: Palgrave Macmillan, 2000. Print.

Part I
Redefining Genres

1. In the Zone:
Topologies of Genre Weirdness

Roger Luckhurst

Gothic science fiction? Can there be such a thing? If I were to adopt, for a minute, a relatively standard position from science fiction criticism, such a hybrid causes all kinds of problems. A meaningful taxonomy cannot have the adjectives *Gothic* and *Science* pre-modifying the same noun, *Fiction*. Darko Suvin, the eminent theorist of science fiction, defined science fiction as a literature of cognitive estrangement, a genre in which the reader enters an imaginative world different or estranged from his or her empirical world, but different in a way that obeys rational causation or scientific law: thus, it is estranged cognitively. For Suvin, the genres of the Gothic, along with horror fiction, fantasy or fairy tales, might well offer estranged worlds, but they are far from cognitive: these are not scientific but magical genres, where the causations are folkloric, irrational or arbitrary. Science fiction projects a future by the rational extrapolation of the present: it is thus a critical, potentially utopian, but always political genre. The Gothic has the present irrationally dominated by the resurgence of the past, which is apprehended only by overwhelming and disabling affect, typically of paralysing horror. Therefore, in Suvin's view, it can only be politically conservative. Any science fiction that veers towards horror or fantasy is, according to Suvin then, not only committing 'creative suicide' and degenerating into a 'sub-literature of mystification', but will become 'obscurantist and reactionary at the deepest level' (*Positions* 71).

This condemnation seems early, strategic and positional, a way of legitimating the value of science fiction by abjecting its allied genres. Yet this view remains largely unchanged in Suvin's later work. The critique that science fiction readers apparently demand is always juxtaposed in Suvin to the 'narcotized dreamers' who passively read fantasy ('Considering the Sense of "Fantasy"' 237). Fredric Jameson repeats this distinction whenever he contrasts science fiction and fantasy, genres which have, he claims, entirely different readerships. Science fiction, Jameson argued, was fundamentally historicist, whilst fantasy was modelled on mythology or theology and therefore intrinsically 'incompatible with history'. For any historical materialist the genre of fantasy must, in its entirety, be dismissed as 'palpably reactionary' ('Radical Fantasy' 277). In *Archaeologies of the Future*, Jameson's long opening reflection on genre, fantasy is 'essentially infantile' and 'narcissistic' and has to be 'radically distinguished from the historicisms at work in the science fiction tradition, which turn on a formal framework determined by the concepts of the mode of production rather than those of religion' (58). These sweeping statements are often the result of an allergy to the Christian conservatism of J. R. R. Tolkien and C. S. Lewis, held to embody an entire genre. Here too, this logic would extend to the Gothic. To modify science fiction with Gothic would be to have a regressive genre burst from the chest of a progressive one. The progressive host, needless to say, is killed at once.

The fact that it is of course possible to entertain the notion of a 'Gothic science fiction', ascribe a meaning to it and even rapidly sketch out a basic bibliography and filmography, is something that – at least in science fiction criticism – has only recently become thinkable. Writing on genre has been obsessed with borders, the risk of invasion and protocols for de-contamination. This is particularly the case with genres perceived as having low cultural value. For abjected or ignored genres, defences have been mounted by narrow definitional work that usually preserves – as in Suvin's case – a tiny cadre of fictions that fulfil a circumscribed political purpose for the genre. The rest? The rest can go to hell.

In the past decade, however, criticism has emerged that resists fixed spatial categories for genre. Instead, it has thought of genre as a continuously unfolding process that is generated not by 'pure specimens' but which advances through 'crossbreeds and mutants' (Altman 16).[1] These critics have relaxed genre strictures and begun to ask the question, as formulated by Istvan Csicsery-Ronay, 'What might serious critical theory look like if the border guards went home?' ('Lucid Dreams' 290). This has been in response to what has come to be termed the 'post-genre fantastic', evidence of a rapid hybridization between horror, Gothic, science fiction and the relatively new label 'dark fantasy'. The appearance of these hybrid texts has accelerated in the last few years, producing new terms like 'slipstream' or 'span' fiction and even movements and manifestos, such as the arrival of the New Weird in 2002, associated with the group of neo-Gothic writers like China Miéville, M. John Harrison, Steph Swainson and others.[2] That name, the New Weird, evokes the Weird Tales of the 1920s, and suggests that different histories might emerge that no longer separated apparently cognitive and affective strands of the fantastic. Thinking weirdly offers an account of the imbrication of Gothic and science fiction, right from the very start, in the very DNA of genre codes.

The post-genre fantastic is, Gary Wolfe proposes, 'recombinant genre fiction: stories which effectively decompose and reconstitute genre materials and techniques together with materials and techniques from a variety of literary traditions, even including the traditions of domestic realism' (415). Rather than trying to establish quarantined genre traditions, defined by rigid structural antipathies, we have seen the beginnings of attempts to think relationally about modes of the fantastic as different fractionations of a spectrum of responses to modernity. As John Clute puts it, in his suggestive book *The Darkening Garden*, 'the genres of the Fantastic began to be invented in tune with the changing world after 1750, and … the story devices of the fantastic constitute a series of exorbitant utterances of that change' (53). To have divided them into separate genre spaces was an artificial act of 'fence-building', which 'fatally scants the constant mutation of story among all the genres of the fantastic'. 'Genres change', Clute says, 'as the world calls for them to change' (*Darkening Garden* 61).

Although it would be necessary to sketch a genealogy of these hybrids back into the 'weird' fictions of the late nineteenth century, a defining text of the particular genre mutation we are calling 'Gothic Science Fiction' would inevitably have to be Ridley Scott's film *Alien* (1979). Massively influential, the film redirects the science-fictional energies of the extensive or expansive sublime towards the horrors of the intensive, bodily grotesque – and gets stuck about half-way, in some hybrid space between. The grotesque is defined by its boundary violation, the feeling, as Geoffrey Harpham describes it, 'that something is illegitimately in something else … the sense that things that should be kept apart are fused together' (qtd. in Csicery-Ronay, 'On the Grotesque' 73). Monsters are the products of taxonomical confusion, and the alien is a being we can never quite grasp, at once mechanical and organic, primitive and advanced, male and female, horror and science fiction. We have merely to account for when and where and why it erupts in this grotesque form.

In this essay, I want to explore two elements in relation to this post-genre fantastic, or generic pile-ups. Many of the texts I want to look at involve a passage through strange spatial zones, weird topologies that produce anomalies, destroy category and dissolve or reconstitute identities. In a way, these zones are meta-critical commentaries; they re-mark on their own dissolution of the law of genre.[3] In other words, many of these fictions thematize their own generic hybridity. This will take us all the way from Pynchon and the Strugatsky brothers to the recent fiction of M. John Harrison, Justina Robson and China Miéville. But rather than proposing some abstract condition of the always-already impure, I later want to offer some historical speculations on why we have had this intensive phase of genre recombination in contemporary genre fiction. This will lead us from hybrid texts to the hybrid assemblages that increasingly litter our contemporary world.

Zones are never easy spaces to occupy: they are often unnerving and transitional, places where the usual laws are suspended. There are De-Militarized Zones, liminal spaces that exist between warring states, where different and temporary laws of engagement apply. Primo Levi suggested that the universe of the concentration camp was a 'Grey Zone', where all ethical determinations of being human were suspended the instant one passed through the gate. In the Green Zone in Baghdad a surreal pretence of ordered colonial government unfolds behind the most heavily fortified borders on the planet – borders that are nevertheless fatally permeable.[4] These are all oneiric and utterly deadly twilight zones. Yet the liminality of the zone can also present possibilities, opportunities for new combinations. Mary Louise Pratt defined the colonial encounter as a contact zone, a social space which often produces violent exercises of colonial power, but it is also the space of surprising or unexpected exchange where neither colonizer nor colonized dominates but a hybrid knowledge emerges from the 'interactive' and 'improvisational' nature of contact (*Imperial Eyes* 6–7). If you think of cultures or literatures as discrete, coherent and monolithic, Pratt argues, then the hybrid works that emerge from the contact zone seem 'anomalous or chaotic'. 'Autoethnography, transculturation, critique, collaboration, bi-lingualism, mediation, parody, denunciation, imaginary dialogue, vernacular expression – these are some of the literate arts of the contact zone,' Pratt states, before adding: 'Miscomprehension, incomprehension, dead letters, unread masterpieces, absolute heterogeneity of meaning – these are some of the perils of writing in the contact zone' ('Arts of the Contact Zone' 11).

The idea of a literature of the Zone immediately makes me reach for J. G. Ballard and his obsession with liminal zones of the dissolution and radical extinction or reinvention of subjectivity, a plot he restages over and over again. In Ballard's story 'The Zone of Terror', the blank Modernist spaces of a retreat in the desert provide a 'supposed equivalence to psychic zero' in which Larsen's self begins to fragment into uncanny doubles that multiply, persecute and supersede him (123). Ballard turns whole zones of Shanghai and then of the post-war era itself into indeterminate and suspensive zones in *The Empire of the Sun* and *The Kindness of Women*. The most significant rendition of the post-1945 world as a suspensive Zone of contending powers is Thomas Pynchon's *Gravity's Rainbow*. By part three, Tyrone Slothrop has left behind his libidinal mappings of London and enters a Germany now divided into Zones of the rival post-war superpowers. Somewhere in that Zone, at Potsdam, the geopolitical regime of the post-war world is being decided. But as yet, the Zone is suspended, as John Jonston puts it, between the Zero of Old Europe and the One of the Rocket-State, 'a space of ruins and the allegories they spawn, where geographies are mental maps and vice versa, but above all a space of indeterminacy and singularity, where no patterns converge' (Johnston 103). In Pynchon's Zone, there are not events so much as 'movements, flows, and a kind of de-differentiated flux of people, object, signs and representations' (Johnston 104). Between zero and one, the binary codes of either/or or on/off, the Zone is the instant of both/and, that passage of undecidability just before decisions are made and determinate forces come back into play. 'Separations are proceeding', it is ominously announced. 'Each alternative Zone speeds away from all the others, in fated acceleration, red-shifting, fleeing the Center' (Pynchon 519). Pynchon therefore sets up the zone as at once dystopian, where the powers of the future Rocket State are beginning to organize the engines of global capitalism, but also as shot through with utopian possibility, since the Zone carries the fugitive evidences of what is called the Counterforce.[5] Tyrone Slothrop, the central character of *Gravity's Rainbow*, simply disappears in the Zone, dispersed into its contradictory flows. We are left in a state of indecision: has the dystopian Rocket State successfully disassembled his subjectivity, or has Slothrop exited this nightmare of history, and thus escaped the totalitarian potentialities burgeoning for the world that will come after the Zone?

Pynchon's Zone is also a meta-critical space, commenting on its own generic indeterminacy. This is one of the reasons we used to call it post-modern, when we still had a use for that term. The epigraph for the section entitled 'In the Zone' is from *The Wizard of Oz* – 'We're not in Kansas anymore' – and we have indeed entered instead a technicolour, hallucinatory and utterly camp extravaganza, complete with full singing and dancing numbers. Pynchon's Zone is both a real space and a phantasmagoric site, both a historical mapping and a generic pile-up, where the Realism meant to record the unfolding of the post-war moment suffers insistent intrusions of the spectral, the fantastic and the science fictional. It's a kind of pile-up that Pynchon enacts again in *Against the Day* (2006), a pastiche of the late nineteenth-century boy engineer tales that soon splintered into pulp science fiction, with Westerns, ghost stories, Vernean adventures, Riemann mathematics and a fair amount of pornography. This is what I mean by such spaces re-marking on their own status: when a Zone appears in a text, it marks out a space of generic hybridization too.

For the history of science fiction, Pynchon's *Gravity's Rainbow* has been perhaps less important than another seminal text of the 1970s, *Roadside Picnic* by Arkady and Boris Strugatsky, published in 1972 and first translated from the Russian in 1977. In this puzzling and enigmatic novel, the Zone is a forbidden site, full of detritus left by an advanced extra-terrestrial race. A black market in artefacts produces huge leaps in technology and is fed by a group of illegal traders called Stalkers who are prepared to risk the threats of the Zone. The things pulled out of the Zone make no sense; no one knows how they work, or why, since they violate every principle of physics. The book is called *Roadside Picnic* because someone speculates this material is the rubbish left behind by a brief alien stopover for lunch on the way to somewhere more interesting. The geography of the Zone shifts randomly and to deathly effect; Stalkers suffer strange wasting diseases, and odd effects develop in the communities that exist in the penumbra of the Zone. If those present at the time of what is called the Visitation try to leave the area, they seem to take something of the Zone with them: 'One of them decides to emigrate', explains a stalker.

> Your most typical man in the street ... He moves, say, to Detroit. He opens up a barbershop and all hell breaks loose. Over ninety per cent of his clients die during a year: they die in car crashes, fall out of windows, are cut down by gangsters or muggers, drown in shallow waters, and so forth. A number of natural disasters hit Detroit and its suburbs. Typhoons and tornadoes ... appear in the area. And all that kind of stuff. And such cataclysmic events take place in any city, any area where an emigrant from a Zone area settles. (108)

The Stalkers who enter the Zone suffer unpredictable effects too: 'Everyone who spends enough time with the Zone undergoes changes, both of phenotype and genotype,' Valentine the Stalker explains. 'You know what kind of children stalkers can have and you know what happens to the stalkers themselves. Why? Where is the mutation factor? There is no radiation in the Zone' (Strugatsky 108–9). The central character is forced to stalk again and again into the Zone in pursuit of an object that might cure his mutant daughter, and engineers the death of an innocent to get at it.

It is inevitable that one wants to read this novel allegorically, and in fact Fredric Jameson provides two slightly different accounts in *Archaeologies of the Future* in the different halves of the book (the latter half collects essays that are separated by twenty years or so from the long opening essay on utopia). The Zone, Jameson suggests, 'is at one and the same time the object of the most vicious bootlegging and military-industrial Greed, and of the purest religious – I would like to say Utopian – Hope' (294). He also reads the Zone as a topography that is a self-referential reflection on genre, 'its narrative production determined by the structural impossibility of producing that Utopian text which it nonetheless miraculously becomes' (295). In his earlier essay, Jameson ends on the moment of utopian expression in the Zone, a technology that might provide 'Happiness for everybody!'

In the later essay, Jameson gives greater emphasis to the Zone's sliver of utopian possibility being cynically cancelled by destructive and possessive human behaviour and generically by the text's 'reconfirmation of SF's reality principle' (*Archeologies* 76).

Perhaps these Zones are less utopias, cancelled or not, than heterotopias, Foucault's suggestive term for real spaces that nevertheless act as imaginative counter-sites to the dominant society. These work, Foucault suggests, to 'suspect, neutralize or invert the set of relations that they happen to designate, mirror or reflect', thus constituting 'a sort of simultaneously mythic and real contestation of the space in which we live' ('Of Other Spaces' 24). Kevin Hetherington in *Badlands of Modernity* regards heterotopias as Zones that offer glimpses of alternate social ordering: 'they organize a bit of the social world in a way different to that which surrounds them' (viii). This is similar to the anarchist theory of Temporary Autonomous Zones, proposed by Hakim Bey, a transitory happening or 'guerrilla operation which liberates an area (of land, of time, of imagination) and then dissolves itself to reform elsewhere, elsewhen, before the State can crush it' (*Temporary Autonomous Zone*). If the Zones of the post-genre fantastic are never straightforwardly utopian, perhaps it is because they are chaotic and disordered as a means of evading the dangers of a static utopian topology, fenced off and guarded from transgressors. They do not elaborate a separate order, but work to set up interference patterns with the dominated or policed space that surrounds them. This is something Andrew Thacker emphasizes in his understanding of heterotopia as 'a sense of movement between the real and the unreal; it is thus a site defined by a process, the stress being upon the fact that it contests another site' (25).

It is a quote from *Roadside Picnic* that serves as the first of the epigraphs to M. John Harrison's 2006 novel, *Nova Swing*. This novel is a sort of sequel to *Light* (2002), and both feature incomprehensible technologies which emerge from a Zone called the Kefahuchi Tract. In *Light*, the Tract is an impenetrable limit from which no one has apparently returned. In the hard jargon of space opera, Harrison describes it as 'a broth of space, time, and heaving event horizons; an unpredictable ocean of radiant energy, of deep light. Anything could happen there, where natural law, if there had ever been such a thing, was held in suspension' (*Light* 141). All that is left at its edges are mad technologies and bizarre engineering techniques, testament to millennia of obsession with the Tract by every being that comes across it. In *Nova Swing*, a slice of this Tract has fallen onto a planet, creating a Zone where illicit traders navigate a shifting, incomprehensible space that few survive. 'They died in numbers', the narrator tells us, 'of odd diseases or inexplicable accidents inside and outside the site, leaving wills too exuberant to understand and last testaments tattooed on their buttocks. These treasure maps, whose psychic north pegged itself to equally unreliable features of the Kefahuchi Tract in the night sky above, always proved worthless' (116).

'All stories', John Clute says in his Lexicon of Horror, 'are not only signposts that tell you where you are, but also crossroads: hoverings of the liminal' (*Darkening Garden* 62). It is impossible to find a pure example of a sub-genre of the fantastic, because they are so insistently intermixed. 'From the perspective of taxonomy', to quote Clute again, 'the literatures of the fantastic could be viewed as a tumult of mistakes' (62). Harrison's novels are so immensely challenging because they exemplify this seeming tumult of category errors, from the broadest strokes of their disjunctive interstellar plots, full of jump-cuts and weird left turns, to the smallest non-sequiturs that litter Harrison's truly strange sentences. *Light* has one strand involving a down-at-heel present-day London with two scientists spooked by quantum phenomena emerging in their Gower Street basement laboratory. This is the science that will motor the far future we are reading in parallel, but instead of offering logical, extrapolative causation from the present to the future this story soon morphs into a Gothic tale of haunting, magical conjurations, paranoid persecution and serial killing. The bending of all the known laws of Earth science is envisaged in Gothic terms, as a monstrous obtrusion into the streets of London. The two discoverers of this quantum space will be driven mad by what they see in quantum space: they will eventually be volatilized into light. This is intertwined with two strands from the twenty-fifth century, one of which is a sort of cyberpunk parody, unfolding in a variety of virtual environments, whilst the other uses all the apparatus of the old space opera, a form that Harrison himself had killed off some twenty-five years before in his vicious demolition of the sub-genre in *The Centauri Device* (1975). Harrison proclaimed that he wanted to get back to baseline science fiction, what he called 'big dumb objects and going very fast in space' ('No Escape' 69). *Nova Swing* keeps up the genre-bending, mixing the scenario of *Roadside Picnic* with film noir and hard-boiled detective fiction.

Until the publication of *Light*, Harrison was regarded as a member of the New Wave, that group of writers associated with the avant-garde years of the magazine *New Worlds* in the late 1960s when it was run by Moorcock and Ballard.[6] Harrison shredded conventional genre forms, writing decadent and mannered books as if they were the last entries in the planet's bibliography. He demolished catastrophe fiction and the space opera, before embarking on a sustained, highly self-reflexive critique of the consolations of fantasy in the Viriconium novels. His best deconstruction of fantasy was, confusingly enough, entirely Realist – indeed it was a documentary fiction about the closed, obsessive world of mountain climbers in the Peak District, written at the end of the 1980s, called *Climbers*. He spent the 1990s writing frightening Gothic novels and short stories, queasy depictions of sub-let flats in grubby suburbs of London where atrocious acts of magic invoke monstrous intrusions of other realities into our own. The consolations of fantasy repeatedly morph into persecutory and obscene magical obtrusions. These were sometimes, as in *The Course of the Heart*, explicitly theorized as Lacanian blots of the Real. Harrison's career has therefore been a long meditation on the potentialities of the genres of the fantastic: the Zone of the Kefahuchi Tract is where this meta-critical examination is folded back into science fictional form, a heterotopic space from which genre materials are spewed out in randomized and mystifying ways. He is now the presiding master for a younger generation of English writers intent on fusing genres under the mantle of what Harrison suggested could be called the New Weird. Even so, Harrison was soon doing his best to bury this label and refusing to accept any kind of stable location, writing instead, as he put it, at 'the collapse of the wave front, the point of choice. I don't want to live in models' ('No Escape' 70).[7]

Harrison's most obvious disciple in this fusion is China Miéville, whose works at the border of horror, dark fantasy, science fiction and utopia are exemplary fictions of the Zone. Like Harrison, Miéville's fusions also operate at the very local level of his tortured, baroque sentences, which owe much to that fustian tradition of Arthur Machen, M. P. Shiel or William Hope Hodgson, minor English writers at the turn of the twentieth century who were much admired by H. P. Lovecraft and celebrated in his essay 'Supernatural Horror in Literature'. Miéville is a scholar of the tradition of weird fiction, which he defines as 'breathless and generically slippery macabre fiction' ('Weird Fiction' 510). Miéville describes something in the *Iron Council* as 'a mongrel of whale-shark distended by bio-thaumaturgy' with 'boat-sized fins swinging on oiled hinges, a dorsal row of chimneys smoking whitely' (454). It is difficult to separate science fictional, fantastic or Gothic elements in such sentences, his clatter of over-egged adjectival descriptions continually shifting the frame of reference between the biological and mechanical. At the larger level of plot, the *Iron Council* also explicitly explores the utopian possibilities of Zones that cut into and across dominated social spaces – the spirit of revolt in this case contained in a train in perpetual, revolutionary movement. These interstitial Zones, opening at random, shifting and disappearing from the purview of organized space, recur across Miéville's work – the feral pathways that open up in his unnerving short story 'Reports of Certain Events in London', for instance, or the rat-runs that exist in parallel to ordinary London lives in *King Rat*. The interpenetration of zones becomes the motor of the plot in *The City and The City*, featuring apparently separate cities that occupy the same space and are cross-hatched over each other in complex ways. Border police try and fail to manage movement between the cities with elaborate passport controls. Miéville's zones are 'impossible' non-Euclidean spaces in which, as Laura Salisbury argues, 'generic transgression is figured in terms of topological complexity' (45). Miéville's work might almost be explored as a full-scale imagining of the suggestive, sketchy comments made by Foucault in his lecture on heterotopias: Miéville has based fictions in the tain of mirrors or the hulls of boats, each of which get brief yet unfulfilled passages in Foucault.

A sense of just how exuberant this genre-bending has become is visible in Justina Robson's *Keeping it Real*, a somewhat ironically titled novel. This novel is set in a near future where 'an unknown quantum catastrophe' in a particle accelerator has fractured the unity of the space-time of the Earth, now renamed Otopia. This event has erased any stable sense of history (no one can quite remember what the proper history of the Earth is) and it has opened up relations with five other parallel orders of reality: the world of elementals, elves, demons, faeries and the dead, who occupy Thanatopia. Different physical laws and social logics exist in each of these spaces; but they are no longer easily separable: 'the Bomb', the narrator tells us, 'had peppered the time of all realms with the fragments of things' (44). The elves are portrayed as slightly to the right of Conservatives, intent on closing their borders to further immigration in order to preserve the purity of the race. They've clearly read too much Tolkien. Across these Zones, Robson tracks two hybridized figures: Zal, an elf who thrives on the transgressive knowledge of the contact zone, and Lila, the female bodyguard assigned to him on Earth, a cyborg fusion of human and heavy weaponry. In contrast to the elves, Lila seems to have spent her youth reading Donna Haraway, she literally embodies the anti-essentialism of cyborg life in a post-Edenic world, even as she struggles to master the tension between flesh and metal interfaces. Things become immensely complicated in *Keeping it Real*: we have a post-human cyborg, for instance, tramping through the Tolkienesque landscape of Alfhiem, whilst inhabited by the spirit of a necromancer. Robson's intent in this jeu d'esprit is very clear in such a scene: science fiction melds with fantasy which melds with horror. Robson's Quantum Bomb is a generic bomb that blasts many holes through the boundaries between science fiction, fantasy, horror and the Gothic.

We could say, following the work of Bruno Latour, that these works and other instances of the post-genre fantastic, are nonmodern. In his polemic, *We Have Never Been Modern*, Latour argues that modernity is typified by its obsession with sorting, categorizing and taxonomizing the world into discrete orders: nature and culture, humans and non-humans, subjects and objects, from which come disciplines, specialisms, closed epistemologies. Science is the agent that progressively separates these spheres, until science itself is regarded as abstracted from the vagaries of culture. These spatial orders are then arranged along a single, unified, linear temporality, separating out primitive and advanced, savages and civilizations, East and West. Latour's conception of modernity borrows a lot from Foucault's *The Order of Things*, in which he argued that the tabula or taxnomical grid came to model the world from the late eighteenth century: the grid, Foucault says, 'enables thought to operate upon the entities of our world, to put them in order, to divide them into classes, to group them according to names that designate their similarities and their differences' (xvi). But *The Order of Things* is prefaced by Foucault's laugh, a 'shattering' outburst of laughter that is prompted by reading Jorge Luis Borges' Chinese Encyclopedia, with its bizarre and hidden principles of organization, its apparently random mixing of beasts in a way that transgresses every Western conception of sorting or taxonomy. Foucault describes this anti-Encyclopedia very evocatively as:

> the disorder in which fragments of a large number of possible orders glitter separately in the dimension, without law or geometry, of the *heteroclite* ... In such a state, things are 'laid,' 'placed,' 'arranged' in sites so very different from one another that it is impossible to find a place of residence for them, to define a common locus beneath them all. (xvii–xviii)

This is the moment of seeing beyond the usual sorting machineries to glimpse the non-modern, a space that refuses the spatial and temporal separations of modernity. For Latour, the non-modern means giving up on the spatial and temporal disciplines of modernity that have fatally separated culture from nature, humans from non-humans. Latour instead embraces hybridity in space and polytemporality in time. Beyond the modern, he says, 'everything happens in the middle, everything passes between the two, everything happens by way of mediation, translation, and networks' (*We Have Never Been Modern* 57).

Needless to say, I am leading you towards thinking of texts by M. John Harrison, China Miéville or Justina Robson as instances where the pile-up of genres act out this non-modern hybridization. The spaces of their Zones work like Foucault's 'heteroclite' or Latour's 'network assemblage' – they will appear to be 'illegimate mixtures' in the eyes of a critic of the Modern, obsessively sorting and categorizing like Darko Suvin, but under a different order of things, their hybridity pushes against the tabula that would define them as monstrous. Therefore, a term like Gothic Science Fiction announces not just a conjuncture of spaces, but a temporal pile-up, where different times coexist or slice through each other. If this is a very contemporary literature, mixing posthuman cyborgs, the pastoral Medievalism of a certain strand of fantasy, or the resurgent tyrannies of the Gothic past, that may be because it coincides with Latour's embrace of polytemporality too: 'We have all reached the point of mixing up times. We have all become premodern again' (*We Have Never Been Modern* 75).

Latour's framework begins to suggest some reasons for this explosion of genre at this particular historical conjuncture. Of course, it is demonstrable that there has always been a constant cross-fertilization between genres of fantastic, going on behind the back of any rigid structural definitions, but why should that secret history become so visible now? Why have some writers whose work was seen as embarrassing, chaotic and ill-disciplined – such as H. P. Lovecraft – become so visible, a linch-pin for new kinds of historical and even philosophical work?[8]

For Latour, the so-called Modern settlement, the division of the world into discrete categories that dominated scientific and cultural thought from the Enlightenment, has reached a particular crisis because it has had to acknowledge the proliferation of strange hybrid objects that confound modern categories. In particular, the strict quarantine between the categories of the natural and the cultural has been thrown in question by a series of controversial events. Where, precisely, does the natural end and the cultural begin with things like ozone holes or global warming or AIDS or epidemics of obesity and allergy or hospital superbugs or Asian bird flu or mad cow disease? Are these products of natural or cultural, human or non-human, processes? Is scientific, or sociological analysis better? These phenomena cannot be 'sorted' – categorized or resolved – in any straightforward way. These hybrid objects 'have no clear boundaries, no sharp separation between their own hard kernel and their environment', Latour expands in his *Politics of Nature*: 'They first appear as matters of concern, as new entities that provoke perplexity and thus speech in those who gather around them, and argue over them' (24). Latour suggests we need to think to cast out the binaries that have been unable to grasp this increasingly populated excluded middle, a Zone we might say, in which we need to grasp 'the nonseparability of quasi-objects and quasi-subjects', things once considered monstrous, outside the grid (*Politics of Nature* 66). There are all sorts of science-fictional places to go with such an analysis: one might think, for instance, of Haraway's 'Cyborg Manifesto' for a similar statement about contemporary hybridization, a post-Edenic world where the purity of Nature has long been overthrown by the miscegenation of technics and humanity.

China Miéville once militantly declared the New Weird to be a freeing up of genre constraints that mirrored 'the radicalisation of the world.' 'This', he said, 'is post-Seattle fiction' ('Long Live the New Weird' 3). Elsewhere, trying to forge links between Marxism and the fantastic as a form of ideology critique, Miéville has proclaimed that 'the fantastic, particularly because "reality" is a grotesque "fantastic form," is good to think with' ('Editorial Introduction' 46) – thus trying to treat aggressively the allergy leftist criticism has felt towards the mass cultural genre of fantasy. This attempt to historicize the post-genre fantastic is important. Although, to emphasize again, there was never a prior moment of generic purity, this current wave intermixing invites comment. It brings us back to John Clute's observation: 'Genres change as the world calls for them to change' (62). Latour offers one set of explanations, that the number of anomalous quasi-objects around us is increasing and forcing a recognition of heterogeneity and artifice, that we do not live in discrete natural or cultural worlds but in messy assemblages and improvized networks. But we could also begin to think about other frameworks of explanation: is, for example, the post-genre fantastic the literature of a risk society? In Ulrich Beck's formulation, risk is a result of a reflexive modernization which paradoxically undermines the authority of science and pulls it into realms of social dispute and rival expertise. The Suvinian model of eliding science and cognition cannot work any more: risk contaminates science fiction with Gothic anxieties and dark fantasies of apocalypse. Similarly, we might wonder whether the weird spatial zones of genre pile-up respond to geopolitical transformations in 1989, the collapse of Cold War space and the end of what Michael Denning has called the culture of Three Worlds (3–4). In its place, we exist in something far more confusing and marked by globalized flows, strange interpenetrations and simultaneities. There's lots of work to be done thinking about genre in relation to Manuel Castells' sociological analyses of the Network Society, for instance, and its exploration of the 'space of flows' (453). But finally, we might wonder whether it is possible to historicize this fiction in any straightforward way, given the polytemporal logic of the post-genre fantastic, its contemporaneity literally pulling times together in a riot of competing and often contradictory historical framings, typified most strongly in that conjuncture of past, present and future suggested by the title 'Gothic Science Fiction.' One thing's for sure: we're not in Kansas any more.

Notes

1. Altman's introduction remains one of the best entries into this different way of thinking about genre.
2. 'Slipstream' is the term coined by Bruce Sterling in 1989. 'Span' fiction had a shorter shelf-life, suggested by the critic Peter Brigg.
3. These terms are derived from Jacques Derrida, 'The Law of Genre', which opens with the assertion 'Genres are not to be mixed' before exploring how the purity of genre is always already 'contaminated' by impurity.
4. See, for instance, Rajiv Chandrasekaran.
5. For commentary, see Dale Carter.
6. For commentary on Harrison's career, see Mark Bould and Michelle Reid.
7. Somewhat inevitably, the movement has been formalized in the anthology, *The New Weird,* edited by Ann and Jeff VanDerMeer.

8. The rehabilitation of Lovecraft is signalled not just by the literary defence of his work by Michel Houellebecq's *Lovecraft: Against the World, Against Life*, but also in the serious attempt to formulate a philosophy of 'weird realism' in Graham Harman's 'On the Horror of Phenomenology: Lovecraft and Husserl.'

Works cited

Alien. Dir. Ridley Scott. Brandywine Productions and Twentieth-Century Fox. 1979. Film.

Altman, Rick. *Film/Genre*. London: BFI, 1999. Print.

Ballard, J. G. *The Empire of the Sun*. London: Gollancz, 1984. Print.

—. *The Kindness of Women*. London: Harper Collins, 1991. Print.

—. 'The Zone of Terror.' *The Disaster Area*. London: Triad/Panther 1979. 131–142. Print.

Beck, Ulrich. *Risk Society: Towards a New Modernity*. London: Sage, 1992. Print.

Bey, Hakim. *Temporary Autonomous Zone: Ontological Anarchy, Poetic Terrorism*. New York: Autonomedia, 1991. Web. 19 June 2010.

Bould, Mark and Michelle Reid (eds). *Parietal Games: Critical Writings on and by M. John Harrison*. London: Science Fiction Foundation, 2005. Print.

Brigg, Peter. *The Span of Mainstream and Science Fiction: A Critical Study of a New Genre*. Jefferson, North Carolina: McFarland, 2002. Print.

Carter, Dale. *The Final Frontier: The Rise and Fall of the American Rocket State*. London: Verso, 1988. Print.

Castells, Manuel. *The Rise of the Network Society*. 2nd ed. London: Wiley, 2010. Print.

Chandrasekaran, Rajiv. *Imperial Life in the Emerald City: Inside Baghdad's Green Zone*. London: Bloomsbury, 2007. Print.

Clute, John. *The Darkening Garden: A Short Lexicon of Horror*. Cauheegan: Payseur and Schmidt, 2006. Print.

Csicery-Ronay, Istvan, Jr. 'Lucid Dreams, or Flightless Birds on Rooftops?' *Science Fiction Studies* 30.2 (2003): 288–304. Print.

—. 'On the Grotesque in Science Fiction.' *Science Fiction Studies* 29.1 (2002): 71–99. Print.

Denning, Michael. *Culture in the Age of Three Worlds*. London: Verso, 2004. Print.

Derrida, Jacques. 'The Law of Genre.' Trans. Avita Ronnell. *Critical Inquiry* 7.1 (1980): 55–81. Print.

Foucault, Michel. 'Of Other Spaces.' *Diacritics* 16 (Spring 1986): 22–7. Print.

—. *The Order of Things*. London: Tavistock, 1970. Print.

Haraway, Donna. 'A Manifesto for Cyborgs: Science, Technology, and Socialist-Feminism in the Late Twentieth Century.' *Simians, Cyborgs and Women: The Reinvention of Nature*. London: Routledge, 1991. 149–181. Print.

Harman, Graham. 'On the Horror of Phenomenology: Lovecraft and Husserl.' *Collapse IV: Philosophical Research and Development*. Falmouth: Urbanomic, 2008. 333–64. Print.

Harrison, M. John. *The Centauri Device*. St Albans: Panther, 1975. Print.

—. *Climbers*. London: Gollancz, 1989. Print.

—. *The Course of the Heart*. London: Gollancz, 1992. Print.

—. *Light*. London: Gollancz, 2002. Print.

—. 'No Escape.' *Locus* (December 2003): 6–7, 69–70. Print.

—. *Nova Swing*. London: Gollancz, 2006. Print.

Hetherington, Kevin. *Badlands of Modernity: Heterotopia and Social Ordering*. London: Routledge, 1997. Print.

Houellebecq, Michel. *H. P. Lovecraft: Against the World, Against Life*. Trans. Dorna Khazeni. London: Weidenfeld, 2006. Print.

Jameson, Fredric. *Archaeologies of the Future: On the Desire Called Utopia and Other Science Fictions*. London: Verso, 2005. Print.

—. 'Radical Fantasy.' *Historical Materialism* 10.4 (2003): 273–80. Print.

Johnston, John. 'Pynchon's "Zone": A Postmodern Multiplicity.' *Arizona Quarterly* 46.3 (1990): 91–122. Print.

Latour, Bruno. *Politics of Nature: How to Bring the Sciences into Democracy.* Trans. Catherine Porter. Cambridge, MA: Harvard UP, 2004. Print.

—. *We Have Never Been Modern.* Trans. Catherine Porter. Brighton: Harvester, 1993. Print.

Levi, Primo. 'The Grey Zone.' *The Drowned and the Saved.* 1988. London: Abacus, 1989. 22–51. Print.

Lovecraft, H. P. *Supernatural Horror in Literature.* New York: Dover, 1973).

Miéville, China. *The City and The City.* London: Macmillan, 2009. Print.

—. 'Editorial Introduction.' *Historical Materialism* 10.4 (2003): 39–49. Print.

—. *The Iron Council.* London: Macmillan, 2004. Print.

—. *King Rat.* London: Macmillan, 1998. Print.

—. 'Long Live the New Weird.' *The Third Alternative* 35 (2003): 3. Print.

—. 'Reports of Certain Events in London.' *Looking for Jake, and Other Stories.* London: Macmillan, 2005. Print.

—. 'Weird Fiction.' *The Routledge Companion to Science Fiction.* Eds. Mark Bould, Andrew Butler, Adam Roberts. London: Routledge, 2009. 510–516. Print.

Pratt, Mary Louise. 'The Arts of the Contact Zone.' *Professing in the Contact Zone: Bringing Theory and Practice Together.* Ed. Janice Wolff. Urbana: National Council for the Teachers of English, 2002. 1–18. Print.

—. *Imperial Eyes: Travel Writing and Transculturation.* London: Routledge, 1992. Print.

Pynchon, Thomas. *Against the Day.* London: Jonathan Cape, 2006. Print.

—. *Gravity's Rainbow.* London: Picador, 1975. Print.

Robson, Justina. *Keeping it Real.* London: Gollancz, 2006. Print.

Salisbury, Laura. 'Michel Serres: Science, Fiction, and the Shape of a Relation.' *Science Fiction Studies* 33.1 (2006): 30–52. Print.

Sterling, Bruce. 'Slipstream.' *Science Fiction Eye* (1989). Web.

Strugatsky, Arkady and Boris Strugatsky. *Roadside Picnic.* Trans. Antonina W. Bouis. London: Macmillan, 1977. Print.

Suvin, Darko. 'Considering the Sense of "Fantasy" or "Fantastic Fiction": An Effusion.' *Extrapolation* 41.3 (2000): 209–47. Print.

—. 'On the Poetics of the Science-Fiction Genre.' *College English* 34.3 (1972): 372–82. Print.

—. *Positions and Presuppositions in Science Fiction.* Basingstoke: Macmillan, 1988. Print.

Thacker, Andrew. *Moving Through Modernity: Space and Geography in Modernism.* Manchester: Manchester UP, 2003. Print.

VanDerMeer, Ann and Jeff VanDerMeer (eds). *The New Weird.* San Francisco: Tachyon, 2008. Print.

Wolfe, Gary. 'Maleboge, or the Ordnance of Genre.' *Conjunctions* 39 (2002): 405–19. Print.

2. Zombie Death Drive:
Between Gothic and Science Fiction

Fred Botting

'Some of your best friends may be zombies'

Zombies, so George Romero noted, 'are the real lower-class citizens of the monster world' (Beard 30). A lesser type of the undead and very much in the shadow – the very poor relations – of their charming bloodsucking aristocratic cousins, zombies have none of the style, attractiveness or supernatural power of vampires. Nor do they, unlike Frankenstein's monstrous progeny with its curious if lumbering dignity of labour, retain much trace of humanity. On screen, zombies tend not to evoke sympathy or identification: it is difficult to remain unrepulsed by a humanoid creature with half a face slavering over the intestines of a dismembered teenager or enjoy the suffering of a ravenous mass of bloody hands clutching hungrily and with grim inevitability at any living flesh. Physically unprepossessing, intellectually challenged and lacking any social skills or redeeming qualities – thoroughly unromanticizable – the zombies remain at the trashiest end of a trashy genre (or two). Have you ever encountered a sexy zombie, or come across a zombie that exuded that special star quality? While zombies still persist in popular culture to pose important questions in both horrific and comedic modes (*Land of the Dead* [2005] and *Shaun of the Dead* [2004], a couple of recent instances), their place and significance in the canon of both Gothic and science fiction genres remains ambiguous.

Zombies' lack of appeal in studies of cultural texts, however, is more than compensated for by their popularity in philosophical discussions of mind and consciousness. In these numerous studies and thought experiments the zombie is a recurrent figure used to pose questions of interior mental states, of supposedly defining human characteristics like sentience and intentionality. At the core of this line of semi-serious philosophical questioning lies an uncertainty about being able to tell the difference between the self-consciousness, self-possession and auto-centredness of properly human intellectual processes and the merely rehearsed familiar behavioural habits equated with the non-conscious operations of a soulless machine. Steven Pinker neatly summarizes the problematic: 'the philosopher Georges Rey once told me that he has no sentient experiences. He lost them after a bicycle accident when he was fifteen. Since then, he insists, he has been a zombie. I assume he is speaking tongue-in-cheek, but of course I have no way of knowing, and that is his point' (Pinker 147). With philosophical zombies, interiority is evacuated or at least placed in doubt as the site of agency, intentionality and individual identity. External appearance, action and attribution, however, also remain insufficient and doubtful when it comes to understanding consciousness. After defining a philosophical zombie as an entity that 'is or would be a human being who exhibits perfectly natural, alert, loquacious, vivacious behaviour but is in fact not conscious at all, but rather some sort of automaton', Daniel Dennett notes, 'you can't tell a zombie from a normal person by examining external behaviour.' Indeed, he goes on, offering some useful life advice, 'some of your best friends may be zombies' (73). The question of telling the difference becomes even more difficult when one is confronted with a 'complex zombie' – what Dennett calls a 'zimbo' – able to self-monitor and function internally, if unconsciously, at a higher level and display complex behaviour 'thanks to a control system that permits recursive self-representation' (310). Zombies seem to become increasingly indistinguishable from humans, to the point that – in the refrain of *Dawn of the Dead* (1978) and to all pragmatic intents and purposes – 'they're us'.

Pursuing the similarity between zombies and humans in philosophical terms, however, is not the aim of this paper, though questions of difference – differences between human and automata, or between human and zombie in various texts – will be addressed in due course. Dennett's zombies and zimbos and their prevalence in much philosophical, rather than cultural, enquiry resonate strongly with a posthuman tone in contemporary critical work where telling the difference between human and machine is less an issue than the celebration of a general machinism or pervasive cyberneticization of culture as a whole: we are all, so the story goes, already machines, already constructed higher-level functioning units of automatic, informatic, genetic – and indeed corporate – processes beyond our control. The human 'we', indeed, has become little more than a faded illusion in an age of technical prostheses, enhancements and networks: we are all cyborgs now, as Haraway's and Hayles's avatars unceasingly remind us.

Cyborgs, however, do not seem to ask or display any concern with the zombie question – though, notably in the shape of Star Trek's Borg, they are nonetheless effects of it. In contrast to recent philosophy, the zombie question is rarely asked: a ready identification – by Haraway, Sandy Stone and Mark Poster – of cyborgs with souped-up vampires or networked Frankenstein monsters plays on an otherness rendered glamorous and subversive and allows a curious flattening or deletion of the differences supposed to be crucial to posthumanism, engendering instead an all-too-predictable romantic flight beyond differences of humanity, history, or body. Zombies may weigh down posthumanism's linear and ecstatic trajectory beyond modernity and suggest that the monsters and vampires exhumed in posthumanist fantasy are less avatars of the supersession of humanism and as much figures productive of modern humanism in the eighteenth century, forms integral to the production of modern subjectivity and culture: the uncanny and doubles evoke an anxiety about telling the difference between humans and automata, an anxiety that comes to define industrial humanity and its relations to machines – relations that, in the case of Hoffman's 'The Sandman' (1816), lead to automatic enamoration (the hero falls in love with a mechanical doll), delirium and, finally, a dive to death; or, in Frankenstein's early imbrication of Gothic and science fiction, render humanity an effect of monstrosity – with equally fatal results. Zombies, neither living nor dead, premodern throwbacks made by modernity, are part of this questioning of the limits of modern humanity. In attempting to eke out the differences zombies provoke, how they expand and implode upon modernity, this paper will move backwards and leap forwards between speculations on zombie histories and on the zombie futures.

Zombiology for beginners (genre)

Moving outwards and pulling back imitates the ambivalent momentum Freud associates with the death drive. The double movement is also characteristic of science fiction's expansive and implosive gestures, and the prophetic and nostalgic directions the genre opens up (Sterling; Roberts). Gothic, too, is a modern genre, a construction of the Enlightenment's fabrication of a dark prehistory. Where romance and its combination of extrapolated possibilities and technological precautions provides one early form of generic articulation for Gothic and science fiction, horror provides another. Though the genres are often held apart, one trying to shut out the unknown or screen off unconscious forces while the other embraces uncertainty and attempts to engage it consciously, the overlaps for many genre critics are considerable. Noel Carroll argues that 'science fiction films are monster films, rather than explorations of grand themes like alternate societies or alternate technologies' (17). Indeed, when the shiny surfaces of science fiction futures are dispensed with, spectators are often left with horrible visions of psychological and corporeal disintegration in which known boundaries collapse and bodies are transformed. James Whale's 1931 *Frankenstein*, according to Telotte, sets out to 'create horrific recoil' (80), while *The Fly* (1958; 1986) presents the repulsive spectacle of human metamorphosis. *Invasion of the Bodysnatchers* (1956; 1978), in which a small American town's inhabitants are replicated and pacified by seeds from outer space, includes a moment of classic horror: on returning to his hiding place to collect his partner, the hero briefly kisses her. He withdraws as the camera captures his shocked expression in extreme close-up. Horror: the revelation that she has been taken over and now lacks any of the feelings or passions that define humanity (Telotte 20–21).

Susan Sontag – in grouping science fiction and horror movies together as modes of disaster film – suggests that both genres share 'complicity with the abhorrent', even if it is only to neutralize it (437). Her reading finds enjoyment in horror and notes how its cause shifts from an 'upsurge of the animal' – the return of repressed desires and the baser instincts associated with human nature – to locate 'the danger … as residing in man's ability to be turned into a machine' (434). While the opposition between natural and technocultural pressures is significant in the manner it dispenses with the clichés of horror criticism, clichés that claim horror appeals to the worst in all of us and releases 'our most base instincts' and 'our nastiest fantasies' (King 309), it delineates, perhaps, too strict an opposition even as it recognizes the role of technology and culture in the production and purveying of horror. Nature all too often seems an alibi that occludes the cultural limits and taboos as well as the technical and textual effects so crucial in the successful working of the machinery of the genre.

In terms of science fiction's relation to the zombie, however, Sontag's reading is instructive. For her, planetary invaders are 'usually zombie-like' with 'cool, mechanical' or 'lumbering, blobby' movements; like the undead, they perform the roles of 'automatized servant'. The humans who are taken over by technical rather than magical means 'become far more efficient – the very model of technocratic man, purged of emotions, volitionless, tranquil, obedient to all orders' (433–434). Zombies, in this more science fiction mode, move away from themes of monstrosity, sexuality and animality to manifest the 'depersonalizing conditions of modern urban life' (435): they are very modern beings, effects of reason, science and technology, creatures of offices, bureaucracies, factories. In contrast, Gothic renditions of the zombie replay generic distinctions between primitivism and enlightenment, with magic and superstition appealing to a base human nature while rationality and science, almost powerlessly, looks on. In American films of the 1930s and 1940s – *King of the Zombies* (1941), *I Walked with a Zombie* (1943) – these Gothic themes are played out in a racialized context: a displaced South – the Caribbean – provides the setting for a sexualized encounter with an otherness exuding colonial anxieties and demanding to be suppressed. Anne Rice's mythology of the undead, which constructs a genealogy linking zombies and vampires, stages an encounter between New World bloodsuckers and their distant East European forebears. On a grand tour in which they attempt to discover their roots, Louis and Claudia only find a disgusting throwback: 'two huge eyes bulged from naked sockets and two small, hideous holes made up the nose; only a putrid, leathery flesh enclosed his skull, and the rank, rotting rages that covered his frame were thick with earth and slime and blood. I was battling a mindless, animated corpse' (Rice 206–207). Not human, not vampire, this 'creature of the Old World' is the lowest of the low in Gothic terms, a figure of life-death that is less than natural and as far away from supernatural glamour as possible, a zombie born of the abject slime of nature at its most vile and putrescent.

Zombies, from technologically driven space invaders or automatized pod people to the abjection of Gothic undead, occupy a curious and significantly interstitial position, overlooked, perhaps, but all the more interesting for that. Less than natural and also magical and primitive – yet also more than natural in that they defy the line between life and death, zombies come from a buried, archaic past; technological effects of advanced alien rationality or products of modern urban society – the automatized and depersonalized invaders or bodysnatchers of science fiction horror, they also come from outer space or a future that is rapidly collapsing on the present. With a touch of space-race anxiety, *Night of the Living Dead* (1968), though Romero tried to avoid a single cause, explains the zombie contagion as the effect of strange radiation from a Venus probe.

Zombies, it seems, as they are put to work differently in two genres, allow a kind of crossing to occur, a traversal, taking the form of a confounding, that doesn't simply articulate the two ends of a spectrum of horror but, in horror, holds open an aporia between nature and culture, instinct and technology, past and future or death and life (as we don't know it), an aporetic space where various mutations can occur, a multifarious screen for projection, recoil and collapse. The proximities between science fiction and Gothic zombies and their entanglings of past, future, nature and culture, though confounding standard modes of generic systematization, can, in their main period of prominence, the twentieth century, be related to historical and cultural shifts. This is where zombiology takes a political and economic turn before it gets psychoanalytical.

Mass (from white zombies to night zombies)

Victor Halperin's *White Zombie* (1932) looks back, very much in the Gothic mode, dominated as it is by images of darkness, sublimity and gloom. An engaged couple are given the opportunity, on visiting Haiti, to marry in the villa of a rich plantation owner. The latter falls for the bride-to-be and solicits the help of a local voodoo master in order to take possession of her. He administers a powder that renders her unconscious and apparently dead and she is then taken from her tomb to the castle of the voodoo master. Her fiancé, with the aid of a local doctor, sets out to rescue and revive her.

On the surface, *White Zombie* presents a tale of amorous delusion and possession, equating race and sexuality as forms of otherness to be mastered through diabolical possession. Black magic and sexual desire are read in terms of primitivism and superstition that must be overcome by the forces of civilization and reason. First, however, there must be a descent into darkness: the film opens with a nocturnal scene in which the betrothed couple being taken by coach to the plantation encounter a crossroads burial and then some zombies and the zombie master. As the plot moves rapidly through wedding, death and burial, it climaxes in a distinctly Gothic location: the lair of the voodoo master is a ruined medieval castle perched on a clifftop. External sublimity – low shots looking up from the shore at the imposing pile – is reinforced with internal scenes dominated by a grand and gloomy hall, its long, arched windows letting in a chiaroscuro of light; its stone columns supporting a distant ceiling and its stairway decorated with fleur-de-lys carvings. Given the Caribbean setting, the Gothic scene is extremely strange, as is the casting of its lead actor: Bela Lugosi, his face covered in dark rather than ultra pale make-up – plays the voodoo master 'Murder Legendre'. The European émigré and Hollywood's face of Dracula further imposes the Old World on the New in a dark Europeanization of a Caribbean that was still under US occupation. It serves, albeit very oddly, to cast voodoo into a Europeanized, archaic realm of primitive superstition, thereby also serving to occlude the modernity of voodoo as a hybrid religion drawn from African, Christian and pagan sources and associated with the slave rebellion led by Toussaint L'Ouverture (Williams). It also draws attention away from US colonialism in the Caribbean.

The film, however, for all its heavy Gothic images, does not quite manage to cast everything into a past associated with Europe. Looking backwards in an anachronistic and anatopical manner for all its worth, the movie presses forwards to engage with the then modernity of film as, in Benjamin's critique, one of the most striking technical manifestations of crowded urban existence. Murder Legendre is not only a master of voodoo spells and potions who dwells in a Gothic castle: he is also a mill owner who puts his zombies to work carrying sacks of cane and turning the enormous grinding wheel that refines it into sugar. His mill, though lit darkly and shot through railings to suggest the atmosphere of a Piranesi print, is a modern place of industrial production. He even recommends zombies to the plantation owner on commercial grounds: tireless, obedient, slavish, neither eating nor sleeping, they are the ideal workers for the long hours and mechanized routines of industrial labour.

In looking back in its many Gothic images and yet forward, to the context of industrial and cinematic production, *White Zombie* discloses the features of 'Gothic modernism' that Tom Gunning analyzes in Lang's *Metropolis* (1927). Lang's film stages a 'clash' between Gothic and modernity – its very modern images of industrialized society, social control and scientific innovation (especially the scientist Rotwang and his robot double of Maria) disclose its science fiction elements, all signs of a dystopic future; its Gothic images – the dark underworld of the workplaces, the monstrous machines of mechanical production, the sublime sets, the cathedral especially, and the magical-technological transformations – look backwards, presenting the future in terms of a barbaric and inhumane past. The clash is barely resolved in the film, despite the efforts of the romantic middle-class hero, Freder. The images of the workers and the conditions of production offer stark presentations of modern, Fordist productive relations for many critics: Gunning notes how the workers' 'dehumanized mechanical actions' signify that they have become 'soulless slaves' (55); they are slaves to the machine (Telotte 88), 'puppets' worked by a mechanical universe in which 'objects rule – the first men we see are dominated by steel bars, and they themselves are depersonalized, faceless, dressed identically, feeding the machines in columns as angular and rigid as their Ferminger homes which we see next' (Tulloch 41). Zombies, it seems, are effects and mirror images of modern mechanical processes, rather than archaic throwbacks. The spectacle of modern industrial production and the zombification of the working masses so strikingly presented in *Metropolis* bring nineteenth-century accounts of capitalism, Marx's in particular, vividly to the screen. Famously, though without specific mention of zombies, Marx (in *Grundrisse* and *Capital*) used Gothic metaphors (the vampire and werewolf in particular) to describe the operations of capital: living labour (human workers) has the life sucked out of it by dead capital, rendering workers the mere appendages – puppets, automata – to the mechanisms of production, surplus value and exchange. The modernity of the zombie – inscribed by conditions of mechanical production and represented by the most modern mode of mechanical reproduction (cinema) – thus crystallizes as the very image of mass society developing in the early twentieth century. The bulky shape and lumbering slowness of zombies (which is why *28 Days Later* [2002] isn't a zombie movie) describe the inertial lurch of mechanical mass as a grim, relentless and inevitable process.

Marx, *Metropolis*, mass (mass society, mass consumption, mass culture): the pattern is set for future renderings and readings of zombies. Take two of the most influential films of the last forty years – Romero's *Night of the Living Dead* and *Dawn of the Dead* – and some critical interpretations: zombies 'are the silent majority who bought into the ideology of the ruling class' (Rider par. 18); their cannibalism represents the 'ultimate in possessiveness, hence the logical end of human relations under capitalism' (Wood 213); the relentless destructiveness manifests 'the whole dead weight of patriarchal consumer capitalism' (Wood 118); or the way that capital encourages a 'zombiefication of citizens into consumers' (Loudermilk 96). Mass consumption becomes the zombie mirror of earlier images of mass production: 'in *Dawn of the Dead* zombie-shoppers ride the escalators in a lobotomized exaggeration of consumer robots. In this film, the mall is a runaway machine; its escalators, fountains, videogames, the automated voice-announcements continue in endless repetition as the "back-from-the dead" move with equally mechanical motions' (Friedberg 116). It is a 'grotesque parody of conspicuous consumption' (Greenberg 86). Consumerism and leisure, under advanced capitalism, are 'bought at the price of spiritual zombieism' and mass entertainment provides a false pleasure – and false consciousness – that keeps the masses 'unaware of their own desperate vacuity' (Modleski 158).

In Romero's films, 'the attack on contemporary life strikingly recapitulates the very terms adopted by many culture critics', their worst fears visualized in the zombie shopping centre with its 'will-less, soulless masses … possessed by the alienating imperative to consume' (Modleski 160). Indeed, 'these visions of swarming, feeding mallrats were more than the paranoiac fantasies of mass culture critics: they were observable realities' (Latham 45). It is curious, however, that such attacks on mass culture come not from its higher realms, but emerge in one of its lowest and trashiest genres; curious too that a cultural critique is made so evident and yet, as Modleski notes, is ironically turned round to the extent that Dawn 'has become a midnight favourite at shopping malls all over the US' (160). Perhaps the film 'is not a satire on the Fordist consumer society, however much it thinks it is' (Beard 30). It becomes too easy to read Romero's two films as a critique or a satire, thereby missing the disturbing ambivalences engendered by zombies, the ambiguities traversing Romero's films and their contexts and, also, their refusal of any resolution, symptomatic of wider and unresolved cinematic and cultural tensions.

Night of the Living Dead, released in the late 1960s, with a grainy, almost avant-garde documentary style, is overdetermined by its cultural context: the opening scenes in which a brother and sister visit the grave of their father not only signal questions of patriarchal family structure, but with glimpses of the American flag waving in the background, hint at political questions then being raised about conformist patriarchal social structures by the anti-Vietnam and Civil Rights movements. The clean-cut hero of the film is black. The main location – an isolated farmhouse – suggests the last outpost of a Western's defence of individual and family, but the family hiding inside (in the basement, as recommended by Cold War nuclear fears) is torn with antagonisms and anxieties which climax in a zombie daughter consuming her parents. Family, social conformism – 1950s American values seem at once both threat and main danger as a socially heterogeneous group of zombies slowly besiege the house. Internal tensions may be projected outwards, towards the undead, but tensions reappear within. Is mass society the problem or the cure? Mass media are foregrounded in the film: radio and television become a focus for the survivors, who avidly watch news reports and interviews with government officials, scientists and the military arguing over the cause of the phenomenon and the solution. Terms like 'mass murder epidemic' and 'mass hysteria' underline the question of mass culture and conformism – and associate it with zombies – while at the same time the humans remain captivated by the TV screen. The end of the film is equally ambivalent: a sheriff's civil defence posse – on a mission to 'search out and destroy marauding ghouls' – sweeps through, shooting zombies on sight. The black hero remains in the farmhouse, unsure whether they are friend or foe: on seeing a shape at the window, a volunteer shoots him down like a zombie. The film closes in a series of grainy stills of white men in hats parading their rifles over a black man's body pierced with meathooks. He has been carried to the pile to be with the other undead corpses. If the zombie threat is effaced and social order restored, *Night* leaves the audience to consider the price and significance of that closure, leaving a series of unanswered questions about social and familiar structure in a political climate in which the status of the mass (be it culture, conformism or production) is the most uncertain thing of all: is it a reactionary or liberatory idea? Something to be feared, protected or destroyed? Does the film, as Robin Wood suggests, imply that '"liberation" and permissiveness ... are at once inadequate and too late – too feeble, too unaware, too undirected to withstand the legacy of repression', or is it more destructive as a vision of a negativity irrecuperable by a 'dominant ideology' offering 'the recognition of that ideology's disintegration, its untenability, as all it has repressed explodes and blows it apart' (Wood 213–215).

Just as Romero wanted to leave the cause of the zombie outbreak obscure (in one version of there were three different causes), the ending leaves only doubt and uncertainty. Perhaps this is not surprising if one follows the implications in terms of economic tensions and shifts. Where earlier zombie films were not so much concerned with the red menace or McCarthyism as with 'the social conformism demanded by Fordist economic integration', expressing the anxiety 'not that all Americans might be secretly different, but that all Americans might be the obscurely the same – serial instances of such contemporary stereotypes as William H. Whyte's organizational man', Romero's zombies occupy a different historical moment which sees 'the hollowing out of this constituency by a post-Fordist organization of labour' (Beard 30). *Night* appears at the death of mass society, mass production and mass culture; its zombies are the disenfranchized underclass, a new lumpenproletariat, those about to be cast off in the move to a postindustrial, postmodern consumer society, a world, at that time, only vaguely taking shape. Unable to look forward with any great clarity, nor back with any great relish, the indecision, the radical equivocation of the film presents a culture pressed in two directions and by two countervailing tendencies that have economic and psychological dimensions – pleasure and death.

Culture of death

Or, the pleasure principle meets the death drive. Freud, in 'Beyond the Pleasure Principle' (1920), speculates on a force refusing the regulation of the principle of homeostasis that seems to govern all life with the aim of lowering tension and decreasing excitation. Trauma, for example, seems to produce repetitions that defy models of pleasure, repeating distress and disturbance rather than recovering equilibrium. Freud hesitatingly advances an explanation for repeated unpleasurable acts: an 'instinct for mastery' moves the subject from a 'passive situation' in respect of the 'distressing experience' of loss to a position of active control ('Pleasure Principle,' 285). Looking for 'tendencies more primitive' and 'independent' of pleasure, Freud continues his speculations (287). He proposes a 'protective shield' defending consciousness from overstimulation caused by unbound, excitable and anxiety-provoking energies and binding the free-floating cathexes or disturbing energies within the psychical apparatus. Life, in the form of Eros, expands outwards, death, Thanatos, pulls it back. The 'daemonic' power that manifests itself in the compulsion to repeat seems to disclose an instinct, a drive, 'to restore an earlier state of things': it is life's drive to return to 'inertia', to death, through its own 'circuitous' path (308–311). Pulled back, pushing forward, its dual momentum stems from the expansions of Eros and the retractions of Thanatos. The return to inertia, to death, is a restoration to come: death rides with life until its return to ultimate homeostasis arrives from the future, in its own time.

In *Civilization and Its Discontents* (1930), Freud returns to the thesis of 'Beyond the Pleasure Principle' to explain the entire dynamic of social and cultural development, dissolution and change: civilization unites in the manner of Eros, enabling humans 'to be libidinally bound to one another'. It is opposed by 'man's natural aggressive instinct, the hostility of each against

all and of all against each', 'the derivative and the main representative of
the death instinct' which 'shares world-dominion' Eros. 'Why this has to
happen, we do not know' (*Civilisation* 313–314). Binding, combining, expanding, unifying, civilization's 'programme' is undertaken in relation to forces
of unbinding, decomposition and destruction. Neither natural nor cultural,
drive appears (and disappears) in the gap of separation and connection, a
gap that itself gives rise to repetition, to the circulations of representation
and symbolization operating according to the pleasure principle.

In subsequent versions – notably those of Lacan – the death drive moves
in two directions. At an early stage of his thought, up to the 1960s, death
is equated with the symbolic: sacrificing living being in the move to language, the subject finds itself fully determined by the signifier, petrified,
automated, mortified under its power. This version finds further expression
in Pontalis, who, in a discussion of 1950s bureaucracies and institutions,
observes that a 'culture of death' is produced by rigid state apparatuses
and social machineries (90). The strongest critical account following this
line of interpretation – and one invoking zombies and linking psychology
and economy – is made by Deleuze and Guattari: 'The only modern myth
is the myth of zombies – mortified schizos, good for work, brought back to
reason' (335). In *Anti-Oedipus* (1983), Deleuze and Guattari are dismissive
of the death drive: the mechanisms of modern production and ideological
reproduction are traced in almost Marxian lines. Zombies – the drones
of the undead – are the product of Marx's vampire capital sucking the
surplus from living labour and leaving a mindless workforce to lumber
round the closed circuits of pleasure and reason. The death drive is central
to the process: it 'celebrates the wedding of psychoanalysis and capital', an
enterprise designed to absorb all surplus value – biological, economic and
psychic. This 'death condition' – its effusions coordinated by the restraints
of the signifier – forms the empty locus of displacement for a transcendent
distinction from life; it blocks schizophrenic flights (335). Death operates as
one of power's 'order words': it creates voids to stop lines of flight, to trap
and stabilize everything in its mutation machine; 'death, death; it is the
only judgement, and it is what makes a judgement a system' (229; 107).

According to this line of thinking, the death drive corresponds to the
zombie reading of mass culture which mortifies, pacifies and subjugates
its worker-consumers under a regime of Fordist mass production. In later
Lacan – from the 1960s on – the death drive is linked to the seething,
often horrifying excesses of life beyond symbolic parameters, that is, to
an irruption of the real or to bursts of jouissance. An 'encounter with the
real' ('tuche'), a shocking, traumatic, horrifying encounter, the death drive
announces that something, something unknown and unpresentable, lies
'beyond the automaton, the return, the coming-back, the insistence of

the signs, by which we see ourselves governed by the pleasure principle'
(Lacan 53). Here the death drive announces some unsymbolizable excess
within the signifying circulations of pleasure. In this distinction between
the homogeneous pleasures of automaton and the intense and disruptive
unbindings of the death drive, the latter is associated with uncontrolled
and undirected energies, negativity, psychical overload, unproductive expenditures, destabilization and dissolution: it drives beyond the symbolized
frameworks of reality, nature or culture, as a purely destructive 'will for
an Other Thing'.

   Lyotard's account of 'acinema' links the tension between pleasure and
death to an economic distinction between homogeneity or sameness
and heterogeneity or difference: where pleasure circulates productively,
returning to meaning, sense and profitable differences (realist, bourgeois
and narratively closed films), death manifests the wasteful, excessive and
unproductive expenditures of open, artistic and formally challenging works,
a consumption, a burning up of meanings and sense in intensities that
have no aim outside themselves, 'sterile differences leading nowhere',
'uncompensated losses', 'dissipation of energy' (Lyotard 171). Not only
does Lyotard's acinema broach differences in form and effect between
conventional and experimental moviemaking, it also presents a way of
understanding key economic shifts of the last century: the move from
modern industrial production – characterized by mass labour, useful rationality and conservative, prudent morality – gives way to luxurious, wasteful
consumption and non-productive expenditures of credit cards, advertis-
ing sign-exchanges and service industries (Goux). Consumption means
exhausting, using up, destroying things rather than producing sensibly,
rationally or usefully. Significantly, *Dawn of the Dead* appears at the end of
the 1970s, the period when Reagan's and Thatcher's radical economic and
political reconstructions began.

They're us

Horror cinema, too, articulates pleasure and death – in its form as well as its
effects: on the one hand its reactionary mode – purging the threat, killing
the monsters – serves to restore order and police dominant norms with
a final and narrative closure; on the other, leaving endings open – often
with a sequel in mind – it offers the spectacle of an 'unprecedented assault
on all that bourgeois culture is supposed to cherish – like the ideological
apparatuses of the family and the school' (Modleski 165). Such an assault
can tend in semi-progressive directions, posing unresolved challenges
to social norms, expectations and values (Wood). Narrative, character,

identification and plot are regularly sacrificed in the production of formulaic shocks that attacks the eyes and refuses any secure position for a cinematic gaze interested only in maintaining its mastery and visual pleasure. Horror jumps out of the screen in making audiences jump out of their seats, reason and sense by-passed in bodily sensations and visceral reaction, the machinery of generic expectation plugged directly into nervous systems. Here, in the compulsive repetitions of horror viewing, a kind of scopic death drive emerges: unpleasure is heaped upon unpleasure, often with only limited cathartic release; shocks, sudden twists, disturbing shots and camera angles, play with generic expectations in escalating fashion in order to penetrate a psychic shield hardened by repetition. The curious pleasure – or jouissance – of horror lies in useless expenditure, in 'having the shit scared out of you – and loving it' (Brophy 5). Horror films manifest, so Robin Wood argues, an irrecuperable negativity, a lust for destruction. Movies like *Dawn of the Dead* exemplify a 'cinema of nihilism' (Cook and Bernink 204), a 'cruel cinema' which, like trash TV, inures and desensitizes viewers to violence (even, perhaps, with the war cry of relentless consumption, making them demand 'more'): they are less 'polemics against capitalism' and more its 'artistic derivatives', at best 'sullied jeremiads', at worst signs of its 'callous manipulations', manipulations that 'have brought us to the point of universal ambiguity, destructiveness and despair' (Greenberg 103).

In a TV studio at the start of *Dawn of the Dead*, a commentator speaks of the 'social apocalypse' brought about by the advent of zombies. Another reporter notes 'our responsibility is at an end' as the station prepares for evacuation and goes on automatic. It is, however, an apocalypse without revelation, without a new dawn or any promise of a new responsibility or new freedom. Police crews fail to keep control as they attempt to clear a housing project of zombies and resistant residents. Scenes of mass media failure and social breakdown precede the famous centrepiece – the shopping mall. On arriving at the zombie-filled mall, the small group of survivors surveys the scene of shambling, animated corpses in bemusement as much as fear: 'what are they doing; where are they going?' asks one: their origins obscure, their amblings senseless, their otherness briefly intact. Another replies with a phrase that becomes the film's refrain: 'they're us', just doing what they used to do in an important place in their lives, directed by the residues of memory and instinct. 'They're us': like the zombies window shopping around the mall, the survivors do the same. 'Let's go shopping first', one says, before clearing the mall for themselves. 'They're us': the zombie consumer identification is reinforced by shots of survivors exchanging looks with zombies through shop windows, one group the mirror of another. Visual commentary is interjected with shots of survivors and zombies intercut with shop-window dummies, all mannequins enslaved to the image of consumption. The survivors enjoy more fully all the opportunities of mindless consumption offered in the mall: fine dining, clothes, jewellery, hairdressing salons, frocks and make-up mirror the patterns of postmodern consumption; their hideaway filled with the expensive furnishings, hi-fis and gadgets of a full consumer lifestyle. Such fullness is underwritten by emptiness as they lapse into frustration, bickering, anxiety and dissatisfaction. They're us; we're them. They're zombies too, nagged by a lack of gratification, imploding on themselves. But the very act of identification discloses a difference, minimal though it may be, a recognition that includes an element of counteridentification manifested in that small degree of the self-consciousness ordinary zombies are supposed to be lacking.

This difference, a hint of ironic self-consciousness, is important in both the movie's representations of zombies and their contextualization, that is, in its overt visual statements and equivalences and in the enunciative differences it discloses, that is, at the level at which the film is consumed. When the survivors turn on the automated facilities of the mall and the lights, escalators, announcements, decorative foundations and, as a comic soundtrack, the muzak all start working, the zombies who had previously been gloomy and threatening shadows are rendered figures of fun: their lack of coordination and appropriate reflexes and ungainliness is exaggerated, their inability to negotiate their environment played up as they fall over, fall into fountains and fall off escalators. Buffoons, clowns, lumbering fools, these consumer zombies are thrown by a world of postmodern automation, hapless in the face of the simplest machinery. Later, when a group of bikers invade the mall in a shopping and shooting spree, they treat the zombies as 'comic stooges' (Harper): squirting them with soda siphons and pressing custard pies in their faces in the traditional humour of the circus clown (Harper). Comedy turns horror to laughter. Both modes, however, display forms of unproductive expenditure, expelling uncomfortable otherness and assuaging or abjecting internal anxieties.

They're us. Something unbearable underlies identification and recognition. What are the anxieties that emerge in *Dawn of the Dead's* depictions of its humans and zombies? They're us, but not quite. Straddling circuits of automated pleasure touched by a dull, relentless and dissatisfying sameness, zombies, beyond life-death seek a fullness, a jouissance, in habits they cannot renounce, clinging to an imploding possibility of carnal gratification that is never gratifying enough. Between pleasure and the finality of death, their perambulations continue, a repetition of the same always and never quite turning into a repetition that discloses the otherness of a radically negative difference, always on the point of an ultimate expenditure, a zombie jouissance compelled to repeat ad nauseam. Zombies are aimless,

useless, senseless, destructive; they have 'no positive connotations whatsoever', their negativity associated, in terms of the skill sets of post-industrial
corporate capital, with 'already-exhausted sources of value': they are the
'dead weight' of a labour force of no use to manufacturing in an age
of outsourced production and high staffing costs; lumbering, redundant,
they slow down capital's investments and returns; they are those workers
'consumed and cast aside' by the move towards post-industrial consumer
services, a 'universal residue' (Shaviro 283–286). Humans – like the animal
trophies shot in horror close-up on the farmhouse walls of *Night* and on
the hardware-store walls in *Dawn* – are stuffed monsters. Zombies manifest
the fate of the modern human figure – as Virilio and Serres imagine it:
the socially abjected, the economically outcast, the homeless, workless,
wretched, materially bound casualties of technocapitalist innovations. They
are the 'disenfranchised underclass of the material world ... a projection
of postmodern capitalism's anxiety about *itself*' (Beard 30, emphasis original). Compare Romero's zombies to the fast, sophisticated, adaptable and
sexy cyborg-vampires celebrated in the flight to posthuman virtuality. In
Latham's account of the vampire-cyborg, youth culture comes to the fore
in a different version of the mall:

> Some accounts suggested that video games were producing new forms
> of consciousness in kids, hyperkinetic attunements of perception and
> reflex reminiscent of the preternatural sensory-motor apparatus of
> Anne Rice's vampires ... while others depicted violence-addled teens
> as stupefied as the zombies shambling through George Romero's 1979
> classic film of mall life, *Dawn of the Dead*. (Latham 138)

Prized for its agility, for coping with speed and constant change, for its
independence, freshness and creativity, the promotion of youth simultaneously advocates the vocational skills of the new, networked creative and
cultural economy of impermanent self-employment, flexibility, technological innovation, risk, mobility and enterprise.

Zombies – figures of unproductive expenditure – are precisely those ex-
pended, rendered expendable in the process. They're us. Hence the anxiety.
A repulsion remains in the horror of and laughter at the zombie – an
unbearable recognition and disavowal of ourselves as too slow, lumbering
and inflexible to cope, too corporeal and disconnected to be anything other
than the jetsam of a virtual dematerialization ... or, in horror, in recognition and repulsion of our zombie fate, with a counteridentificatory leap,
spectators can reject and cast aside the zombie, becoming cyborg instead
in a differentiation and re-pulsion that recognizes and effaces the very
obsolescence of the zombie.

Conclusions are irrelevant

Zombies look back – mirrors of the ragged residues of modern humanity; the anxiety and horror they embody, in contrast, evokes a dematerializing forward momentum – very peculiar angels of history. They are curiously gothicized in a relation to science fiction that is less about iconic images of an expansive utopia and more concerned with the imploding biotechnological dystopia of cyberpunk: the wretched humans of *Terminator*'s (1984) future, trampled by merciless machines; the wrecked bodies among the urban ruins of *Blade Runner* (1982) or the expendable crew and meat by-products of *Alien* (1979). Zombies only intensify the dissolution, figures of economic, technological and social obsolescence. Their sell-by date, it seems, should be long passed. Yet, in terms of science-fiction television, zombies, in the shape of *Star Trek*'s Borg, have proved the most popular of all the *Next Generation*'s future villains. Dressed in dark body armour, covered in mechanical whirring enhancements, grey skin and soulless eyes, and moving with that slow, lumbering gait, Borg drones assimilate Frankenstein's monster, undead zombies, robotic aliens and pod people. The anachronism of their appearance is extended by their collective and biotechnological powers: they are the most advanced species in the galaxy, capable of razing entire worlds and fleets, relentless, implacable and irresistible. If not in appearance, in their organization, technical capacities and their corporate ethos, they represent 'an alterity that is genuinely other', simply negating every value upheld by the Federation (Roberts 164–165). Borg is a collective consciousness, a hive mind interacting in subspace communicational networks, with no concept of or consideration for individual identity, social hierarchy or difference. These are, quite simply, 'irrelevant'. As are notions of freedom, self-determination, strength and, even, death. Resistance, too, 'is futile'. All they do is assimilate technological and cultural 'distinctiveness' – the rest is discarded or erased. Unthinkably advanced, their ethos is utterly alien and totally antithetical to the cosy, familial and romanticized humanism of the Federation. So why, as Adam Roberts notes, do they look so 'old-fashioned' with their 'retrograde' styling, their tubes whirring devices and 'the tiny little revolving satellite dishes on the top of their heads'? Roberts suggests that the oddness of their look re-enacts 'the fertile contradiction at the heart of SF, the collision of future and past, of prophetic and nostalgic modes' (163). But the styling of the Borg (associated as they are with cyborg, corporate posthumanism in its most disturbing and alien form) might also look back in order to screen off, with familiarly archaic monsters, that monstrous future rapidly collapsing on the present, diverting attention from the pervasive mobile, interactive and surveillance technologies that already control the networked transnational new world order: we have already been Borged. In this respect, the styling of the Borg operates according to cybergothic principles in which terminators, replicants, wireheads, meaties are 'camouflaged' in familiar science fiction and Gothic forms as vampires, zombies, monsters, but operate according to inhuman, anorganic and machinic protocols, a machinic desire that

> Rips up political cultures, deletes traditions, dissolves subjectivities, and hacks through security apparatuses, tracking a soulless tropism to zero control. This is because what appears to humanity as the history of capitalism is an invasion from the future by an artificial intelligent space that must assemble itself entirely from its enemy's resources. (Land, 'Machinic Desire' 479)

The process is driven by a headless and immanent drive – synthanatos – an artificial death drive (as if the drive were ever natural) which manifests 'the terminal productive outcome of human history as machinic process' (474). What emerges is 'affirmative telecommercial dystopianism', 'voodoo economics', 'v(amp)iro finance', 'lateral webs of haemocommerce' (Land, 'Cybergothic' 80; 86–87). Resistance is futile.

Works cited

28 Days Later. Dir. Danny Boyle. 20th Century Fox, 2002. Film.

Alien. Dir. Ridley Scott. 20th Century Fox, 1979. Film.

Beard, Steve. 'No Particular Place to Go.' *Sight and Sound* 3.4 (1993): 30–31. *Periodicals Archive Online*. Web. 17 October 2010.

Benjamin, Walter. *Illuminations*. Trans. Harry Zohn. London: Fontana, 1973. Print.

'The Best of Both Worlds. Part 1.' *Star Trek: The Next Generation*. Paramount Television. 19 June 1990. Television.

Blade Runner. Dir. Ridley Scott. Warner Bros, 1982. Film.

Brophy, Philip. 'Horrality: The Textuality of Contemporary Horror Films.' *Screen* 27.1 (1986): 2–13. *Oxford Journals*. Web. 17 October 2010.

Carroll, Noel. *The Philosophy of Horror*. New York: Routledge, 1990.

Cook, Pam and Meike Bernink (eds). *The Cinema Book*. London: British Film Institute, 1999.

Dawn of the Dead. Dir. George A. Romero. UFDC, 1978. Film.

Deleuze, Gilles and Felix Guattari. *Anti-Oedipus*. Trans. Robert Hurley, Mark Seem and Helen Lane. Minneapolis: U of Minnesota P, 1983.

Dennett, Daniel. *Consciousness Explained*. Oxford: Oxford UP, 1991.

The Fly. Dir. Kurt Neumann. 20th Century Fox, 1958. Film.

The Fly. Dir. David Cronenberg. Brooksfilms, 1986. Film.

Frankenstein. Dir. James Whale. Universal, 1931. Film.

Freud, Sigmund. 'Beyond the Pleasure Principle.' 1920. *On Metapsychology*. Trans. James Strachey. Harmondsworth: Penguin, 1984. Print.

—. *Civilization and its Discontents*. 1930. *The Standard Edition of the Complete Psychological Works*. Trans. James Strachey. Vol. XXI. London: Hogarth, 1955. 57–145. Print.

Friedberg, Anne. *Window Shopping: Cinema and the Postmodern*. Berkeley: U of California P, 1993. Print.

Goux, Jean-Joseph. 'General Economics and Postmodern Polemics.' *Yale French Studies* 78 (1990): 206–224. Print.

Greenberg, Harvey R. 'Reimagining the Gargoyle: Psychoanalytic Notes on *Alien*.' *Close Encounters*. Ed. Constance Penley et al. Minneapolis: U of Minnesota P, 1991. 83–104.

Gunning, Tom. *The Films of Fritz Lang*. London: BFI, 2000. Print.

Haraway, Donna J. 'A Cyborg Manifesto: Science, Technology, and Socialist-Feminism in the Late Twentieth Century.' 1985. *Simians, Cyborgs, and Women: The Reinvention of Nature*. London: Routledge, 1991. 203–230. Print.

Harper, Stephen. '"They're Us": Representations of Women in George Romero's "Living Dead" Series.' *Intensities: The Journal of Cult Media* 3 (2003). Web.

Hayles, N. Katherine. *How We Became Posthuman: Virtual Bodies in Cybernetics, Literature, and Informatics*. London: U of Chicago P, 1999. Print.

Hoffmann, E. T. A. 'The Sandman.' *The Golden Pot and Other Tales*. Trans. Ritchie Robertson. Oxford: Oxford UP, 1992.

Invasion of the Body Snatchers. Dir. Don Siegel. Wanger Productions, 1956. Film.

Invasion of the Body Snatchers. Dir. Philip Kaufman. Solofilm, 1978. Film.

I Walked with a Zombie. Dir. Jacques Tourneur. RKO, 1943. Film.

King of the Zombies. Dir. Jean Yarbrough. Monogram, 1941. Film.

King, Stephen. 'Why We Crave Horror Movies.' *Longman Reader*. Ed. Judith Nadell, John Langan, and Eliza A. Comodromos. 9th ed. Boston: Longman, 2011. 307–309. Print.

Lacan, Jacques. *The Four Fundamental Concepts of Psychoanalysis*. Trans. Alan Sheridan. London: Penguin, 1977. Print.

Land, Nick. 'Cybergothic.' *Virtual Futures*. Ed. Joan Broadhurst Dixon and Eric J. Cassidy. New York: Routledge, 1998. 79–87. Print.

—. 'Machinic Desire.' *Textual Practice* 7.1 (1993): 471–482. Print.

Land of the Dead. Dir. George A. Romero. Universal, 2005. Film.

Latham, Rob. *Consuming Youth*. Chicago: U of Chicago P, 2002. Print.

Loudermilk, A. 'Eating "Dawn" in the Dark: Zombie Desire and Commodified Identity in George A. Romero's *Dawn of the Dead*.' *Journal of Consumer Culture* 3.1 (2003): 83–103. *Sage Journals Online*. Web. 15 October 2010.

Lyotard, Jean-Francois. 'Acinema.' *The Lyotard Reader*. Ed. Andrew Benjamin. Oxford: Blackwell, 1989: 169–80. Print.

Marx, Karl. *Capital: Critique of Political Economy*. 1867–94. 3 vols. Trans. Ben Fowkes, 1976. David Fernbach 1978, 1981. London: Penguin, 2004–6. Print.

—. *Grundrisse: Foundations of the Critique of Political Economy*. 1953. Trans. Martin Nicolaus. 1973. London: Penguin, 2005. Print.

Metropolis. Dir. Fritz Lang. Parufamet, 1927. Film.

Modleski, Tania. 'The Terror of Pleasure: The Contemporary Horror Film and Postmodern Theory.' *Studies in Entertainment: Critical Approaches to Mass Culture*. Ed. Tania Modleski. Bloomington: Indiana UP, 1986. 155–166. Print.

Night of the Living Dead. Dir. George A. Romero. Continental, 1968. Film.

Pinker, Stephen. *How the Mind Works*. London: Penguin, 1997. Print.

Pontalis, J.-B. 'On Death-Work in Freud, in the Self, in Culture.' Trans. Susan Cohen. *Psychoanalysis, Creativity, and Literature*. Ed. Alan Roland. New York: Columbia UP, 1978. 85–95. Print.

Poster, Mark. '*High-tech Frankenstein*, or Heidegger Meets Stelarc.' *The Cyborg Experiments: The Extensions of the Body in the Media Age*. Ed. Joanna Zylinska. London: Continuum, 2002. 15–32. Print.

Rice, Anne. *Interview with the Vampire*. London: Futura, 1977. Print.

Rider, Shawn. 'The Silenced Majority: Colonization of the Mind and the Flesh Eating Zombie.' Shawn Rider, 1999. N. pag. Web. March 2004.

Roberts, Adam. *Science Fiction*. London: Routledge, 2000. Print.

Serres, M. *Angels: A Modern Myth*. Trans. F. Cowper. Paris: Flammarion, 1993. Print.

Shaun of the Dead. Dir. Edgar Wright. Focus Features, 2004. Film.

Shaviro, Steve. 'Capitalist Monsters.' *Historical Materialism* 10:4 (2002): 281–290. Print.

Sontag, Susan. 'The Imagination of Disaster.' *Film Theory and Criticism*. Ed. Gerald Mast and Marshall Cohen. New York: Oxford UP, 1974. 422–437. Print.

Sterling, Bruce, ed. *Mirrorshades*. London: HarperCollins, 1994. Print.

Stone, Roseanne [Sandy] Allucquere. *The War of Desire and Technology at the Close of the Mechanical Age*. Cambridge, MA: MIT Press, 1995. Print.

Telotte, J. P. *Science Fiction Cinema*. Lexington: U of Kentucky P, 2001. Print.

The Terminator. Dir. James Cameron. Orion, 1984. Film.

Tulloch, John. 'Mimesis or Marginnality? Collective Belief and German Expressionism.' *Conflict and Control in the Cinema*. Ed. John Tulloch. Melbourne: Macmillan, 1977. 37–68. Print.

Virilio, Paul. *The Art of the Motor*. Trans. Julie Rose. Minneapolis: U of Minnesota P, 1995. Print.

White Zombie. Dir. Victor Halperin. Perf. Bela Lugosi. United Artists, 1932. Film.

Williams, Tony. '*White Zombie*: Haitian Horror.' *Jump Cut* 28 (1983): 18–20. Print.

Wood, Robin. *Hollywood from Vietnam to Reagan*. New York: Columbia UP, 1986. Print.

Part II
Biopower and Capital

3. 'Death is Irrelevant': Gothic Science Fiction and the Biopolitics of Empire

Aris Mousoutzanis

It is fairly easy to see why science fiction and the Gothic have been tradition-ally seen as very different genres. The futuristic spaceships, alien creatures and the faith in science and technology that feature among the prominent features of the former would seem to be in stark contrast to the haunted houses, vampires and the belief in the supernatural and the occult of the latter. And yet, it is equally easy to identify instances where the two genres have interacted with each other during important stages of their history, according to a process of convergence that has only accelerated during the last two centuries. Connections can be traced, for instance, in texts as early as Mary Shelley's *Frankenstein* (1818), which has been seen as the first modern science fiction text, even if it was previously approached as a classic Gothic novel often read in conjunction with the first major cycle of Gothic writing – a group of texts ranging roughly from Horace Walpole's *The Castle of Otranto* (1765) to Charles Maturin's *Melmoth the Wanderer* (1820). Furthermore, the same cultural moment witnesses the production of the earliest modern narratives of futuristic fiction, such as the anonymous *Reign of King George VI* (1763) or Sebastien Mercier's *L'An 2440* (1771), which have been seen as 'the beginnings of a vast new literature of anticipation' (Clarke 2) that prepared the ground for the emergence of modern science fiction. Even if we follow those critics who consider science fiction to be a thoroughly modern genre, only to emerge in its recognizable form in the late Victorian period, the early works of H. G. Wells, such as *The Time Machine* (1895), *The Island of Doctor Moreau* (1896) and *The War of the Worlds* (1897) stand as exemplary in this respect. Their themes of time travel, genetic experimentation and alien invasion that have by now become conventional science fiction tropes were intertwined with a focus on the grotesque and the monstrous, as, for example, in the cannibalistic Morlocks, the vampiric Martians and the hybrid animals of Moreau, thus betraying a simultaneous influence of the Gothic tradition. The Gothic was also going through its next major cycle of writing at the time, whose representative texts by writers such as Bram Stoker, Robert Louis Stevenson, H. Rider Haggard and Arthur Machen, amongst others, were distinguished from their predecessors for their increasing reliance on contemporary technoscientific discourses in a way that would become much more typical of what would later crystallize into 'science fiction'. The late twentieth century, finally, is the most recent period to witness the proliferation of popular narratives from fiction, film and television that consciously breach the boundaries of and combine elements from the two genres, such as the popular narratives of the 1990s on which I will be focusing in this discussion, like Chris Carter's *The X-Files*, the *Blade* film trilogy and the *Star Trek* storyline featuring the cybernetic race of the Borg.

The two genres have therefore always found themselves in a dialectic relationship of reciprocal influence, which consists largely in a combination of references to contemporary technoscientific formations and a simultaneous focus on the corporeal, the monstrous and the grotesque. I will be discussing this preoccupation with the encounter between contemporary technoscience and monstrous corporeality by focusing on their shared status as two genres that respond to the formation and entanglement of modern discourses of knowledge and power, and particularly those that participated in the emergence of what Michel Foucault has termed 'biopower'. Foucault discussed the concept of biopower as part of his analysis of the ways in which modern power mutated into more sophisticated formations from the eighteenth century onwards. Unlike the classical age, when sovereign power was exercised through a juridical model relying on the right of the ruler to decide over the life and death of individuals and populations, the period of modernity, for Foucault, witnessed the gradual emergence of an internalized model of power exercised not under the threat of death but in the name of life itself – in Foucault's words, a 'biopower' whose 'highest function' was 'no longer to kill, but to invest life through and through' by way of 'numerous and diverse techniques for achieving the subjugation of bodies and the control of populations' (*History of Sexuality* 138, 140), such as policies to intervene on birth rates, interventions in cases of morbidity and disease that endanger public health and hygiene, measures to coordinate medical care, and mechanisms of insurance on old age and accidents, amongst others. This is a form of power that is 'situated and exercised at the level of life, the species, the race, and the large-scale phenomena of population' (*History of Sexuality* 137) and operates through a network of institutions, mechanisms and practices seeking to monitor, interpret, organize, optimize and control health and life itself.

Foucault's analysis of biopower is relevant to a discussion of Gothic science fiction insofar as the two genres have found themselves at a stage of mutual interaction to a higher degree during periods that witnessed major developments and fluctuations in the trajectory of modern biopower and specifically, I will be arguing, its increasing association with contemporary discourses of imperial sovereignty. This argument applies particularly to two important periods: the late Victorian era and, the main focus of this discussion, the late twentieth century. Critics such as Judith Wilt have already underscored the significance of imperialist discourses for the convergence of the two genres during the *fin de siècle*: the publication of *Dracula* and *War of the Worlds* in December 1897 was a turning point where 'Victorian gothic changed – into Victorian science fiction', a transformation whose 'fairy godfather' was 'Victorian imperialism, that march of mind and militia whose confident momentum concealed anxieties which the literature of the time faithfully, if often obscurely, recorded' (618). In staging the invasion of Britain by creatures whose project has been seen as a 'reverse colonization' (Arata), these narratives articulate anxieties regarding the status and integrity of the British Empire during a cultural moment often described as the 'New Imperialism', whose 'newness' consisted just as much in its more aggressive, competitive nature as in the increasing reliance on contemporary technoscientific formations for the perpetuation of imperial hegemony. The British Empire, in particular, occupied more than a fifth of the globe and a quarter of its people by the end of the nineteenth century and, in a climate of increasing patriotic fervor, imperialism had become 'one of the pivotal facts of the late Victorian and Edwardian years' as 'British society was saturated with nationalist and militarist ideas' (Macdonald 4, 2). The increasing patriotic feeling and jingoist fervor, however, were accompanied by undercurrent anxieties on the prospect of imperial decline, which popular narratives such as the above were articulating in staging 'the return of the repressed', whereby disruptive figures seek to migrate from the peripheries of the Empire to the imperial metropolis in a 'fearful reversal' whereby 'the colonizer finds himself in the position of the colonized, the exploiter is exploited, the victimizer victimized' (Arata 108).

It is important to underline, however, that in these texts colonial otherness is marked by reference to contemporary scientific discourses, such as, for instance, those on the potential degeneration of the human race to a lower species in the chain of evolution, on which narratives by Stoker, Wells and Haggard relied by identifying symptoms of degeneration in their representatives of otherness. Generally, the late Victorian period is marked by a dialectic process of interaction between discourses of scientific knowledge and imperial power: on the one hand, the 'enormous empire', Bruce Hunt has already demonstrated, 'provided one of the principal contexts for Victorian science' (312) in granting access to resources, environments and specimens from diverse remote areas of the globe previously inaccessible. On the other hand, scientific discourses like those of evolution, degeneration, socio-biology and eugenics were appropriated to legitimate and expand imperial hegemony in their identification of symptoms of degeneration in marginalized individuals and communities of different sexualities, classes and 'races' or national identities and their promotion of health and fitness for the imperial body and the perpetuation of the Empire. Under this discursive formation, the human body became a 'medical Dark Continent' that, for Athena Vrettos, 'seemed to offer boundless territory for exploration, a physiological empire to be conquered by the boldest scientific minds' (171). From this perspective, it is hardly surprising that major texts of *fin-de-siècle* Gothic, in their simultaneous preoccupations with colonial otherness and monstrous corporeality, have been allocated to subgenres of both the 'imperial Gothic' (Brantlinger) and the 'somatic Gothic' (Hurley), an aspect of these narratives that further underscores the status of Gothic science fiction as symptomatic of crucial transmutations in contemporary sites of biopolitical production.

This approach seems even more viable when focusing on the next period to witness a major convergence between the two genres, the late twentieth century. The emergence of the genre of 'horror science fiction' in film, probably epitomized by the work of David Cronenberg, its transcoding on television with shows like Chris Carter's *The X-Files*, the movement of cyberpunk in science fiction – and even more its offshoot, 'splatterpunk' – all these are instances of a set of narratives exhibiting a renewed fascination with the body, its (mal)functions, transmutations and boundaries within a cultural landscape permeated by technoscientific discourses and formations. This stage of convergence may, again, be seen as responsive to contemporary biopolitical formations determined by a number of processes and developments in postwar technoscientific discourses: the inauguration and consolidation of information theory and cybernetics from the late 1940s onwards and their discursive dissemination across various diverse disciplines, from biology to psychology and from economics to social science; the emergence of molecular biology after the decoding of the human DNA, as well as ongoing discussions on concerns of the 'new biology' in the 1960s, such as *in vitro* fertilization, abortion, contraception and reproduction rights; relevant technoscientific developments such as cosmetic and prosthetic surgery; and an increasing preoccupation with viral outbreaks and diseases such as the AIDS epidemic.

This biopolitical regime has been seen as the result of a convergence of discourses of knowledge and power integral to emerging formations of imperial sovereignty at, first, the decline of classical imperialism and, later, the alleged 'end of the nation state' at the end of the Cold War and the emergence of discourses of globalization. The text that directly comes to mind is Antonio Negri's and Michael Hardt's *Empire* (2000), in which the authors announced the advent of a new form of sovereignty composed of a network

of national and supranational organizations, media institutions, technological networks and multinational corporations that form a 'decentered and
deterritorializing apparatus of rule that progressively incorporates the entire
global realm within its open, expanding frontiers' (xii). Importantly, Negri
and Hardt persistently underline 'the biopolitical nature of the new paradigm of power' (23). For them, Empire represents 'the paradigmatic form of
biopower', a form of power that 'can achieve an effective command over the
entire life of the population only when it becomes an integral, vital function
that every individual embraces and reactivates of his or her own accord' (24).
Power under the new global order operates through more internalized and
'democratic' mechanisms 'through the brains and bodies of the citizens':

> Power is now exercised through machines that directly organize the
> brains (in communication systems, information networks, etc.) and
> bodies (in welfare systems, monitored activities, etc.) toward a state
> of autonomous alienation from the sense of life and the desire for
> creativity. (23)

Negri and Hardt thus locate the emergence of their new imperial paradigm
precisely at networks of bodies and machines or, in other words, at the
interstices of information and communication technologies and sites of
biopolitical production. 'Hardt and Negri', Jodi Dean confirms, 'understand
the absorption of media and mediation in the productive machine brought
about by communicative capitalism as a merging of the communicative and
the biopolitical' (275).

It is hardly surprising then that Lee Quinby has suggested that Hardt
and Negri's model of global sovereignty seems to be 'much indebted to *Star
Trek*'s apocalyptic concept of the Borg' (251), for '[l]ike the Borg, Empire is
an elaborate network of hybridity that incorporates organic life forms into
its neural web' (251). The *Star Trek* storyline of the Borg, part of the group of
the late-twentieth-century narratives mentioned above, is indeed exemplary
of the ways in which the convergence of the two genres is symptomatic
of shifts in the relations between contemporary imperial and biopolitical
discourses. I discuss further the ways in which that narrative articulated
anxieties related to these shifts, below, after providing the cultural and
generic context within which that storyline may be placed.

Horror science fiction and 'alien pervasion'

One of the most popular media texts that may be seen as part of that group
of Gothic science fiction narratives of the 1990s discussed in this paper is
Chris Carter's *The X-Files*, a show that managed to respond to and feed back

on the contemporary appeal of conspiracy theories and alien abductions, with a combined focus on the monstrous and the grotesque that may be seen as an influence of the 'body horror' film that was increasing in popularity since the 1970s. Linda Badley in particular has seen the body horror of the show to be in line with 'the 1980s postfuturist science fiction film, which has turned away from themes of space exploration and alien invasion' (149) to an increasing preoccupation with the economy of the body. The turning-point for the emergence of these films would be the release of Ridley Scott's *Alien* (1979), a film whose importance lies precisely in its combination of elements from the science fiction film and the horror movie. If the horror film, from the 1970s onwards, was characterized by 'a further hyperbole of the body – a meticulous lingering upon the destruction or transformation of the human body' (Bukatman 265), the 'structuring principle of the science fiction film' was, according to Scott Bukatman, the 'separation of (rational) technology and (slimy) biology' (266). What was radical about *Alien* was its disruption of the boundaries between the biological and the technological in its humanoid machines, like the robot-crewmember Ash, and silicon-based life forms, like the alien itself, which was almost blending with the organic-like environment of the spaceship Nostromo. *Alien* was therefore a text that was staging 'the return of the repressed – the body – to the space of the science fiction film' (Bukatman, 1993, 262). For Bukatman, 'this flood of bodily fluids ... separates *Alien* from the antiseptic and virginal spaces of the science fiction cinema':

> The pronounced, indeed hyperbolic, transition from science fiction to horror actually marks a profound moment in the history of the genre: *Alien* is the film in which the body invades the pristine and sexless rational spaces of the science fiction films. The genre hasn't been the same since. (266–267)

The release of Scott's film, then, together with that of *Halloween* in 1978, signalled both a rebirth of the horror movie and a shift to a more corporeal orientation in science fiction cinema. One distinctive feature of the hybrid genre is what Philip Brophy terms 'horrality' to denote the emphasis on '[t]he act of showing over the act of telling' and 'the photographic image versus the realistic scene' (286, 2). What is distinctive about these films, for Brophy, is that they tend to play 'not so much on the broad fear of Death, but more precisely on the fear of one's own body, of how one controls and relates to it' (8). Cronenberg's films *Scanners* (1981), *Videodrome* (1983), *Dead Ringers* (1988) and *Crash* (1996) are probably the most widely known examples, but even more indicative of this shift are the contemporary remakes of films from the 'Golden Age' of science fiction cinema of the 1950s: Philip Kaufman's 1978 remake of Don Siegel's *Invasion of the Body*

Snatchers (1956), John Carpenter's 1982 remake of Howard Hawks's *The Thing from Another World* (1951) and Cronenberg's 1986 remake of Kurt Neumann's *The Fly* (1958). Unlike the original films, which only hint at any monstrous transformations occurring off screen, the remakes focus on the visualization of hideous bodily mutations on screen through the employment of elaborate special effects.

The importance of corporeality in these popular texts has been seen by Badley as symptomatic of 'a cultural moment in which bio-power is the issue' (151). Technoscientific discourses such as information theory, cybernetics and biogenetics have turned the human body into either a resource or a commodity, thus alienating it from traditional understandings of the 'self' and rendering it as 'alien.' For Badley,

> The emphasis on visualization, mapping and surgical manipulation of the body led to what Foucault would term our modern 'technologies of the body,' a discourse of bio-power, whose terms were bodily fluids, organs, and parts, and identification of the human with the machine. (155)

The X-Files is a narrative produced precisely in these terms, even as numerous episodes feature institutions that have been seen by Foucault as integral to the emergence of modern biopower: psychiatric wards and prisons, leper colonies and refugee camps, fertility and abortion clinics, military bases and biochemistry labs, and so on. From this perspective, one of the distinctive aspects of the show is its engagement with the already-established science fiction motifs of alien invasion and alien abduction, with a simultaneous focus on the theme of 'alien autopsy' which, for Badley, is the obverse of the theme of alien abduction:

> the alien abduction/autopsy scenario provides a metaphor for the way we perceive human and other biology at this particular cultural moment, as a 'rebirth of the clinic.' Ultimately it is a metaphor for the present fragility of the self, which biology, psychology, and cybernetics increasingly pronounce an illusion. (154)

The reference to a 'rebirth of the clinic' is an allusion to Foucault's archaeology of 'the medical gaze', *The Birth of the Clinic* (1973), in which he discusses the ways in which the establishment of clinical medicine from the late eighteenth century onwards brought about 'the constitution, at state level, of a medical consciousness whose constant task would be to provide information, supervision, and constraint' (*Birth of the Clinic* 26). The birth of the clinic alienated the human subject from the body, which was now envisioned as a conceptual inner space to be colonized by medical science. Accordingly, Badley sees the increasing emphasis on corporeality and the persistent restaging of the pathological body under the surveillance of medical technologies in these narratives as a response to advances in technoscientific discourses such as the above, which have brought about a 'rebirth of the clinic'. It is for this reason that these films have moved away from a previous insistence on the theme of alien invasion, to an increasing preoccupation with that of 'alien pervasion', whereby '[b]iological space is pervaded and negotiated through exchanges of genetic data' (Badley 149). Badley is following Vivien Sobchack at this point, who has suggested that under the conditions of a postmodernity,

> the 50s concept of 'invasion' loses much of its meaning and force. The new electronic space we live and figure cannot be invaded. It is open only to 'pervasion' – a condition of kinetic accommodation and dispersal associated with the experience and representations of television, video games, and computer terminals. (229)

What is distinctive about these narratives in relation to their predecessors is their representation of the grotesque and the monstrous as the result of the encounter of the human subject with contemporary technologies. It is for this reason that the figure of the cyborg has a central place in these narratives, as Bukatman seems to confirm when he suggests that what was at stake in these films was 'no longer the fusion of beings and the immortality of the soul, but the fusion of being and electronic technology in a new, hard-wired subjectivity' (244).

One of the most indicative recent examples of such fusion is the *Star Trek* storyline involving the Borg: a cybernetic race in a state of Collective existence. What renders the worst villains of *Star Trek* iconic of the processes discussed above is that the Borg are not only cyborgs, but also vampires; the Borg not only conquer alien races but also 'assimilate' them into their Collective by injecting cybernetic implants in their victims' bodies that turn them into Borg and deprive them of their 'individuality'. As only one of many examples of 'cyber-vampirism' that emerged during the period, the Borg stand as indicative both of the convergence of the Gothic and science fiction and of the contemporary biopolitical discourses to which these hybrid narratives respond.

Cyber-vampirism in the 1990s

One version of the cyber-vampirism that emerged in popular narratives of the 1990s may be found in the *Blade* film trilogy. The first film stages the fight of half-human, half-vampire super-hero Blade against vampire 'sects' who intend to bring about a human Armageddon after summoning the vampire god La Magra, who will empower the vampires to conquer the world, after taking all the power from 'the chosen one' – Blade himself. Blade is a hybrid creature not just because he is half-human, half-vampire, but also because he is 'made into a cyborg', according to John Jordan, 'a creature that seamlessly blends flesh and technology together into an other-worldly being' (9). The hi-tech weapons and accessories that Blade uses are integral to the character: he does not use wooden stakes or silver crosses to destroy vampires, but futuristic weaponry which blends 'so seamlessly into his body armor that it is difficult to discern where the vampire ends and the technology begins', and it is to this extent that he 'is revealed as the vampire cyborg' (Jordan 11). The indebtedness of the film to contemporary technoscientific discourses, however, extends even further, in the representation of Blade's vampirism with recourse to biogenetics: his vampirism is a 'genetic defect', in the words of Blade's associate, Karen Jenson, a chemical change in his DNA because of his exposure to vampire blood before his birth, which made him undergo 'some genetic changes', as his other associate, Abraham Whistler, puts it. The plot of the sequel, *Blade II* (2002), on the other hand, revolves around the efforts of the vampire overlord, Eli Damaskinos, to conduct genetic experiments for the creation of a day-walking, 'pure' vampire race. The 'purity' of the blood of the trilogy's own version of Dracula, Drake, is also seen as the source of his tremendous power in the third film, *Blade: Trinity* (2004). The importance in this plot of the project of the 'vampire final solution', which involves 'blood-farming' facilities where humans are kept in a coma as live bloody resources, only underscores further the impact of contemporary biopolitical discourses, like biogenetics and cybernetics, on the production of Gothic science fiction narratives in the 1990s, and renders the 'cyber-vampire' as a figure literally embodying these discursive convergences and interactions.

The 'cyborg' has by now turned not only as one of the most recognizable science fiction figures but also as an icon epitomizing human subjectivity within a technologically saturated postmodernity. First theorized in a paper by Manfred Clynes and Nathan S. Kline on the use of 'self-regulating man-machine systems' in space exploration (30), the half-human, half-machine hybrid creature received increasing critical attention in the humanities after the publication of 'A Manifesto for Cyborgs' by Donna Haraway in 1984. Haraway saw the cyborg both as a metaphor for the increasing dependence on contemporary technologies in Western industrialist societies and as a subversive icon whose hybrid status destabilized a series of binary opposi-tions that have historically served as a basis for repression and exploitation, such as 'human'/'animal,' 'human'/'machine,' and 'male'/'female'. 'Cyborg imagery', for Haraway, could suggest 'a way out of the maze of dualisms in which we have explained our bodies and our tools to ourselves' (181).

Critics have accordingly followed Haraway's approach in their discussion of fictional cyborgs, such as the Borg, like Katrina Boyd, who has suggested that the Borg, 'with their interchangeable parts and interlocking circuits, counter the image of the holistic self possessed of a consistent identity' (107). However, *Star Trek*'s representation of cyborg subjectivity has evolved in a way that does not fulfil the 'subversive' identity politics envisioned by Haraway. Boyd has demonstrated how the transformations that the Borg undergo during their various appearances in different episodes 'reveal the difficulty of representing radical difference' (96): their initial lack of sex gave way to a gendering of the race, their representation as a decentred network of bodies and machines was replaced by the central positioning of a Borg Queen, whereas they were also shown as having children growing in 'maturation chambers', according to a gradual process of 'humanization' that the race underwent through its different appearances over the years. In fact, the representation of the race rather demonstrates an indebtedness to Foucault's analysis of biopower, one of whose major mechanisms 'centered on the body as a machine: its disciplining, the optimization of its capabilities, the extortion of its forces, the parallel increase of its usefulness and its docility' and 'its integration into systems of efficient and economic controls' (Foucault, *History of Sexuality* 138) – the belief in 'perfection' and 'efficiency' that drives the cybernetic race is only one proof of the validity of such a reading.

However, Boyd's description of the Borg as 'a postmodern version of radical difference' (95) seems to miss the fact that, during its engagement with this storyline, *Star Trek* persistently blurs the boundaries between the Federation and the Borg, self and other. What the Borg do is not that 'radically different' from what the Federation does: both of them assimilate other races within their structures through political and military practices that are 'inverse reflections of one another' (Russell and Wolski). As Lynette Russell and Nathan Wolski have underlined:

> An intrinsic part of the assimilation process is the adoption of a false consciousness by the one who is to be assimilated. Within Starfleet, many races come together and work as part of the Federation. Although cultural difference is accepted for the most part, it is subverted to allow the dominant human culture to prevail. In order to exist within the Federation, alien cultures must be assimilated.

The *Star Trek: Next Generation* episode to feature the first major confrontation with the Borg, 'The Best of Both Worlds', is only one instance that reveals this peculiar relationship between the Borg and the Federation: Jean-Luc Picard is 'assimilated' and transformed into 'Locutus of Borg', who serves as a mouthpiece for the cybernetic race. As Locutus, the expressions that he uses are very similar to the kind of language that Picard uses when he encounters new civilizations: expressions such as 'We mean you no harm' or 'We only wish to raise the quality of life for all species' are only 'harsh parody of white assimilationist and colonialist practices' (Wilcox 79). Later episodes underline the uncanny relationship between the two political structures even further. In a *Star Trek: Deep Space Nine* episode titled 'For the Cause', when former Starfleet officer Ettington joins the renegade group of the Maquis, he challenges Captain Sisko: 'In some ways you're even worse than the Borg. At least they tell you about their plans for assimilation. You assimilate people and they don't even know it.' However, it was *Voyager* that most persistently blurred the distinction between the Borg and the Federation. In 'Scorpion', while considering an alliance with the Borg – who, Captain Janeway comments, 'are no different to us – they are just trying to survive' – the crew discover a human female 'drone', designated Seven of Nine, who was assimilated at a very young age. By the end of the story, Janeway and her crew have managed to rescue the drone from the Collective, with the intention of restoring her individuality. Having grown up as a Borg, Seven initially resists Janeway's attempts and when Janeway refuses to give her the choice to return to the Borg, Seven responds: 'You are no different than the Borg.'

This uncanny echo between totalitarian and Western imperial rhetoric demands that we move beyond existing interpretations of the politics of the cybernetic race that rely on earlier twentieth-century political realities. Taylor Harrison, for instance, has read the Borg as a metaphor for Nazism, as they are seen as 'pure totalitarian power incarnate' who inflict 'diaspora, destruction, death' (247), whereas Boyd has associated the Borg with 'a 1950s nightmare of communism as envisioned in the original *Invasion of the Body Snatchers* (1956)' (107). A reading that particularly relies on Cold War dialectics does not seem satisfactory in itself, not only because it is in conflict with the constant uncanny conflation of self and other discussed above, but also because the first appearance of the Borg, in the episode 'Q Who?', was in August of 1989, and the first major battle, in 'The Best of Both Worlds', in June 1990, that is, after the collapse of Communism. Instead, Russell and Wolski's discussion of the Borg as 'a "post-colonial" mirror held up to reflect the nature of colonization and assimilation' invites a reading of the uncanny relation of the two political structures that paves the way for a discussion of the cybernetic race in terms of the theory of global sovereignty formulated by Hardt and Negri. From such a perspective, the Federation and the Borg emerge as different structures of imperial control. The Federation, on the one hand, is a hegemonic political structure alluding to classical nineteenth-century modes of imperialism which manages to maintain its political power through an adherence on hierarchy and rank. Generally speaking, the utopian future of *Star Trek* is based on a 'nineteenth-century faith in progress, human perfectability, and expanding frontiers' (Boyd 151). Alluding to the phrases used to describe the show in its earliest beginnings in the late 1960s, such as 'wagon train to the stars' or 'Hornblower in space', Michèle and Duncan Barrett point out that '[m]aritime exploration and the technological superiority of the ships in which modern western powers "discovered" and colonized "new worlds" are themes played on and replayed in *Star Trek*'s imagination of space' (viii). The persistent use of technical terminology in dialogue relies on a lexicon that is 'specifically drawn from the age of exploration and conflict by sailing ship' (13). Federation hegemony rests on traditional attitudes towards technology, then, on a view of technology as 'not as important in itself', in Gene Roddenberry's own words, 'but as a tool with which we humans can better reach for our dreams' (v). The Borg, on the other hand, represent a form of imperial power where the relations between technology and empire are of a different balance. In 'Q Who?' the omnipotent creature Q explains to Picard that the Borg are 'not interested in political conquest, wealth or power as you know it. They're simply interested in your ship, its technology. They've identified it as something they can consume.' From their very first appearance in *Star Trek*, then, the primacy of technological hegemony over traditional politics is underscored for this race which does not negotiate but assimilates. In contrast to the Federation, imperial expansion and hegemony does not rest on hierarchical structures but on networks of bodies and technologies. The Borg enact a form of colonization that relies almost exclusively on biopolitical discourses, because 'the Borg colonize from within, by injecting microscopic nanoprobes into the body of their prey' (Russell and Wolski). Theirs is a form of power that emerges at the interstices of the technological and the biopolitical, in a manner that alludes to models of global sovereignty such as the one by Hardt and Negri, who have described life under the rule of Empire as 'a great hive in which the queen bee continuously oversees production and reproduction' (32).

The conservative politics of *Star Trek* may account for its 'othering' of a race emblematic of processes integral to novel forms of imperial power. It is quite indicative, for instance, that the Borg Queen may be read as an embodiment of what Barbara Creed has described as 'the monstrous feminine' to refer to representations of pre-Oedipal archetypes of 'archaic' motherhood which, in patriarchal discourses, are constructed as monstrous and evil. One important aspect of the monstrous feminine for Creed is its 'merging together of all aspects of the maternal figure into one – the horrifying image of woman as archaic mother, phallic woman and castrated body represented as a single figure' (135). In patriarchal narratives, the complexity of the figure is reduced to the more recognizable image of the pre-Oedipal phallic mother, who is rendered monstrous in her desire to have the phallus. A reading of the Borg Queen as the monstrous feminine is illustrated by the opening scene of a *Voyager* episode called 'Unimatrix, Zero One'. In her search of a group of resister 'drones' who struggle to regain their individuality, the Queen has one of them captured, interrogated and finally mutilated and salvaged of his 'functional components' for other drones. The significance of the imagery of mutilation and castration for representations of monstrous motherhood, however, becomes more obvious when focusing on the ways in which the 'patriarchal signifying practices' that reproduce these representations are embedded in contemporary biopolitical discourses that inevitably inform their method of signification, such as, in the case of the Queen, her appropriation of cybernetics. In the case of *Star Trek*, the monstrous representation of the Borg Queen is part of the show's general attempt to demonize and defeat the political structures of which she is the major representative. From this perspective, the fact that the Queen acquires a prominent role in a show like *Voyager* seems in line with this argument. Primarily a narrative of 'homecoming', the major narrative drive of that show is precisely the 'erasure' of the unhomely – in Homi Bhabha's terms, 'the paradigmatic colonial and post-colonial condition' (9) – that *Voyager* engages with in terms of a conflict between a monstrous Borg matriarchy and a conservative matriarchy represented by Captain Janeway in her struggles to bring her crew back to the patriarchal 'home' of the Federation. The Queen's destruction, in the finale of *Voyager*, 'Endgame', further encourages such a reading: the Queen and the Borg network are destroyed at the same time as the Federation starship finally reaches home, the child of two crew members, B'Ellana Torres and Tom Paris, is born, and Seven has her final cybernetic implants removed in order to live with Commander Chakotay. In a gradual process of transition from cyborg monstrosity to patriarchal subjectivity, the show therefore posits the 'family' as an antidote to the monstrous matriarchy of the Borg. The closure of *Voyager* thus enacts a conservative attempt to erase the 'unhomeliness' of the postcolonial days of global Empire, in a nostalgic gesture towards more traditional patriarchal political structures.

The narratives chosen are far from exhaustive, let alone isolated, instances of contemporary narratives that stand at the interstices of the Gothic and science fiction. The discussion could have been extended to discuss the ways in which the entanglement of technoscientific, imperial and biopolitical discourses affect the narratives of cyberpunk novelists such as William Gibson, contemporary feminist science fiction writers of the time such as Octavia Butler, the work of David Cronenberg, or even the ways in which these themes, issues and preoccupations have been transcoded in more recent films such as the *X-Men* trilogy, and TV shows such as *Heroes*, *The 4400* and *Fringe*. The fact that contemporary popular texts that may qualify as

'Gothic science fiction' still demonstrate a fascination and concern with the themes and processes discussed in this paper only underscores the extent to which this subgenre is responsive to shifting processes and relations of contemporary formations of knowledge and power.

Works cited

Alien. Dir. Ridley Scott. 20th Century Fox, 1979. Film

Anonymous. *The Reign of King George VI. 1900–1925; A Forecast Written in 1763*. London: W. Niccoll, 1763. Print.

Arata, Stephen. *Fictions of Loss in the Victorian Fin de Siècle*. Cambridge: Cambridge UP, 1996. Print.

Badley, Linda. 'The Rebirth of the Clinic: The Body as Alien in *The X-File*', *Deny All Knowledge: Reading The X-Files*. Eds. D. Lavery, A. Hague and Maria Cartwright. London: Faber and Faber, 1996. 148–167. Print.

Barrett, Michèle and Duncan Barrett. *Star Trek: The Human Frontier*. Cambridge: Polity, 2001. Print.

Bhabha, Homi K. *The Location of Culture*. London: Routledge, 1994. Print.

Blade. Dir. Stephen Norrington. Marvel Enterprises, 1998. Film.

Blade II. Dir. Guillermo del Toro. Marvel Enterprises. 2002. Film.

Blade: Trinity. Dir. David. S. Goyer. Marvel Enterprises. 2004. Film.

Boyd, Katrina G. 'Cyborgs in Utopia: The Problem of Radical Difference in *Star Trek: The Next Generation*.' *Enterprise Zones: Critical Positions on Star Trek*. Eds. T. Harrison, S. Projansky, K. A. Ono and E. R. Helford. Oxford: Westview Press, 1996. 95–113. Print.

Brantlinger, Patrick. *Rule of Darkness: British Literature and Imperialism, 1830–1914*. London: Cornell UP, 1998. Print.

Brophy, Philip. 'Horrality – the Textuality of Contemporary Horror Films', *Screen* 27.1 (1986): 2–13. Print.

Bukatman, Scott. *Terminal Identity: The Virtual Subject in Postmodern Science Fiction*. Durham: Duke UP, 1993. Print.

Clarke, I. F. *The Pattern of Expectation 1644–2001*. London: Jonathan Cape, 1979. Print.

Clynes, Manfred and Nathan S. Kline. 'Cyborgs and Space', 1960. *The Cyborg Handbook*. Eds. C. H. Gray, H. J. Figuera-Sarriera and S. Mentor. London: Routledge, 1990. 29–33. Print.

Crash. Dir. David Cronenberg. Alliance Communications Corporation, 1996. Film.

Creed, Barbara. '*Alien* and the Monstrous-Feminine.' *Alien Zone: Cultural Theory and Contemporary Science Fiction Cinema*. Ed. A. Kuhn. London: Verso, 1990. 128–141. Print.

Dead Ringers. Dir. David Cronenberg. Téléfilm Canada, 1988. Film.

Dean, Jodi. 'The Networked Empire: Communicative Capitalism and the Hope for Politics', *Empire's New Clothes: Reading Hardt and Negri*. Eds. P. A. Passavant and J. Dean. New York: Routledge, 2004. 265–288. Print.

'Endgame', *Star Trek: Voyager*. Paramount. 23 May 2001. Television.

'For the Cause', *Star Trek: Deep Space Nine*. Paramount. 8 May 1996. Television.

Foucault, Michel. *The Birth of the Clinic*. Trans. A. M. Sheridan Smith. London: Tavistock, 1973. Print.

—. *The History of Sexuality: Volume I: An Introduction*. Trans. R. Hurley. Harmondsworth: Penguin, 1978. Print.

Halloween. Dir. John Carpenter. Compass International Pictures, 1978.

Haraway, Donna J. 'A Cyborg Manifesto: Science, Technology, and Socialist-Feminism in the Late Twentieth Century.' *Simians, Cyborgs, and Women: The Reinvention of Nature*. London: Free Association, 1991. 149–181. Print.

Hardt, M. and A. Negri, A. *Empire*. London: Harvard UP, 2000. Print.

Harrison, Taylor. 'Weaving the Cyborg Shroud: Mourning and Deferral in *Star Trek*: The Next Generation.' *Enterprise Zones: Critical Positions on Star Trek*. Eds. T. Harrison, S. Projansky, K. A. Ono and E. R. Helford. Oxford: Westview Press, 1996. 245–257. Print.

Hunt, Bruce J. 'Doing Science in a Global Empire: Cable Telegraphy and Electrical Physics in Victorian Britain.' *Victorian Science in Context*. Ed. B. Lightman. Chicago: U of Chicago P, 1997. 312–333. Print.

Hurley, Kelly. *The Gothic Body: Sexuality, Materialism, and Degeneration at the Fin de Siècle*. Cambridge: Cambridge UP, 1996. Print.

Invasion of the Body Snatchers. Dir. Don Siegel. Wanger Productions, 1956. Film.

Invasion of the Body Snatchers. Dir. Philip Kaufman. Solofilm, 1978. Film.

Jordan, John J. 'Vampire Cyborgs and Scientific Imperialism: A Reading of the Science–Mysticism Polemic in *Blade*.' *Journal of Popular Film and Television* 27.2 (1999): 4–15. Print.

MacDonald, R. H. *The Language of Empire: Myths and Metaphors of Popular Imperialism, 1880–1918*. Manchester: Manchester UP, 1994. Print.

Maturin, C. R. *Melmoth the Wanderer*. 1820. Ed. Victor Sage. London: Penguin, 2010. Print.

Mercier, Sebastien. *L'An 2440*. 1771. Geneva: Slatkine Reprints, 1979. Print.

'Q Who?', *Star Trek: The Next Generation*. Paramount, 10 May 1989. Television.

Quinby, Lee. 'Taking the Millennialist Pulse of Empire's Multitude: A Genealogical Feminist Diagnosis.' *Empire's New Clothes: Reading Hardt and Negri*. Eds. P. A. Passavant and J. Dean. New York: Routledge, 2004. 221–251. Print.

Roddenbery, Gene. Introduction to *Star Trek: The Next Generation Technical Manual*, by Rick Sternback and Micahel Okuda. New York: Pocket, 1991. Print.

Russell, Lynette and Nathan Wolski. 'Beyond the Final Frontier: *Star Trek*, the Borg, and the Post-Colonial.' *Intensities: The Journal of Cult Media* 1 (2001): n. pag. Web. 1 August 2010.

Scanners. Dir. David Cronenberg. Canadian Film Development Corporation, 1981. Film.

'Scorpion', *Star Trek: Voyager*. Paramount, 21 May 1997. Television

'Scorpion, Part II', *Star Trek: Voyager*. Paramount, 3 September 1997. Television.

Shelley, Mary. *Frankenstein*. 1818. New York and London: W. W. Norton & Co, 1996. Print.

Sobchack, Vivien. *Screening Space: The American Science Fiction Film*. 2nd ed. New York: Ungar, 1993. Print.

Stoker, Bram. *Dracula*. 1897. London: Penguin, 1993. Print.

'The Best of Both Worlds', *Star Trek: The Next Generation*. Paramount. 20 June 1990. Television.

'The Best of Both Worlds, Part II', *Star Trek: The Next Generation*. Paramount, 26 September 1990. Television.

The Fly. Dir. Kurt Neumann. 20th Century Fox, 1958. Film.

The Fly. Dir. David Cronenberg. Brooksfilms, 1986. Film.

The Thing from Another World. Dirs. Christian Nyby and Howard Hawks. Winchester Pictures Corporation, 1951. Film.

The Thing. Dir. John Carpenter. Universal Picturs, 1982. Film.

'Unimatrix, Zero One', *Star Trek: Voyager*. Paramount, 4 October 2000. Television.

Videodrome. Dir. David Cronenberg. Canadian Film Development Corporation, 1983. Film.

Vrettos, Athena. *Somatic Fictions: Imagining Illness in Victorian Culture*. Stanford: Stanford UP, 1995. Print.

Walpole, Horace. *The Castle of Otranto*. 1765. London: Penguin. 2010.

Wells, H. G. *The Island of Doctor Moreau*. 1896. London: Penguin, 2007.

—. *The Time Machine*. 1895. London: Penguin, 2007.

—. *The War of the Worlds*. 1897. Harlow: Pearson, 2005.

Wilcox, R. V. 'Dating Data: Miscegenation in *Star Trek*: The Next Generation.' *Enterprise Zones: Critical Positions on Star Trek*. Eds. T. Harrison, S. Projansky, K. A. Ono and E. R. Helford. Oxford: Westview Press, 1996. 69–92. Print.

Wilt, Judith. 'The Imperial Mouth: Imperialism, the Gothic and Science Fiction.' *Journal of Popular Culture* 14.4 (1981): 618–628. Print.

The X-Files. Fox. 1993–2001. Television.

4. 'A Butcher's Shop where the Meat Still Moved': Gothic Doubles, Organ Harvesting and Human Cloning

Sara Wasson

Doubles are a long-standing motif in Gothic, and literary criticism has traditionally interpreted doubling as symbolic of a self divided. Persuasive though these readings are, seeing the double as an echo of an original's psyche can elide the potential social impact of the trope. Recent science fiction of human cloning featuring clones used for organ harvesting challenges us to re-imagine the traditional Gothic trope of the double. Rather than reading these clone-doubles as mirrors of an original self, I ask what human interactions are evoked by such doubling, and ultimately I suggest that the doubling in these particular science fictions can be read as a scathing critique of a conceptual binary at the heart of contemporary organ transplant practice. Greg Egan's short story 'The Extra' (1990), Michael Marshall Smith's novel *Spares* (1996) and Kazuo Ishiguro's novel *Never Let Me Go* (2005) all depict clones bred for organs. The monstrous body glimpsed through these texts is the body of the organ *recipient*, a body monstrous in its artificially enhanced ability to assimilate the tissue of others. In these texts, originals devour their doubles. Such bodies are not fictional: innovations in immunosuppressant drugs over the last two decades have made them a reality.

This work is a contribution to the emerging field of medical humanities, a field sited on the cusp between medical science and the humanities. I note elsewhere that literary criticism brings alertness to narrative structure to such explorations, most notably in the way that scientific discourse itself decrees narratives for patients (e.g. Wasson, 'Olalla's Legacy'). Scholars of the Gothic have valuable contributions to make to the field of medical humanities in a range of ways, but, I suggest, particularly in our alertness to the ways that language can enact abjection.

Doubles and the Gothic

Doppelgängern are long-standing figures of classic Gothic texts, and hitherto much literary criticism has tended to read doubling as symbolic of a divided self. Such analysis can be underpinned by a range of critical theory, but is particularly characteristic of psychoanalytically inflected literary criticism in which a double can be read as embodying repressed desires not admitted to the daylight of consciousness, or as demonstrating a mind fracturing under modernity's pressures (Botting 11–12, 111; Gilbert and Gubar; Dryden). As Avril Horner and Sue Zlosnik note, doubling is one of the most Gothic of tropes, 'in which we are invited to read [a novel's] protagonists as aspects of each other, a strategy of doubling which emphasises the instability of the boundaries of the self' (84). Either way, such approaches read the double through the lens of a single self – a tormented, Romantic self. One of the earliest exercises in psychoanalytic literary criticism was Otto Rank's *The Double* (1914), which argues that the literary double symbolizes a narcissistic longing to escape death, to preserve a self intact. Sigmund Freud agrees, noting that 'the "double" was originally an insurance against the destruction of the ego, an "energetic denial of the power of death," as Rank says; and probably the "immortal" soul was the first "double" of the body' (356). Freud and Rank suggest that a double can be a defence mechanism to bolster a sense of self. At the same time, however, the otherness of the double is inevitably testament to a fracture within that cherished self. Bronfen captures the paradox of the narcissistic double:

> The double is an ambivalent figure of death since it signifies an insurance that one will continue to live, that the soul is eternal even as the body decomposes and as such signifies a defense against death. The composition of representation serves as a triumph over and against material decomposition in the real or system of the real. However, the double is by definition also a figure for a split or gap, a figure signifying that something that was whole and unique has been split into more than one part (114).

In other words, while a double might enable the fantasy of immortality for the self, that fantasy is simultaneously undermined by the very fact of a split between the self and its double. Either way, however, these approaches approach the double as a version of the self, explaining the double through an original's internal psychic drama.

The clone doubles I will discuss in this article make the theories of double-as-immortality-bringer literal, for the very *raison d'être* of these hapless duplicates is to let their originals cheat death. In each of the three texts discussed, the clones are created in order that the originals can raid the clones' organs and tissues when their own wear out on account of dissipated living, illness or age. As such, these texts tempt us to neatly reapply the established literary critical analysis mentioned above: to read the 'doubles' of these clone texts as representing repressed or divided aspects of an original self. Instead, I argue something quite different: that these texts invite us to activate another, slightly more slender body of criticism, that which sees doubles as commenting on the dynamics of class exploitation (e.g. McClintock 95–97). These science fiction texts demand that we read the doubles *not* as dramatizing a single mind's internal drama, but rather as dramatizing exploitative social processes – specifically, the horror of the black market trade in human tissue. No mere futuristic speculative fantasy, this trade is already very real and benefits thousands of people, particularly in the West, at the expense of those poorer than they. The way this trade is structured is highly problematic, and these texts in the Gothic mode argu-ably dramatize the emotional manoeuvres that underpin such exploitation. In addition, this approach to doubling gives an opportunity to re-examine the political potential of the Gothic.

'Bloody harvest': trade in human tissue

Science fiction and other speculative genres have long engaged with the idea of organ harvesting, such as the organ banks of Larry Niven's *The Patchwork Girl* (1980), in which criminals are raided for organs, the 'slaughterhouse' of *Blake's 7* season 2 and 3 in which people are paralysed and then dissected for spare parts (1978–80) and of the *Star Trek: Voyager* episode in 1995 which features a species who trawl the galaxy, ripping tissue from other species and grafting it to their own continually deteriorat-ing bodies ('Phage'). Today, organ harvesting is increasingly topical, with mainstream media increasingly exposing organ harvesting issues. Most of the scandals that preoccupy media in the UK and USA involve body snatchers desecrating corpses for long bones, corneas and other tissue ('US Undertakers Admit Corpse Scam'; Pilkington), and China's highly controversial post-execution organ harvesting has received particular at-tention (e.g. Kilgour and Matas). Similarly, fictional representations of organ harvesting abound, with a surge in fictions and films grappling with the issue, such as the horror musical *Repo! The Genetic Opera* (2008) and CSI episodes in 2004 and 2009 ('Harvest'; 'CSI: Trilogy'). Even young adult fiction grapples with the notion, such as Neal Shusterman's chilling *Unwind* (2007), which describes teenagers being disassembled for parts. Science fiction about organ harvesting does not always involve human clones, but what is particularly fascinating about fiction that combines cloning and organ harvesting is the way it highlights the horror of the cost and the irrefutable humanity of the tissue donor.

The current market for organ harvesting has been called a 'form of late modern cannibalism' (Scheper-Hughes, 'Bodies for Sale' 1). Several villages in India have been nicknamed 'kidney village' by virtue of the proportion of inhabitants who have submitted to nephrectomies (Warren), and China's extensive government-regulated organ trade has been called a 'holocaust', in which dissidents and minorities are highly vulnerable (Milne; Kilgour and Matas). Over 15,000 kidneys are trafficked illegally per annum globally (Organ Watch par. 5), and numerous sources document black market trade in human tissue (Allison; Bowcott; Handwerk; Hughes; Milne; Parry; Roy).

The Bellagio Task Force created by the United Nations identified that the most impoverished people in a society are by far the dominant sellers of organs, most notoriously in India but also in Western countries. It noted: 'In all, inequities in political power and social well-being remain so profound that the voluntary character of the sale of an organ remains in doubt' (Rothman et al. 2742). Scheper-Hughes notes that the most common explanation given by kidney sellers worldwide is the desire to feed the family ('Bodies for Sale' 1). In the illegal markets, donors are often medically neglected after the tissue removal, and many suffer ill-health and even death. But even in legal tissue transfer, such as paid transfer in Iran or unpaid transfer in Britain and America, all evidence demonstrates that 'donor' and recipient often inhabit a colonizing binary, human tissue flowing from East to West, from poor to the wealthy, from female to male, from children to parents and from marginalized to powerful.[1]

This vast market has been made possible by progress in immuno-suppression biotechnology. Until recently, tissue transplantation was fraught with peril for the recipient and almost all attempts were doomed to fail. Tsuyoshi Awaya points out that human tissue transfer is not new: teeth, hair and bones have been transferred since ancient times (par. 2). What is new, however, is transfer of tissue of ontological significance, i.e. tissue necessary for existence (Waldby and Mitchell 84–85). In such tissue transfer, the human body's immune system actively seeks out and attacks the foreign tissue. Immunologically speaking, identity literally inheres within every cell, in that each cell's surface contains macromolecules that allow the body's immune system to recognize the tissue as belonging to the body. If the signature macromolecules are different, the immune system will destroy the tissue, causing the recipient's death through both organ failure and necrosis (Waldby 248). As a consequence, tissue transfer initially relied on tissue matching, in the hope that the transplanted tissue would be less likely to provoke fatal immunological response. Such matching required connecting the tissue of two very particular individuals, and as such generated detailed data about both 'donor' and recipient.

The advent of immunosuppressant drugs like cyclosporine revolutionized the way that recipient relates to harvestee. Immunosuppressants disable the body's recognition system so that alien tissue is not attacked. As Lawrence Cohen notes, this meant the industry of human tissue exchange 'could shift from an unwieldy biopolitics of recognition, mobilizing large populations and searching for identifiable tissue matches within it, to a more pragmatic biopolitics of suppression, disabling the recognition apparatus' so that willingness to sell becomes 'the criterion of the match' (11). The disturbing consequence is that the donor is now often nameless and effaced in medical discourse, while the transplant recipient is extensively documented and cherished. Extending the cannibal metaphor, Scheper-Hughes argues, 'Global capitalism and advanced biotechnology have released new medically-incited "tastes" (a New Age gourmet cannibalism, perhaps) for human bodies, living and dead, for the skin and bones, flesh and blood, tissue, marrow and genetic material of "the other"' ('Commodity Fetishism' 54). With regard to media coverage of the 9/11 deaths, Judith Butler has offered the concept of 'ungrievable lives', lives a particular society does not recognize as fully human:

> Violence against those who are already not quite living, that is, living in a state of suspension between life and death, leaves a mark that is no mark. There will be no public act of grieving [for such dead] … If there is a 'discourse,' it is a silent and melancholic one in which there have been no lives, and no losses; there has been no common bodily condition, no vulnerability that serves as the basis for an apprehension of our commonality. (36)

This concept is also helpful in the context of organ transfer. We can say that the organ market constructs tissue-givers as similarly ungrievable, as abject non-persons. When a life is not recognized as human, then its death or impoverishment leaves a mark that is no mark.

The term 'donor' is dominant in discussions of legal and illegal organ transfer, but this deceptive noun implies full agency. I will opt instead for the candour of 'harvestee', which makes the agency of the action clearer. (The ethics of unpaid organ donation are more complex, but as I will later show, even these are not straightforward.) One (black market) organs broker describes his practice in benevolent terms: 'Don't think of me as an outlaw … Think of me as a new version of the old-fashioned marriage broker. I locate and match up people in need, people whose suffering can be alleviated by the other' (Scheper-Hughes, 'Commodity Fetishism' 42). The metaphor is disingenuous, obscuring the unequal power balance in the exchange and the suffering of the harvestee (Davis 52).

Scheper-Hughes' horrifying metaphor of scientific advancement facilitating human cannibalism is a dramatic example of the dread that technology can accrete in science fiction (Luckhurst, *Science Fiction* 5). However, the literary texts I will discuss are chilling not because of any inherent menace in the technology. Rather, the horror in these fictions derives from the rapacious flesh of the recipient, engineered to devour. Locating the horror *there*, in the body of the receiver, draws the eye to the human interaction itself in a way which requires us to question the ethics of the act. The technology is disturbing in that it is allied with the violence to bodies done by capitalist systems. These science fiction texts depicting circulations of human flesh illuminate some of the darkest circulations of capital. I suggest that these literary texts depict imaginative processes equivalent to cyclosporine for the mind (Joralemon 336), showing how a society can empty a 'donor' of human identity and degrade them into waste so that the raid of their organs causes no emotional rejection on the part of the receiver. In these novels and in the twentieth-century globalized tissue marketplace, relabelling human tissue as 'waste' is a necessary legal step before the tissue can enter legal channels of exchange. I read these science fiction texts not as allegories of surgical suffering but rather as nightmarish representations of a social reality, a reality in which we minimize ethical qualms over tissue trade by constructing the 'donor' as ripe for harvest.

Rendering the harvestee abject

Copies are often assumed to be deficient by comparison with originals. This idea of the wounded copy recalls Walter Benjamin's 'Work of Art in the Age of Mechanical Reproduction', which maintained that technological duplication deprives a work of the unique and precious 'aura' of the original (215). The negative valence of 'copy' is reflected in copious early cloning science fiction, where clones are depicted as maimed copies. The clones of Aldous Huxley's 1932 novel *Brave New World*, for example, tend to inspire revulsion. Mass produced and deliberately brain damaged, the cloned classes are violently shaped by pre- and post-natal manipulation to be obedient, sub-human slaves. Their mass-produced origin – in which embryos are literally carried on conveyer belts through a factory for nine months – makes them seem less human, more like manufactured products. Although the embryos of all classes are manufactured this way, only the lower caste of embryos are cloned. Their relentless sameness is just one of a constellation of lacks that makes them objects of repulsion for one character, who is haunted by 'the nightmare of swarming indistinguishable sameness ... like maggots they had swarmed' (165). By metonymic association, their cloned status acquires connotations of mental retardation. Similarly, in Kate Wilhelm's story 'When Late the Sweet Birds Sang', a character opines that the clones 'all had something missing, a dead area' (246). For several decades, this maimed quality of the clone was often associated with threat. These representations of clones inspire revulsion and fear, with part of the dread stemming from an intuition that they are damaged in ways which might make them dangerous (Wasson, 'Love in the Time of Cloning'). Recent cloning fiction, however, recuperates the trope of the damaged copy into very different narratives. In these texts, the reader's sympathies are with the clones, who are vulnerable, exploited and brutally damaged – psychologically as well as physically – into submissive, helpless living organ banks, tortured by vivisection.

The societies in these texts inscribe the harvestees as waste in multiple ways. In Greg Egan's story 'The Extra', the world's wealthiest people own 'stables' (57) of congenitally brain-damaged clones, used as organ banks, guinea pigs for medical experiments and vessels for brain transplant after which the clone's original brain is discarded as medical waste. Clones are marked off as subhuman legally, sartorially and linguistically. The courts have defined them as subhuman: '[T]ime and time again the highest courts had ruled that the Extras were not human beings. Too much cortex was missing; if Extras deserved human rights, so did half the mammalian species on the planet' (57). They are not killed, but 'put down', like animals (57). They are even denied the dignity of clothing, because 'even the slightest scrap of clothing made them look too human' (56). But it is in language that their plight is most clear. Because of their brain damage they will never learn speech, and they have no names, being produced in batches and merely having an identifier number tattooed on the sole of one foot.

The clones of Marshall Smith's *Spares* are not cerebrally mutilated but are treated so viciously from birth that the effect is the same. Never taught to speak or think, they are stored in box-like tunnels, forty 'spares' to a chamber eight feet square: 'Living in tunnels waiting to be whittled down … while mangled and dissected bodies stumped around them … a butcher's shop where the meat still moved occasionally, always and forever bathed in a dead blue light.' Again, they are repeatedly likened to animals: their tunnels are a 'farm', and 'In the blue, the bodies staggered and crawled like blind grubs, disturbed by the periodic moans of the spare who'd had part of his face ripped out' (42). As well as conveying the bodily damage to the clone, *Spares* conveys the damage done to the clones' capacity for interaction and fellowship. They have 'no family. They're like dead code segments, cut off from the rest of the program and left alone in darkness' (45). Naked, speechless and nameless, the clones of these two texts convey the horror of what David Kilgour and David Matas have called the 'bloody harvest' of non-consensual organ harvesting.

Looking at contemporary tissue transfer practices outside these texts, it may seem that requiring informed consent would overcome the ethical problems with the process, but even consensual and legal organ trade is highly problematic. The binaries remain disturbingly constant, tissue moving from poor to wealthy, marginalized to powerful. Even in intra-family donation, the psychological pressures can be highly suspect. Ishiguro's and Egan's texts connect with a disturbing trend in Western transplant practice. In the last decade, there is evidence that increasing pressure is being put on younger generations to donate organs to parents (Scheper-Hughes, 'Tyranny'). In the 1970s, less than 1 per cent of legal worldwide living kidney donation was from children to parents, but by 2003, 57 per cent of legal worldwide living kidney donation was from adult children to parents (Fox and Swazey 386 n.6; Scheper-Hughes, 'Tyranny' 510). The complexities of voluntary organ donation are seen most clearly in recent discussions of 'saviour siblings', children conceived specifically with a view to having them donate tissue to a sick sibling ('Concern over "Spare Part" Babies'; Picoult; Scheper-Hughes 'Tyranny'; Spriggs; Weathers). The UK government's recent Human Fertility and Embryology Bill controversially made saviour siblinghood legal, although the most publicity went to the human–animal gene admixture component of the bill. The growing mind of the child conceived in order to donate tissue to another would be shaped towards such sacrifice from birth. Kazuo Ishiguro's haunting novel *Never Let Me Go* helps us to imagine the way covert lifelong pressure in such a relationship could shape a mind into unwilling surrender. Its first-person narrator describes the experience of growing up and gradually learning that her body is essentially an object owned by others, destined to be disassembled and consumed by them.

The novel is narrated by Kathy H., aged 31, looking back on her life growing up at a private English boarding school called Hailsham. As the story progresses, we gradually realize something is profoundly amiss. Parents – or the lack thereof – are never mentioned, the students live in the school from infancy and they never leave the grounds. All the students have oddly truncated names – Reggie D., Alice B. – and all but one of the student initials is between A and K, suggesting they are number 1 to 11 of a particular model. Their names are truncated, like their lives. The school seems friendly enough despite being unusually rich in medical surveillance, but odd stories evoke a dreadful menace beyond the boundaries. A wooded hill overhangs the school, and inspires ghost stories:

> There were all kinds of horrible stories about the woods. Once, not so long before we all got to Hailsham, a boy had had a big row with his friends and run off beyond the Hailsham boundaries. His body had

been found two days later, up in those woods, tied to a tree with the hands and feet chopped off. (50)

This story is symbolically true: outside the Hailsham boundaries the students are indeed not safe, and in fact they are destined to have their limbs severed and their organs taken away. The raw horror of the surgical wound is at the centre of the book. After Tommy gashes an arm, he takes off the dressing 'to reveal something at just that stage between sealing and still being an open wound. You could see bits of skin starting to bond, and soft red bits peeping up from underneath' (83). Their awareness of the impending threat of surgical organ removal is betrayed in jokes. Tommy, for example, is teased that his whole skin could be unzipped and his skeleton flop out, and a running joke develops among the students about how they all plan to unzip themselves and extract an organ that way, when the time comes (84). The students intuit a link between donating organs and being devoured, and try to discourage each other from eating with the joke of unzipping themselves and putting an organ on a plate. In one extraordinary example, Kathy recalls, 'I remember once Gary B., who had this unbelievable appetite, coming back with a third helping of pudding, and virtually the whole table "unzipping" bits of themselves and piling it all over Gary's bowl, while he went on determinedly stuffing himself' (86). Only half a joke, the mime illustrates the way they will be consumed when they leave.

The clones of Ishiguro's novel are also distanced from their bodies by being taught to see their relationship to their own bodies as custodial. Every student gets a medical exam each week (13), they are lectured about smoking and sexually transmitted disease as if they are the single most dreadful evils anyone could perpetrate (67) and they are even warned against sharing Walkman earphones in case they get ear infections (101). Their bodies are not their own. Language is warped to give a similar message, to make organ harvesting seem natural and right. 'Donor' implies that they give their organs willingly, when in fact they have been taught from birth that they have no choice. The hospitals where they live between donations are called 'recovery centres'. Most powerful of all, instead of 'dying' the donors 'complete', a verb implying that dying in the service of donation is the fulfillment of their lives' purpose. 'Fourth donation' is the terrifying culmination of a donor's career: we never hear of a fifth, and many die after first or second. Such language encourages the clones to internalize the values of those who exploit them. Kathy H. admits the strangeness of this, noting:

> this odd tendency among donors to treat a fourth donation as some-
> thing worthy of congratulations. A donor 'on a fourth,' even one who's
> been pretty unpopular up till then, is treated with special respect. Even

the doctors and nurses play up to this: a donor on a fourth will go in for a check and be greeted by whitecoats smiling and shaking their hand. (273)

Most poignant of all, the children learn that their bodies are disposable. The first time we encounter the word 'clone' is in an impassioned harangue by one character, Ruth, after the protagonists have reached adulthood and left Hailsham:

> 'We're modeled from *trash*. Junkies, prostitutes, winos, tramps. Convicts, maybe, just so long as they aren't psychos. That's what we came from. We all know it, so why don't we say it? ... [I]f you want to look for possible [originals] ... then you look in the gutter. You look in rubbish bins. Look down the toilet, that's where you'll find where we all came from.' (164, emphasis in original)

These texts depict the work of language in rendering organ harvestees abject, leaching away their value. These are those whose death leaves a mark that is no mark.

Gothic politics?

One must be wary of seeing texts in the Gothic mode as having a straightforwardly progressive political agenda. Most eighteenth- and nineteenth-century Gothic, for example, ends by reinstating the world of daylight order and rationality. In addition, Gothic has been implicated in creating and perpetuating docile submission to bourgeois capitalism. Franco Moretti, for example, argues that the primary political effect of classic Gothic was to pacify audiences' anxieties, conditioning them to subject themselves to capitalist structures (107–108). On the other hand, the Gothic can also be a subversive form with a politically revolutionary valence. Such defences of the Gothic's political potency typically hinge on the argument that the uncanny can be a political tool, in that it destabilizes the certainties that underpin structural oppressions. Alex Link, for example, notes that 'modernist Gothic narratives are often fuelled by the anxiety that citizens are owned, controlled, and consumed by the structures of capitalist urban space', and that work in the Gothic mode can challenge those oppressive structures by offering alternative histories and uncanny resistance: 'the unruly play' of Gothic 'rais[es] the uneasy possibility that historical progress is an illusion; and third, that the complexity of urban codes opens a space for a multiplicity of ... histories' (521). Similarly, Luckhurst has suggested that 'unearthing Gothic fragments might contribute to an aesthetics of resistance' ('Contemporary London

Gothic' 533). Such an argument implies that the shocking imagery of the Gothic may break the lullaby of capitalist docility in the same way that surrealists sought to use dream imagery to foster revolution.

In a similar vein, Val Scullion has offered a valuable theoretical model for considering Gothic's political potential. Coining the term 'Gothic Brechtianism', Scullion suggests that Gothic can trigger the same cognitive moves that Bertoldt Brecht sought to achieve in his revolutionary theatre performances. Brecht wished to estrange his audiences, shocking them out of passive identification with the scenes they viewed and in so doing to make them aware of their own powers of revolutionary resistance. Scullion suggests the same effects can be elicited by Gothic, particularly in its more visceral and grotesque forms. Scullion notes that the Gothic often features both disgust and empathy: the disgust alienates the viewer, as Brecht wishes, and thus stops straightforward empathy, but there is empathy too with the suffering depicted. Scullion argues that 'The reader/viewer response of disgust and rejection, followed by recognition and empathy, is a defining characteristic of the Gothic' (7). This movement between revulsion and sympathy similarly characterizes these science fiction texts, a discomfiting, convulsive response challenging the reader to face the ethics of the processes depicted.

These fictions, then, outline some of the imaginative moves required of a society in order for some of its members to be raided as living organ banks. Yet these fictions also give a platform for imagining resistance, for the fact that the clone is a double emphasizes the kinship between harvester and harvested, and thus demonstrates visibly that the harvester is implicated in the tissue economy. Some of the most disturbing comments recipients commonly make about paid organ consumption are those in which an organ recipient chooses to take an organ from an anonymous person instead of family member and then justifies that choice in moral terms: 'Why should I put a family member at risk when I can just buy a kidney?' (Cohen 22–23). Such formulations deny the reality of the donor's body. By contrast, these gruesome cloning fictions force us to acknowledge the way organ transplant raids the bodies of real people. A double can be dismissed as a mirror-image or reflection of an original – less corporeal – but in these fictions, the visceral reality of the clones' suffering bodies is undeniable. The Gothic doubling within these texts helps us to rethink the place of corporeality in the language of the posthuman, specifically by restoring attention to the way that body augmentation with organic tissue has a very real cost. The cannibal doubles are those who consume them, and those who bolster that practice by emptying the other's body of difference.

This chapter does not imply that we should idealize bodily boundaries and revalorize discrete identities. Haraway, Halberstam and other theorists of the posthuman rightly celebrate the extent to which posthuman discourse threatens nostalgic, idealized visions of the body as self-contained and discrete. This work, too, requires us to resist nostalgic and essentialist rhetorics which imply that identity inheres in flesh. I do not seek to resurrect reverence for boundaries. However, we must also acknowledge that immunosuppressant blurring of body boundaries has combined with late capitalism to permit terrible violence on the bodies of the marginalized. These texts dramatize the imaginative moves that enable that violence.

Notes

1. For evidence of gender disparity in tissue transfer (predominantly female to male, in both paid and unpaid donations) see Scheper-Hughes ('Tyranny of the Gift' 508); A. Ojo and F. K. Port; Nikola Biller-Andorno; Parviz Khajehdehi; D. S. Zimmerman et al.; and Liise Kayler et al. For evidence of children increasingly donating to parents, see Scheper-Hughes ('Tyranny of the Gift') and Sharon Kaufman et al.

Works cited

Allison, R. 'Doctor in Organ Sale Scandal Struck Off.' *Guardian* 31 August 2002: 7. Print.
Awaya, Tsuyoshi. 'The Human Body as a New Commodity.' World Congress of Bioethics, Nihon University Hall, Tokyo, Japan, 4–7 November 1998. Conference paper. Web. 17 April 2008.
Benjamin, Walter. 'The Work of Art in the Age of Mechanical Reproduction.' Trans. Harry Zohn. *Illuminations*. Ed. Hannah Arendt. London: Fontana, 1992. 211–244. Print.
Biller-Andorno, Nikola. 'Gender Imbalance in Living Organ Donation.' *Medicine, Health Care and Philosophy* 5.2 (2005): 199–204. Print.
Blake's 7. Dir. Terry Nation. Season 2 and 3. BBC. 1978–1980. Television.
Botting, Fred. *Gothic*. London: Routledge, 1996. Print
Bowcott, O. 'World Scramble for Kidneys Exploits Poor: Disciplinary Hearing Sheds Light on Third World Market which Makes Peasants and Criminals Hostages to Advances in Medical Science.' *Guardian* 5 April 1990: 4. Print.
Bronfen, Elisabeth. *Over Her Dead Body: Death, Femininity and the Aesthetic*. 1992. Manchester: Manchester UP, 1996. Print.
Butler, Judith. *Precarious Life: The Powers of Mourning and Violence*. London: Verso, 2004. Print.
Cohen, Lawrence. 'The Other Kidney: Biopolitics beyond Recognition.' *Commodifying Bodies*. Ed. Nancy Scheper-Hughes and Loïc Wacquant. London: Sage, 2002. 9–29. Print.
'Concern over "Spare Part" Babies.' *BBC News*. BBC, 31 January 2006. Web. 17 August 2009.
'CSI: Trilogy.' By Anthony E. Zuiker, Carol Mendelsohn and Ann Donahue. CBS Paramount, Alliance Atlantis and Arc. 9–12 November 2009. Television.
Davis, Emily S. 'The Intimacies of Globalization: Bodies and Borders On-Screen.' *Camera Obscura: A Journal of Feminism, Culture, and Media Studies* 21.62 (2006): 33–73. Print.
Dryden, Linda. *The Modern Gothic and Literary Doubles: Stevenson, Wilde and Wells*. Basingstoke: Palgrave Macmillan, 2003. Print.
Egan, Greg. 'The Extra.' 1990. *Clones*. Ed. Jack Dann and Gardner Dozois. New York: Ace, 1998. 55–73. Print.
Fox, R. and J. P Swazey. *The Courage to Fail: A Social View of Organ Transplants and Dialysis*. Chicago: U of Chicago P, 1978.

Freud, Sigmund. 'The Uncanny.' 1919. *Art and Literature: The Penguin Freud Library*, Vol. 14. Ed. Angela Richards. London: Penguin, 1985. 336–76. Print.

Gilbert, Sandra and Susan Gubar. *The Madwoman in the Attic: The Woman Writer and the Nineteenth-Century Literary Imagination*. New Haven: Yale UP, 1979. Print.

Graham, Elaine. *Representations of the Post/Human: Monsters, Aliens and Others in Popular Culture*. New Brunswick, NJ: Rutgers UP, 2002. Print.

Halberstam, Judith and Ira Livingston (eds). *Posthuman Bodies*. Bloomington, IN: Indiana UP, 1995. Print.

Handwerk, Brian. 'Organ Shortage Fuels Illicit Trade in Human Parts.' Nationalgeographic. com. *National Geographic*, 16 January 2004. Web. 15 July 2009.

Haraway, Donna. 'A Cyborg Manifesto: Science, Technology, and Socialist-Feminism in the Late Twentieth Century.' *Simians, Cyborgs and Women: The Reinvention of Nature*. New York: Routledge, 1991. 149–181. Print.

'Harvest.' By Judith McCreary. Dir. David Grossman. *CSI: Crime Scene Investigation*. Season 5 Episode 1. CBS Paramount, Alliance Atlantis and Arc. 4 October 2004. Television.

Horner, Avril and Sue Zlosnik. 'Strolling in the Dark: Gothic *Flânerie* in Djuna Barnes' *Nightwood*.' *Gothic Modernisms*. Ed. Andrew Smith and Jeff Wallace. Basingstoke: Palgrave Macmillan, 2001. 78–94. Print.

Hughes, C. 'Egypt's Desperate Trade: Body Parts for Sale.' *New York Times* 23 September 1991, sec. A: 8. Print.

Huxley, Aldous. *Brave New World*. 1932. London: Chatto and Windus, 1939. Print.

Ishiguro, Kazuo. *Never Let Me Go*. London: Faber, 2005. Print.

Joralemon, Donald. 'Organ Wars: The Battle for Body Parts.' *Medical Anthropology Quarterly* 9.3 (1995): 335–56.

Kaufman, Sharon, Ann J. Russ and Janet K. Shim. 'Aged Bodies and Kinship Matters.' *American Ethnologist* 33.1 (February 2006): 81–99. Print.

Kayler, Liise K., Cynthia S. Rasmussen, Dawn M. Dykstra, Akinlolu O. Ojo, Friedrich K. Port, Robert A.Wolfe and Robert M. Merion. 'Gender Imbalance and Outcomes in Living Donor Renal Transplantation in the United States.' *American Journal of Transplantation* 3.4 (April 2003): 452. Print.

Khajehdehi, Parviz. 'Living Non-Related versus Related Renal Transplantation: Its Relationship to the Social Status, Age and Gender of Recipients and Donors.' *Nephrology Dialysis Transplantation* 14.11 (November 1999): 2621–2624. Print.

Kilgour, David and David Matas. 'Bloody Harvest: An Independent Investigation into Allegations of Organ Harvesting of Falun Gong Practitioners in China.' 31 January 2007. Web. 15 July 2009.

Link, Alex. '"The Capitol of Darknesse": Gothic Spatialities in the London of Peter Ackroyd's Hawksmoor.' *Contemporary Literature* 45.3 (Fall 2004): 516–537. Print.

Luckhurst, Roger. 'The Contemporary London Gothic and the Limits of the "Spectral Turn."' *Textual Practice* 16.3 (Winter 2002): 527–546. Print.

—. *Science Fiction*. Cambridge: Polity, 2005. Print.

Marshall Smith, Michael. *Spares*. 1996. London: Harper Collins, 1998. Print.

McClintock, Anne. *Imperial Leather: Race, Gender and Sexuality in the Colonial Contest*. London: Routledge, 1995. 95–97. Print.

Milne, Celia. 'Canadian MD-Activist Likens Chinese Organ Trade to the Holocaust.' *The Medical Post* 11 March 2008. Web. 15 July 2009.

Moretti, Franco. 'Dialectic of Fear.' 1983. Trans. David Miller. *Signs Taken for Wonders: On the Sociology of Literary Forms*. 2nd ed. London: Verso, 2005. 83–108. Print.

Niven, Larry. *The Patchwork Girl*. 1980. New York: Ace, 1984. Print.

Ojo, A. and F. K. Port. 'Influence of Race and Gender on Related Donor Renal Transplantation Rates.' *American Journal of Kidney Disorders* 22.6 (December 1993): 835–841. Print.

Organ Watch. '15,000 Kidneys Trafficked Each Year: Organ Watch.' *MSN News*. MSN, 15 February 2008. Web. 15 July 2009.

Parry, G. '"Broker" Accuses Other Doctors.' *Guardian* 5 April 1990: 4. Print.

'Phage.' *Star Trek: Voyager*. By Timothy De Haas. Adapt. Skye Dent and Brannon Braga. Dir. Winrich Kolbe. Season 1 Episode 5. 6 February 1995. Television.

Picoult, Jodi. *My Sister's Keeper*. London: Hodder and Stoughton, 2004. Print.

Pilkington, Ed. 'Up to 54 Years in Jail for Tissue Harvest Ringleader Who Stole Alistair Cooke's Corpse.' *Guardian Unlimited*. Guardian, 20 March 2008. Web. 30 March 2008.

Rank, Otto. *The Double*. 1914. Trans. Harry Tucker, Jr. Chapel Hill: U of North Carolina P, 1971. Print.

Repo! The Genetic Opera. Dir. Darren Lynn Bousman. Twisted Pictures, 2008. Film.

Rothman, D. J., E. Rose, T. Awaya, B. Cohen, A. Daar, S. L. Dzemeshkevich, C. J. Lee, R. Munro, H. Reyes, S. M. Rothman, K. F. Schoen, N. Scheper-Hughes, Z. Shapira and H. Smit. 'The Bellagio Task Force Report on Transplantation, Bodily Integrity, and the International Traffic in Organs.' *Transplantation Proceedings* 29.6 (September 1997): 2739–2745. Print.

Roy, Anirban. 'A Nepal Village that's a Kidney Bank.' HindustanTimes.com. *Hindustan Times*, 10 February 2008. Web. 15 July 2009.

Scheper-Hughes, Nancy. 'Bodies for Sale: Whole or in Parts.' *Commodifying Bodies*. Ed. Nancy Scheper-Hughes and L. Wacquant. London: Sage, 2002. 1–8. Print.

—. 'Commodity Fetishism in Organs Trafficking.' *Commodifying Bodies*. Ed. Nancy Scheper-Hughes and Loïc Wacquant. London: Sage, 2002. 31–62. Print.

—. 'The Tyranny of the Gift: Sacrificial Violence in Living Donor Transplants.' *American Journal of Transplantation* 7.3 (2007): 507–511. Print.

Scullion, Val. 'Invasion of the Head: Gothic Dissent in Dennis Potter's *Cold Lazarus*.' *Gothic Studies* 10.1 (May 2008): 4–13. Print.

Shusterman, Neal. *Unwind*. 2007. London: Simon and Shuster, 2008. Print.

Spriggs, M. 'Commodification of Children again and Non-Disclosure Preimplantation Genetic Diagnosis for Huntington's Disease.' *Journal of Medical Ethics* 30.6 (2004): 538. Print.

'US Undertakers Admit Corpse Scam.' *BBC News*. BBC, 19 October 2006. Web. 19 September 2008.

Waldby, Catherine. 'Biomedicine, Tissue Transfer and Intercorporeality.' *Feminist Theory* 3 (2002): 235–250. Print.

Waldby, Catherine and Robert Mitchell. *Tissue Economies: Blood, Organs, and Cell Lines in Late Capitalism*. Durham: Duke UP, 2006. Print.

Warren, Lynne. 'Inhuman Profit.' *National Geographic* 204.3 (September 2003): 26–29. Libezproxy.open.ac.uk . Web. 15 July 2009.

Wasson, Sara. 'Love in the Time of Cloning: Science Fictions of Transgressive Kinship.' *Extrapolation* 45.2 (Summer 2004): 130–144. Print.

—. 'Olalla's Legacy: Twentieth Century Vampire Fiction and Genetic Previvorship.' *The Journal of Stevenson Studies* 7 (2010): 55–81. Print.

Weathers, Helen. 'I Had a "Saviour Sibling" to Cure My Desperately Ill Son – But Now I''ve Found Out My Newborn Daughter Can't Save His Life.' Mail Online. *Daily Mail*, 1 April 2008. Web. 17 August 2009.

Wilhelm, Kate. 'Where Late the Sweet Bird Sang.' 1974. *Clones*. Ed. Jack Dann and Gardner Dozois. New York: Ace, 1998. 203–254. Print.

Zimmerman, D. S., J. Donnelly, J. Miller, D. Stewart and S. E. Albert. 'Gender Disparity in Living Renal Transplant Donation.' *American Journal of Kidney Disorders* 6 (2000): 534–540. Print.

5. Guillermo del Toro's *Cronos*, or the Pleasures of Impurity

Laurence Davies

There are things in the wood that are older, stranger, and wickeder than us. They have been here before. (del Toro, 'La noche de los Gotham', 23)[1]

We must all face and integrate the profane and the sacred, market economics and state interventionism, nationalism and globalism. Ruins and garbage stare at us: being Walter Benjamin's angel, facing all of history as ruins, is perhaps better, if crueller, than ending contentedly in the junkyard. (Fuentes 196)

Pan's Labyrinth (*El laberinto del fauno*, 2006) aside, Guillermo del Toro's wood is chiefly metaphorical; his ghosts and monsters inhabit such locations as the arid plateau of central Spain (*The Devil's Backbone / El espinazo del diablo*, 2001), or the sewers, streets, and libraries of Manhattan (*Mimic*, 1997, *Hellboy*, 2004), or the Giant's Causeway (*Hellboy II*, 2008). In *Cronos*, his first full-length film as a director, the locale is Mexico City. It went into production in 1992, at a time of intense debate about the North American Free Trade Agreement (NAFTA), which had not yet been ratified.[2] After a prologue set partly in 1537 or thereabouts and partly in 1937, the rest of the film takes place during the last two days of 1996 and the beginning of 1997.[3] From what we see of it, this capital of the imminent future is not a happy place. The screen play sets the scene:

> Opening credits. Beneath them we see Mexico City, a compact mass of urban putrefaction. Grey house walls and retaining walls, endless rows of TV aerials, a still life lit by a drab brown, timid sun. This is a post Free Trade Agreement Mexico. (del Toro, *La invención de Cronos* 17)[4]

The Spanish equivalent of 'still life', be it noted, literally means 'dead nature'. In the film itself, there is garbage everywhere, much of it the detritus of Christmas celebrations. Some of the houses are well on their way to ruin. The word *basura* (garbage, rubbish, trash), applied at large to people and to things, echoes throughout (e.g. 22, 31, 84), and the antique shop of Jesús Gris is popularly known as *El Basurero* (The Dump).

In the quotation above, Carlos Fuentes, like Walter Benjamin's Angel of History, is looking backwards. He surveys the nineties – the period not only of NAFTA, with its disruptions of economy and culture, but of the indigenous revolt in Chiapas, and the abrupt decline of the paradoxically named Institutional Revolutionary Party (PRI) after decades of power unassailable.[5] His book speaks of crises, existential and material. His distinction between rubbish and ruin acknowledges the condition of living in an age of throwaways, while implying that ruins carry the greater cultural charge and the greater consolation. To put the difference another way, ruins speak to a Gothic sensibility and rubbish to a postmodern. This is not to deny that Gothic and postmodern may make lively bedmates – provided the parties don't become too giggly or too cynical. I am not making an aesthetic judgement here, but thinking of aesthetic challenges. If Gothicism sees the value and the beauty of dilapidation and decay, postmodernism does the same for destruction and its aftermath – as, for example in Fernando Arrabal's play *The Car Cemetery* (*Le cimetière des voitures*, 1960) or Donald Barthelme's story 'The Indian Uprising' (1968), or even 'The Tree' ('An Crann', 1986), Nuala Ní Dhomhnaill's poem about the fairy woman with the Black and Decker chainsaw. One of the forces that make Guillermo del Toro's work so electrifying is the tension between multiple versions of cultural entropy and persistence.

His films are gleefully impure. Thanks to the breadth of their allusions, literary, graphic, and cinematic, they are not easily boxed into any one genre or mode, 'high' or 'low'. Among other sources, they draw on alchemy, martial arts, comic books, antiquarian ghost stories, symbolist painting, Christian and Pagan iconography, Mexican popular culture, and an encyclopaedic array of international cinema. The mix varies from film to film but typical ingredients include horror, science fiction, fantasy, and the Gothic. *Cronos*, also known as *La invención de Cronos* (*The Cronos Device*), sets the pattern.[6] Fantasy is certainly not the word for the grungy near-dystopia of the city, but the story of the device itself and its horrific effects on those who covet it can be read as Gothic narrative or science fiction – preferably both.[7]

It was the screenplay's cultural impurity that made it hard to win financial backing from IMCINE (Instituto Mexicano de la Cinematografía), the government body producing or co-producing artistically ambitious films.[8] In November 2003, recalling his efforts in the mid-1980s, del Toro told Jason Wood: 'When I first presented the film to IMCINE, they complained that it wasn't an art movie, it was a vampire film, and that I should go and get some

private money. I disagreed, I said it was an art film and horror can also be art'
(Wood 38). He was also told that the project 'wasn't essentially Mexican' (del
Toro, *Cronos* Director's Commentary). Eventually the Instituto relented, and
with some backing from the University of Guadalajara, some from Larson
Sound Center and Ventana Productions (both in California), and a great deal
of personal debt, the film at last went into production in 1992. In 1993 the
film had a one-week run at a Mexico City cinema and an unfunded showing
at the Cannes Festival, where it won the Critics' Prize. Subsequently, the
Academia Mexicana de Cine de Artes y Ciencias Cinematográficas gave the
film nine Ariel awards (among them one for best original story), but in
some quarters the suspicion has smouldered, flaring up every time del Toro
works with a US studio, that he compromises overmuch with Hollywood
money and Hollywood tropes (Lázaro-Reboll 44–45).[9] In some other critical
versions, there is a good del Toro who makes remarkable films in Spanish
exploring history, politics, culture, cruelty, and suffering, and a naughty one
who tries to shock and scare his English-speaking audiences with monsters
out of Lovecraft. All this is far too Manichaean, I believe. We have here a
director fertile in paradox and contradiction: an obsessive auteur who insists
on getting every angle, every colour right, yet always acknowledges his
collaborators warmly (Wood 31–38); a cineaste whose extraordinary sense
of visual splash and detail is joined to a love of spoken words. Unlike some
cinematic purists, he does not put his trust in sight alone.[10]

   While this essay may sometimes veer towards biography, it isn't anchored
there. The critical challenge is the work itself. Even mapping its boundaries
requires safe passage through the theoretical reefs. Like most screenplays,
this one differs considerably from the final, cinematic cut, but its ongoing
fascination lies more in the energy and specificity of its language and the
imagination of details almost or actually invisible to the cinema-goer than
in the smudges of erased ideas. Scene 36, for instance, showing the insect
imprisoned within the Cronos device, did not feature in the film (perhaps on
account of sporadic cash flow), though two briefer appearances of the captive
mite do. Here is just one segment of the description: 'Along its sides, six
short and useless legs are moving rapidly, blood swells its belly, folds of aged
skin thick with warts fill out, bloating almost to the point of explosion. In its
translucent intestines, blood filters, changes shade, turning darker, almost
black' (del Toro, *La invención* 48).[11] In a case like this, I prefer to think of the
relation of published text to released film as a timeless continuum or a state
of mutual supplementarity in which early and late keep changing places.

   Like many literary Gothic narrratives, the film opens with a prologue,
formally different from what is to come in its use of voice-over, yet linked to
the rest by motifs such as bandaged hands and mottled skin. The narrator
tells us how the device came into being, the creation of the alchemist Uberto

Fulcanelli, who fled to what is now Mexico in 1536, under the shadow of
the Inquisition, his right hand seared by a cruciform branding iron.[12] He is
first shown breaking the device's mould, still hot from the furnace. Then, a
leap across four centuries. In 1937, the roof of a church has caved in during
a night-time service.[13] Among the dead and dying is a man with skin like
moonlit marble. His heart has been pierced by a metal shaft, and his last,
gasped words are in Latin: 'Suo ... tempore' ('In his ... time)' (15). These
are the only words he utters in the film. The police find his lodgings: bowls
full of blood are laid across the floor, above them the body of a naked man
suspended by his ankles; because he is filmed from behind, we can't see
whether, like the Hanged Man in the Tarot, he is smiling.

The Gothicism of all this is inescapable. Like a vampire, Fulcanelli can only
die when pierced through the heart, and he has gone to the church under
cover of darkness. His very name has an occult resonance as the pseudonym
of a French alchemical writer of the early twentieth century, author of *Le
Mystère des cathédrales*. Alchemists often figure in Gothic fiction – by Percy
Shelley, W. Harrison Ainsworth, Bulwer Lytton, Balzac, Hoffmann, and
Hugo, for example, and we might recall that Victor Frankenstein's false start
in science begins with reading Paracelsus and Albertus Magnus. Alchemical
laboratories are a great opportunity for literary or painterly chiaroscuro,
and lost or forbidden texts are perfect plot-initiators. In Mary Shelley,
especially, alchemy is associated with unhallowed desire and furtiveness.
Her 'Mortal Immortal' has been the sole helper of Cornelius Agrippa: 'my
friends implored me not to return to the alchymist's abode. I trembled as I
listened to the dire tale they told; I required no second warning; and when
Cornelius came and offered me a purse of gold if I would remain under
his roof, I felt as if Satan himself tempted me' (220). I shall defer further
discussion of the Gothic elements, however, until turning to the device's
effect on the Gris and De La Guardia families in the film as seen in the
context of the 1990s. First it is necessary to establish the less obvious links
with science fiction.

The Cronos device is seductive, pulling the initiate-victim into an intensely
sexual dependency, a *folie à un*, not just a desiring machine but a machine
desired. Craving it, or in the case of Jesús Gris even having the temerity
to be curious, results in agony. At rest, it resembles a golden scarab or a
Fabergé egg. Its surface is incised with alchemical signs and emblems such
as Ouroboros, the serpent who bites its own tail in token of eternal return
and immortality. An amber vitrine allows a glimpse of the mechanism
within. When it is wound up, six articulated legs extend, each with a sharp
prong or claw capable of embedding itself in flesh; when the right moment
comes, a seventh limb extends, poised to stab, to suck, to inject. Inside, we
see tiny shafts and cogs revolving, and, at the very centre, the insect through

whose body the victim's or, better, the devotee's blood is filtered. Thus the device can be seen as literally inscribed by the occult, but also as a machine which encases a living being. This machine has a manual, glimpsed at two moments in the prologue and several times more during the struggle to possess the device itself; crowded with beautifully penned diagrams, notes, and anatomical drawings, its pages resemble the notebooks of Leonardo da Vinci. In Scene 100, Dieter De La Guardia, the decrepit industrialist who will do anything to possess the device, announces that he's eaten them: 'The best meal I've had in years. Very good for the memory' (del Toro, *La Invención* 98).[14] Black humour, yet another display of voraciousness, and an allusion to the Renaissance *ars memoriae*: the name of this film is legion. The alchemical quest for immortality, the transmutation of base metals, and the secret of the alkahest – the universal solvent – is both nefarious and bold, a transgression of divine law and a protoscientific enterprise.[15] The man dangling head down over a bowl of blood is an experimental subject, a victim of nefarious arts, and a vampire's milch cow.

When viewing *Cronos* on the science fiction frequencies, Darko Suvin is an indispensable guide. He has long argued, in the spirit of Shklovsky and Brecht, that science fiction is a literature of cognitive estrangement, and its intellectual field 'distinguished by the narrative dominance or hegemony of a fictional "novum" (novelty, innovation) validated by cognitive logic'. This novum is 'born in history and judged in history' (67, 86). Although Suvin does not make this argument, it is thus possible to consider as science fiction a narrative that starts at an imaginary cultural bifurcation sometime in the past. Samuel R. Delany's essay 'About 5,750 Words' probes the 'subjunctivity' of different kinds of fiction with a set of variations on grammatical tense and mood. Thus the defining statement about fantasy is that these events 'could not have happened'; naturalistic fiction deals with 'events that have not happened', but so, in a much stronger sense, does 'that SF speciality, the parallel-world story, whose outstanding example is Philip K. Dick's *The Man in the High Castle*' (11) – a novel posited on the victory of Japan and Germany in the Second World War. Another version of this mode is the steampunk narrative, as in Gibson and Sterling's *The Difference Engine* (1990), posited on the invention of steam-powered computing in the Victorian era. These are not so very far from the 'what if' scenarios favoured by some historians. *Cronos* itself can be seen as alternative history, while having affinities with the hypotheticals that medico-legal ethicists pose when dealing with such issues as xenotransplantation (the transference of cells from one species to another) or the prolongation of life by heroic means. Indeed there are echoes in the script itself of medical discourse; four centuries ago, 'The genius of the alchemist created a kind of primitive dialysis, a strange living filter' (48).[16]

Does it make sense then to think of the device as a cyborg, a working partnership of flesh and metal? Donna Haraway's influential definition begins: 'A cyborg is a hybrid creature, composed of organism and machine. But, cyborgs are compounded of special kinds of machinery and special kinds of organisms appropriate to the late twentieth century' (*Simians* 1). She has also argued that 'The cyborg is a creature in a post-gender world' (*Simians* 1; *Modest_Witness*); that is clearly the case for the creature and its golden carapace, though the point seems to have escaped those poster artists who show the device pricking the exposed breast of an ecstatic woman – a scene quite unlike anything in the film itself (IMDb). For Anne Davies, the device is transnational, portable across borders (401–02). Kantaris refers to the Cronos entity as 'a pre-modern prototype cyborg adrift in a completely irresolvable postmodern timeframe'. This remark fits well with the idea that the alchemist's invention originated in an extrahistorical novum. This temporal slippage, moreover, is a means of cognitive estrangement, and thus another marker of science fiction. The invention is not only an ancient (and ingenious, and beautiful) artefact, but a disturber of present-day desires and narratives. It is also nothing like the engine of liberation that Haraway envisages.[17] Chained to an alien mechanism for centuries, the insect is a victim, with a good chance of regular nourishment, but an exploited captive nevertheless. In terms of science-fictional parallels, it is much more like the prisoners of the vindictive computer AM in Harlan Ellison's story 'I Have No Mouth and I Must Scream' (1967) than the 'shell people' of Anne McCaffrey's *The Ship Who Sang* (1969), who are empowered by their work as 'brains' connected to spaceships or entire cities.

The subject of exploitation brings us back to Mexico in the 1990s. Desiring Cronos reshapes the lives of two families. Jesús and Mercedes Gris are taking care of their granddaughter Aurora (I shall take up the tricky matter of naming later). Jesús has a small shop, called The Grand Bazaar, packed with old things, particularly clocks all ticking away at their own pace. Mercedes teaches tango, an art requiring precise timing and a link with another part of the Hispanic world; she is much preoccupied with death and has accumulated a great pile of clipped obituaries. Aurora is eight years old, but (or so) turns out to have a remarkable tolerance of odd events. Dieter De La Guardia is the boss of a family firm (products unspecified) and riddled with cancer, living in an ultra-sterile apartment at his factory, a Howard Hughes-like recluse surrounded by bottles stuffed with his surgically excised organs. Kantaris describes him as 'clearly a cyborg composite, dependent upon biomedical technology to keep himself alive, and as such he is the post-modern double of the insect cocooned inside the pre-modern Chronos device'. He uses his nephew Angel as an envoy, nurse, and hitman. They are foreigners, and since they have the same name as one of New York's airports, we may assume they come from the US, and are thus benefiting from the uneven terms of NAFTA. Del Toro told Jason Wood: 'I wanted to show the vampiric relationship between the nephew and the uncle and, of course, the vampiric relationship between Mexico and the United States' (Wood 33). The nephew would always rather speak in English than in Spanish, reads self-improvement books, and has an obsession with his battered nose; he carries round with him a set of cards modelling perfect ones. The uncle's determination to stay alive at all costs, and his confidence in the power of medical technology, suggest that del Toro's critique of *norteños* is cultural as well as economic. The De La Guardias come from the land of cryonics and expensive cosmetic restorations of the dead.[18] Until he breakfasts on it, Dieter has the manual, while Jesús has the device itself, which he has found hidden in the base of a wooden sculpture; it has been scarred by age, but is still recognizably the statue of the Archangel Michael slaying the Satanic serpent that first appeared in the prologue. Dieter has long been searching for this particular statue, for along the length of his living quarters hang scores and scores of similar statues, all bagged in plastic like a gangster's victims, and a fitting representation of his painstaking ruthlessness and utter indifference to anything in any way numinous.

In the narrative of these two somewhat eccentric families, the discourses both of science and of Gothicism lead to violence and horror.[19] Those whose blood has passed through the device experience the symptoms of vampirism: photophobia, burning thirst, a longing for blood, rejuvenation, a high resistance to death and the ability to survive in an undead state. Only the traditional piercing of the heart can kill for good. Once he has been unintentionally, so to speak, initiated, Jesús starts to look and act younger and is sexually reinvigorated. His thirst for blood is abject. In one of the film's most notorious scenes, he attends a New Year's Eve celebration with Mercedes and Aurora, who are dressed in green; the ball room is decorated with blue and white balloons. A fellow reveller develops a nose bleed. Jesús follows him into the men's lavatory, a space all black and white – dinner jackets and immaculate formal shirts, black and white marble fittings. The only colour is that of blood. With the side of his hand, Jesús starts to make a little pool of the already clotting liquid. He starts back as another man enters, grizzling about the illegal immigrants from elsewhere in Latin America who must have made this mess. When the man leaves, Jesús sees splashes of blood on the floor. He prostrates himself and starts to lick it up. Worse is to come. Angel arrives, kicks him into unconsciousness, drives him away, pushes the car over a cliff, and leaves Jesús to die. He will, however, come back, undead, find his own obituary in a dustbin, and shelter in Aurora's toy-chest like a pet animal.

In terms of reading vampirism as a metaphor of economic exploitation, del Toro has already done the work for us with his remarks on the chain of dependencies that binds the insect to Jesús Gris and the De La Guardias, and his visual presentation of Dieter's massive factory. The metaphor goes back at least as far as Marx and still has life in it.[20] Kraniauskas cites a Zapatista manifesto from 1994 insisting that 'Chiapas blood flows as a result of the thousand fangs sunk into the throat of southeastern Mexico' (143). A Marxist reading of *Cronos*, though, faces a few difficulties. There are three practising vampires in the narrative: Gris, Fulcanelli, and the hapless insect. Jesús operates a one-man business, Fulcanelli was an intellectual who made a living as a craftsman-servant of the colonial state, and the insect is enslaved. The only full-blown capitalist in the cast is Dieter, who, in the literal sense, isn't a vampire, but badly wants to be one. In the metaphorical sense, the main example of vampiric behaviour is his contemptuous treatment of Angel, his own nephew. None of this lends itself easily to a match between class and supernatural status. It isn't especially productive to present a capitalist who wants to be a metaphor of himself.[21] A capitalist is a capitalist is a capitalist, and a capitalist like Dieter by any other name would smell no worse. A simple Marxist reading, in other words, is too blatant. We can contrast such an interpretation of the film with the jolt of finding Franco Moretti's version of Bram Stoker's Count Dracula as a 'rational entrepreneur' and a 'saver, an ascetic, an upholder of the Protestant ethic' (84, 91). We might want to challenge this reading, but it gives the pleasure of surprise.[22]

I do not want to deny that the shadow of NAFTA falls across this film, nor overlook the sheer voracity of Dieter De La Guardia, but a base-and-superstructure model or even a Gramscian one can't necessarily do justice to the cultural issues. Here we come back to the supposed lack of 'Mexicanness' about which some cultural bureaucrats complained. Reasonably enough, Ann Marie Stock observes that *Cronos* 'defies containment within extant critical categories that privilege formal purity and national authenticity' (276). She quotes del Toro in support of her case: '"People are going to say [that it] is a Mexican, Catholic, vampire movie with mariachis."' No mariachis, thank goodness, but it is a Mexican movie with ranchero music, a Latin American movie with *cumbias* and tangos, and a movie by a lapsed Catholic who has never quite washed away the influence of a grandma who believed in the redemptive power of pain and made him put upturned bottle-tops in his shoes. Two scenes from the film serve to illustrate these presences – and here we might recall the reference at the head of this essay to 'the profane and the sacred' as forces in Mexican life that need somehow to be brought together (Fuentes 196). During the first scene in *El Gran Bazar*, a middleman delivers the statue of the archangel. Jesús unwraps it, and then, as Aurora plays a board game, sings a cradle song about a baby opening its eyes, which are windows to look at God. The song is interrupted as first one, then dozens, then hundreds of cockroaches skitter from the statue's eyes. Taking off a shoe, Aurora hammers the creatures with gusto. 'It's worse if you provoke them, Aurora,' Jesús warns her.[23] As Aurora watches, her grandfather starts to open the base of the statue, where the device lies hidden. This scene does much to establish the warmth that they feel for each other, and Aurora's wide-eyed openness to unnerving experience. The statue of the victorious archangel has survived time and termites, and its gaze might be taken as melancholy, serene, or interrogative. Once we know more about the device it shelters, we might wonder whether the roaches and the imprisoned mite have some uncanny rapport. In any event, the sight of insects pouring out of a holy statue is a shocker, not unlike the scene in Buñuel's *Viridiana* where the would-be nun peels apples with a tool that is both knife and crucifix.

This episode raises a more general issue in connection with the Gothic. Until at least the middle of the nineteenth century, the Anglophone tradition is heavily anti-Catholic, as is its pre-Gothic ancestry in Jacobean drama. By the end of that century, a cautiously ecumenical spirit is spreading, as when Stoker, an Irish Protestant, imagines his company of Germanic gentlemen going on the attack with crucifixes and consecrated hosts. Nevertheless, such invocations of the sacred (or as a sceptic might put it, the magical) and the sacrilegious have more resonance in Mexico or the Philippines than they do among Protestant or outright secular audiences.[24]

The scene with the cockroaches, then, touches on a question of cultural embedding germane to a range of societies inflected by Roman Catholicism. The scene at the mortuary is better stocked with what many would argue is distinctively Mexican in its familiarity with death.[25] It is imbued with macabre humour. The central figure is Tito, who doubles as cosmetic artist and furnace operator. He wears a large crucifix over the singlet which forms the top half of his working clothes, but his language is profane. A wizard with rouge, needle, mouth guard, and stapler, he knows just how to make a corpse presentable for its *velorio* (wake), and reacts angrily when he learns that he's wasted his artistry on Jesús, who is going to be cremated. As he works, he eats bananas and listens to *cumbias*. In his quarters, votive candles burn before miniature altars. Like one of those cameo purveyors of 'comic relief' in Shakespeare, he likes gruesome jokes. When Angel De La Guardia arrives to gloat over the body of the stubborn antique dealer, Tito says 'Why not. Medium or well done?'[26] and leads him over to the furnace. The now undead Jesús has already slipped out of his coffin, but neither of them knows this. The whole scene is not too far removed from the *calavera* tradition embodied in the skull-shaped sweeties given to children during the Days of the Dead and the skeleton figures drinking, or shooting pool, or playing in jazz bands inspired by Posada's prints.[27] Those readers who find these connections a little too folkloric might reflect on what del Toro says of Aurora: "'the girl who does not mind dying is the truly immortal character. [...] Immortality doesn't mean you live longer; it means you are *immune* to death'" (Kermode 24). This is the counterpoise to Dieter De La Guardia's cult of death postponed indefinitely. Moreover, Aurora lives because her grandfather would rather die a second death than sacrifice her life. The final scenes of the film might be taken as a refraction of Murnau's *Nosferatu*, originally called *A Symphony in Grey* (in Spanish *Gris*), in which the vampiric Count Orlok can be sent into oblivion only by a pure-hearted woman, but Aurora's strength lies in acceptance of what is rather than in fairy-tale spotlessness. This is a girl who bashes cockroaches.

Another feature of Tito the mortuary attendant's working quarters is a mask. It is the mask of Santo (Saint), freestyle wrestler and star of 52 movies in which he defeats mummies, alien invaders, Men from Hell, the Evil Brain, the Son of Frankenstein, and other monsters. In *Santo versus the Martian Invaders* (*Santo vs. la invasión de los Marcianos*, 1967) the aliens are unusually glamorous. They are all blond, tightly muscled, and have evidently spent their Martian childhoods wearing dental braces. We know where they really live. It is by now an axiom of Anglophone criticism that the Gothic is a manifestation of unending anxiety – about sexuality, reverse colonization, the death of the subject, or whatever. The critics are largely right, of course, but two caveats are necessary. One: it is often the function of Gothic narratives to provoke anxiety only to allay it; even in *Dracula* there are elements of reassurance: the dictaphone, the panoply of religious ritual, and the stalwartness of the Anglo-Saxon race are more than a match for the Transylvanian. Two: even in the supposedly ever-worried world of English-speakers, there is a robust tradition of Gothic as satire, Gothic as resistance.[28] As there is in Mexico.[29] The most fearful character in *Cronos* is Dieter De La Guardia, who suffers from acute thanatophobia. He and his nephew have a cartoonish affect. The scene in which Angel struggles with Jesús on the factory roof, backed by a colossal neon sign and filmed from a low angle in brilliant primaries, looks like a page from a comic-book. This is not anxiety at work, but ridicule, not existential uncertainty, but rebuttal of a crass and inadequate system of beliefs.[30]

To characterize this film, though, as any sort of allegory – political, cultural, sexual, or religious – goes against its grain. Its moods are mercurial, its modes elusive. One of its presiding beings is the Archangel Michael; another, Fulcanelli, a scientist and occultist who has defied the biblical proscriptions on extending life; a third is that connoisseur of weird events, Charles Fort. 'I always look for the Fortean in life,' says del Toro (*Cronos* Director's Commentary). Fort, who recorded countless occurrences of the improbable and inexplicable, is the joker in del Toro's pack. How is it, for example, that the flow of gas to the cremation chamber fails just long enough for Jesús to slip away? In this film, the shifts are more important than the fixities. A suitable analogy would be the instability of perception demonstrated in the Necker Cube, whose facets keep on changing places, or Jastrow and Wittgenstein's tantalizing hybrid the Duck-Rabbit.[31] Even the names are unreliable. Angel – a Spanish name for a man who takes every opportunity to speak English. Jesús Gris – Grey Jesus, but grey in age, or grey in his initial mildness? Mercedes – Mercy or Pity, neither of which appears to be her characteristic virtue. Aurora – Dawn, whose virtue is that she never seems to change. Gothic or science fiction? It is both and more, a rabbit and a duck.

Notes

1. 'Hay cosas en el bosque que son más viejas, más raras y más malvadas que nosotros. Han estado aquí antes.' (Translations from Spanish are by Laurence Davies.) This passage comes from del Toro's notebooks. The bulk of the article is a translated version of an interview with three Mexican directors, Cuarón, Iñárritu, and del Toro, for the PBS network in the United States.
2. There was a ceremonial signing in December 1992, but getting the consent of the Mexican, Canadian, and US legislatures took another year, and the treaty came into effect on New Year's Day, 1994.
3. The voice-over in the initial sequence gives the date of the Alchemist's flight to Mexico as 1536 and implies that he created the device after his arrival. Thus 1537 would make a chronological rhyme.
4. 'Créditos iniciales. Bajo éstos vemos la ciudad de México, masa compacta de putrefacción urbana. Muros y paredones grises, interminables hileras de antenas de televisión, naturaleza muerta iluminada por un sol pardo y tímido.[…] Éste es un México *post*-Tratado de Libre Comercio.'
5. For its specific effects on Mexican cinema, see Wood (38–40).
6. Earlier versions were called *El vampiro de Aurelia Gris* and *Sangre gris* (García Tsao 8).
7. His work is not unique in this respect. As the missing sequences of Fritz Lang's *Metropolis* resurface, the Gothic tendencies of both the film and Thea von Harbou's script become more and more evident.
8. For the complex history of public and private cinema funding in Mexico, see Maciel, Mora, and Turrent. At the time del Toro sought help, audiences were shrinking: between 1989 and 1991, 992 cinemas closed and 10,082 video clubs opened (Turrent 111).
9. In fact, del Toro, an admirer of such earlier masters as Hitchcock, has repeatedly complained about the stultifying demands of contemporary big studios, not least their reliance on focus groups (e.g. 2007). Lázaro-Reboll's discussion of reception, specifically of *El espinazo del diablo* (*The Devil's Backbone*), is nuanced and wide ranging. For *Cronos* as a 'cross-Border' film, see Stock. It is also worth remarking that several recent academic studies of contemporary Mexican cinema find no room for del Toro (Foster, Noble, Schaefer).
10. Del Toro has also said that 'the perfect movie has no dialogue' (Earles 29), but he makes the most of imperfection. He also understands the power of letting otherwise silent characters such as Fulcanelli and Aurora utter just a few words.
11. 'Seis patas cortas e inútiles se mueven rápidamente a los lados, la sangre hincha su

vientre, pliegues de piel vieja, llena de verrugas, se expanden, se inflan casi a punto de explosión. En sus intestinos traslúcidos se filtra la sangre, cambia de ton, volviéndose más oscura, casi negra.'

12. Fulcanelli is employed as clockmaker to Antonio de Mendoza, the first Viceroy of New Spain (a much larger area than present-day Mexico), who had arrived the previous year.

13. The collapse of the church is left unexplained, but Mexican cinema-goers were likely to recall similar scenes after the dreadful earthquake of 1985.

14. 'La mejor comida que he probado en años. Muy buena para la memoria.'

15. On the complex and fruitful relationship between science and the occult in the Renaissance, see James and Yates.

16. 'El genio del alquimista ha creado una especie de diálisis primitiva, un extraño filtro viviente.'

17. Let alone the posthumanist vision of 'cyborgothic' mothering proffered by Yi (121–44).

18. Starting from Baudrillard's comments on the funeral business, Botting (67–75) offers a suggestive commentary on the sterilization and prettification of death and their relevance to the contemporary vampire. Of course not all US citizens can afford such luxuries or would want them in the first place. Ironically, Americans have often turned to Mexico as a source of cheap or unapproved medicines.

19. For the prevalence of family solidarity in current vampire films and fiction, see Nixon (120–22).

20. During Marx's analysis of factory labour in Chapter 10 of *Capital* this metaphor appears three times; one of them, aptly enough, comes at the start of Section IV, which is about 'Day and Night Work'.

21. See also Zanger on the 'new vampire as sliding into metonymy' (20). Overall, he argues that vampires have become representations of our own ambiguities rather than images of the other, an observation that works better with, say, *The Hunger* or *The Lost Boys* or even Rice's *Vampire Chronicles* than with *Cronos*.

22. In Moretti's version, for example, Dracula is a monopoly capitalist and, by implication, his enemies represent an older, more conservative tradition. Yet this is a reversible equation: one could, with equal justification, see those muscular opponents as representatives of a new bourgeois order who try to stamp out a resurgence of the feudal. This counter-reading lends itself at least as well to historicizing as Moretti's does. All the same, without his reading we'd be much the poorer.

23. 'Si tu provocas, es peor, Aurora.' This line is not in the screen play, and the whole order of scenes in the final cut differs considerably.

24. For more about the international production and reception of horror films, see Schneider.

25. Mexicans, not least del Toro (Wood 28), often lay claim to a distinctive acquaintance with death, intimate and darkly comic. Such an outlook can also be found in Central America – in Guatemala for example. Taking a wider perspective embracing Native American and African cultures, Jewelle Gomez, creator of the lesbian vampire and former slave Gilda, reminds us that 'ecologically, all life is interdependent and death is a natural part of life – not necessarily a separate horror'. She adds: 'If people can donate a pint of blood to the Red Cross and live, they can give it to Gilda' (91).

26. 'Cómo no. ¿Término medio o bien cocido?'

27. See Miliotes, Carmichael and Sayer.

28. A couple of hours with the works of G. W. M. Reynolds would yield plenty of examples. The most accessible source is Trefor Thomas's selection from the first series of the immensely popular *The Mysteries of London* (1844–46).

29. Not to mention the satirical aspects of popular music such as the *corrido*. Another example of popular culture as resistance is the masked figure of Superbarrio, who

made his first appearance in the devastated neighbourhoods of Mexico City after the 1985 earthquake, rallying opposition to a corrupt and heartless government (Hemispheric Institute).
30. Here, in other words, is a lovely example of what Jameson calls 'Media Jujitsu' (328–33). Parody can be a weapon of resistance: consider, for example, the school-girls' mimicry of the police sergeant and the caricatures of colonial officers and their wives in Wole Soyinka's *Death and the King's Horseman*.
31. This inconstant creature originated with the psychologist Joseph Jastrow in 1899 and reappeared in Wittgenstein's *Philosophical Investigations* (II.xi).

Works cited

Arrabal, Fernando. *Plays*. Volume 1. Trans. Barbara Wright. London: Calder & Boyars, 1962. Print.
Barthleme, Donald. *Unspeakable Practices, Unnatural Acts*. New York: Farrar, Straus & Giroux, 1968. Print.
Botting, Fred. *Gothic Romanced: Consumption, Gender and Technology in Contemporary Fictions*. London: Routledge, 2008. Print.
Carmichael, Elizabeth and Chloë Sayer. *The Skeleton at the Feast: The Day of the Dead in Mexico*. London: British Museum, 1991. Print.
Cronos. Dir. Guillermo del Toro. October Films, 1993. Film.
Davies, Anne. 'Guillermo del Toro's *Cronos*: The Vampire as Embodied Heterotopia.' *Quarterly Review of Film and Literature*. 25.5 (October 2008). 395–403. Print.
Del Toro, Guillermo. *La invención de Cronos*. Mexico D.F.: El Milagro, 1995. Print.
—. *Cronos* Director's Commentary. DVD. London: Optimum Releasing, 2007. Video.
—, et al. 'La noche de los Gotham.' *Letras Libres*. Mexico D.F.: 9.100 (April 2007): 20–27. Print.
Delany, Samuel R. 'About 5,750 Words.' *The Jewel-Hinged Jaw*. Middletown, CT: Wesleyan UP, 2009. 1–16. Print.
Devil's Backbone, The. Dir. Guillermo del Toro. London: Optimum Releasing, 2007. Video.
Dick, Philip K. *The Man in the High Castle*. Harmondsworth: Penguin, 1965. Print.
Earles, Steve. *The Golden Labyrinth: The Unique Films of Guillermo del Toro*. Hereford: Noir Publishing, 2009. Print.
Ellison, Harlan. *I Have No Mouth and I Must Scream*. New York: Pyramid, 1967. Print.
Foster, David William. *Mexico City in Contemporary Mexican Cinema*. Austin: U of Texas P, 2002. Print.
Fuentes, Carlos. *A New Time for Mexico*. Trans. Marina Gutman Castañeda and Carlos Fuentes. London: Bloomsbury, 1997. Print.
García Tsao, Leonardo. 'Introducción.' Del Toro 1995. 7–9. Print.
Gibson, William and Bruce Sterling. *The Difference Engine*. London: Gollancz, 1990. Print.
Gomez, Jewelle. 'Recasting the Mythology: Writing Vampire Fiction.' *Blood Read: The Vampire in Contemporary Culture*. Eds. Joan Gordon and Veronica Hollinger. Philadelphia: U of Pennsylvania P, 1997. 85–92. Print.
Haraway, Donna J. *Modest_Witness@Second_Millennium*. London: Routledge, 1997. Print.
—. *Simians, Cyborgs, and Women: The Reinvention of Women*. London: Free Association, 1991. Print.
Hellboy. Dir. Guillermo del Toro. Revolution Studios, 2004. Video.
Hellboy II: The Golden Army. Dir. Guillermo del Toro. Universal Studios, 2008. Video.
Hemispheric Institute of Performance and Politics. 'Superbarrio.' Web. 10 August 2010.

Hunger, The. Dir. Tony Scott. Warner Home Video, 1983. Video.

Internet Movie Database (IMDb). *Cronos*. Web. 2 August 2010.

James, David Gwilym. *The Dream of Prospero*. Oxford: Clarendon Press, 1967. Print.

Jameson, Fredric. *The Geopolitical Aesthetic: Cinema and Space in the World System*. Bloomington: Indiana UP, 1992. Print.

Kantaris, Geoffrey. 'Between Dolls, Vampires, and Cyborgs: Recursive Bodies in Mexican Urban Cinema.' 1998. Web. 20 July 2010.

Kermode, Mark. 'Girl Interrupted.' *Sight and Sound* 16.12 (December 2006): 20–24. Print.

Kraniauskas, John. 'Cronos and the Political Economy of Vampirism: Notes on a Historical Constellation.' *Cannibalism and the Colonial World*. Eds. Francis Barker, Peter Hulme and Margaret Iversen. Cambridge UP, 1998. 152–59. Print.

Lázaro-Reboll, Antonio. 'The Transnational Reception of *El espinazo del diablo*.' *Hispanic Research Journal* 8.1 (February 2007): 39–51. Print.

Lost Boys, The. Dir. Joel Schumacher. Warner Home Video, 1998.

Maciel, David R. 'Cinema and the State in Contemporary Mexico, 1970–1999.' *Mexico's Cinema: A Century of Film and Filmmakers*. Eds. Joanne Hershfield and David Maciel. Wilmington, DE: Scholarly Resources, 1999. 197–232. Print.

Marx, Karl. *Capital*. Volume 1. Trans. Ben Fowkes. Harmondsworth: Penguin, 1976. Print.

McCaffrey, Anne. *The Ship Who Sang*. London: Corgi, 1972. Print.

Metropolis. Dir. Fritz Lang. Wiesbaden: Stiftung F. W. Murnau, 2010. Film.

Miliotes, Diane. *José Guadalupe Posada and the Mexican Broadside*. Chicago: Art Institute, 2006. Print.

Mimic. Dir. Guillermo del Toro. Buena Vista Home Entertainment, 1998. Video.

Mora, Carl J. *Mexican Cinema: Reflections of a Society, 1896–1980*. Berkeley: U of California P, 1982. Print.

Moretti, Franco. *Signs Taken for Wonders*. London: Verso, 2005. Print.

Ní Dhomhnaill, Nuala. *Selected Poems: Rogha Dánta*. Trans. Michael Hartnett. Dublin: New Island, 1993. Print.

Nixon, Nicola. 'When Hollywood Sucks, or, Hungry Girls, Lost Boys, and Vampirism in the Age of Reagan.' *Blood Read: The Vampire in Contemporary Culture*. Eds. Joan Gordon and Veronica Hollinger. Philadelphia: U of Pennsylvania P, 1997. 115–28. Print.

Noble, Andrea. *Mexican National Cinema*. London: Routledge, 2005. Print.

Nosferatu. Dir. F. W. Murnau. Masters of Cinema, 2007. Video.

Pan's Labyrinth. Dir. Guillermo del Toro. London: Optimum Releasing, 2007. Video.

Reynolds, George W. M. *The Mysteries of London*. Ed. Trefor Thomas. Keele: Keele UP, 1996. Print.

Rice, Ann. *Interview with the Vampire*. London: Futura, 1994. Print.

Santo vs. la invasión de los Marcianos. 1967. Kit Parker Films, 2001. Video.

Schaefer, Claudia. *Bored to Distraction: Cinema of Excess in End-of-the-Century Mexico and Spain*. Albany, NY: SUNY Press, 2003. Print.

Schneider, Steven Jay. *Fear without Frontiers*. Godalming, Surrey: FAB, 2003. Print.

Shelley, Mary. *Collected Tales and Stories*. Ed. Charles E. Robinson. Baltimore: Johns Hopkins UP, 1976. Print.

Soyinka, Wole. *Death and the King's Horseman*. London: Methuen, 1975. Print.

Stock, Ann Marie. 'Authentically Mexican? *Mi querido Tom Mix* and *Cronos* Reframe Critical Questions.' *Mexico's Cinema: A Century of Film and Filmmakers*. Eds. Joanne Hershfield and David Maciel. Wilmington, DE: Scholarly Resources, 1999. 267–86. Print.

Stoker, Bram. *Dracula*. Ed. Maud Ellmann. Oxford: Oxford UP, 2008. Print.

Suvin, Darko. 'Science Fiction and the Novum.' 1977. *Defined by a Hollow: Essays on Utopia, Science Fiction and Political Epistemology*. Ralahine Utopian Studies 6. Bern: Peter Lang, 2010. 67–92. Print.

Turrent, Tomás Pérez. 'Crises and Renovations (1965–91).' *Mexican Cinema*. Ed. Paulo Antonio Paranaguá. Trans. Ana M. López. London: British Film Institute, 1995. 94–115. Print.

Viridiana. Dir. Luis Buñuel. Arrow Films, 2006. Video.

Wittgenstein, Ludwig. *Philosophical Investigations*. Translated by G. E. M. Anscombe. Oxford: Blackwell, 1958. Print.

Wood, Jason. *The Faber Book of Mexican Cinema*. London: Faber, 2006. Print.

Yates, Frances A. *Giordano Bruno and the Hermetic Tradition*. London: Routledge, 1964. Print.

Yi, Dongshin. *A Genealogy of Cyborgothic: Aesthetics and Ethics in the Age of Posthumanism*. Farnham, Surrey: Ashgate, 2010. Print.

Zanger, Jules. 'Metaphor into Metonymy: The Vampire Next Door.' *Blood Read: The Vampire in Contemporary Culture*. Eds. Joan Gordon and Veronica Hollinger. Philadelphia: U of Pennsylvania P, 1997. 17–26. Print.

6. Infected with Life: Neo-supernaturalism and the Gothic Zombie

Gwyneth Peaty

In the opening of Danny Boyle's film *28 Days Later* (2002), a team of animal activists are shown breaking into the Cambridge primate research centre. In this dark laboratory they encounter a spectacle of scientific atrocity. Dead chimpanzees, their bloody chests splayed open, lie stretched across operating tables surrounded by test tubes, wires and X-rays. Living creatures scream and beat the walls of small glass cages. A single distraught chimpanzee is strapped down, forced to watch a row of televisions that repeatedly screen violent images of war, pain and human aggression. Unbeknownst to their would-be saviours, the animals in this room represent a dire threat. Like Victor Frankenstein's 'work-shop of filthy creation' (Shelley 50), this laboratory is the birthplace of a human-made horror: the Rage virus. 'The chimps are infected. They're highly contagious', explains the scientist on duty as he tries to stop the intruders. 'The infection is in their blood and saliva. One bite ...'. But it is all too late. A door is opened, and the animal within explodes forth to fix its teeth in the female activist's neck. Within seconds, the woman is making a transition. Writhing, growling, vomiting blood across the floor and into her companion's face, she finally turns to reveal glazed red eyes. She is infected; she has become a zombie. The others are swiftly infected and the apocalypse has begun.

In this introduction the mode of 'living death' associated with the filmic zombie is transformed from a supernatural to a pathological condition; a state of disease. Born of biomedical science, this condition speaks of human technologies spun out of control, generating the very pandemic horrors they are intended to eradicate. Focusing on *28 Days Later*, its sequel, Juan Carlos Fresnadillo's *28 Weeks Later* (2007), and Francis Lawrence's *I Am Legend* (2007), this essay will examine how contemporary zombie films re-imagine the Gothic undead in the context of scientific discourse, and highlight some of the repercussions of this figure's shift from the superstitious margins to the privileged centre: the realm of biomedicine. What makes these particular films significant is not only their focus upon the scientific genesis of 'the Infected', but their investment in the possibility that biomedicine produces a form of living death that can be diagnosed, monitored and ultimately cured using biomedical technologies. In each film such possibilities parallel, or are embedded within, the operation of military forces, offering a suggestive vision of Gothic pathology that simultaneously eludes and is made subject to the institutional regimes of biopower.

28 Days Later follows the story of Jim, a bicycle courier, who wakes from a month-long coma to discover that London is a wasteland inhabited by hordes of Infected. Along with a small group of fellow survivors, Jim follows a radio recording that promises the cure to infection, only to discover that it is a false claim perpetuated by soldiers with no medical knowledge whatsoever. *28 Weeks Later* depicts the American army's attempts to cleanse and rebuild London after the Infected of the previous film have starved to death. This sequel further explores the relationship between science, horror and the military, with the possibility of a cure embodied in the characters of Andy and his mother, Alice, who possess a natural immunity to the virus. Finally, *I Am Legend* likewise portrays a post-pandemic city, New York, where lone survivor Robert fights to survive attacks from the Infected. Unlike in the *28* films, the hope for a medical solution becomes a reality in this scenario when Robert manages to create a cure from his own immune blood. Each of these films draws upon the conventions of both horror and science fiction, and the Infected are understood to emerge from a convergence of these genres.

Kyle Bishop argues that, unlike the vampire, zombies are a distinctly filmic twentieth-century creature: 'the zombie ... has no germinal Gothic novel from which it stems, no primal narrative that established and codified its qualities or behaviors' (13). When he considers the Infected, however, the question of origins becomes more complex. 'This kind of zombie is more frightening than the traditional fantasy monster', because '[it] crosses the genre into science fiction: it could happen' (28). The notion of infection situates the zombie as a medical horror, a laboratory creation whose existence has a prominent forebear. Mary Shelley's *Frankenstein*, as Fred Botting has noted, stands as an influential antecedent to both Gothic horror and science fiction narratives ('Monsters' 113). By 'closing the gap between superstition and rationality, Frankenstein replaces occultism and alchemy with electricity in order to bring his technological creation to life' (Dinello 41). The contemporary zombie film draws much inspiration from this seminal text, reproducing and reformulating its concerns in the context of modern medicine.

Zombie science

It is useful to begin with a consideration of biomedical discourse, for this context produces particular notions of 'the body' as both an object of knowledge and an entity requiring firm administration. Discussing the development of medical practice, Foucault identifies the 'clinical gaze' as that which produces medicalized bodies by mapping human anatomies in terms of culturally determined symptoms and categories. 'A man coughs; he spits blood; he has difficulty in breathing': these facts are not enough, in themselves, to confirm disease (*Birth of the Clinic* 146). They require the clinician's organizing presence, and the application of known definitions. 'Disease', Foucault argues, 'is deprived of being [but] is endowed with a configuration' (*Birth of the Clinic* 146). The doctor's eye 'is the separating agent of truths'; 'a gaze that travels from body to body' imposing taxonomies of deviance and normalcy (*Birth of the Clinic* 147–148). Contemporary biomedicine likewise views the body according to categories of wellness and disease, but does so in the context of new imaging technologies. A mechanized version of the 'clinical gaze' now pierces the skin, magnifying, diagnosing and compartmentalizing the body at the genetic level. Catherine Waldby explains that biomedical technologies involve a mode of scrutiny that 'exposes the bodily interior to new orders of machine vision' (5). This technological gaze 'reads the body's interior as digitized information configured on a computer screen' (5). Thus biomedical practice actively constructs the human body 'as a network of informational systems, working through code, signal, transcription, interference, noise, and the execution of programmes' (25). By situating the Infected within this world, as the subject of a biotechnologized 'clinical' gaze, contemporary films present a medico-scientific vision of the zombie that resonates with larger anxieties regarding possible 'posthuman' futures of the human body.

Notions of a posthuman condition emerge from such conflations of the molecular with the cybernetic. 'In the posthuman', Katherine Hayles states, 'there are no essential differences or absolute demarcations between bodily existence and computer simulation, cybernetic mechanism and biological organism, robot teleology and human goals' (3). The human subject, defined as an informational entity, is disembodied to the extent that, it is imagined, it will eventually transcend its material 'host' body. Such an eventuality is often conceived as a liberation from the realities of a life limited by flesh. As Hakim Bey puts it, 'materiality is such a mess' (2). The Infected are certainly messy, all blood and rage and meat. But these bodies are also posthuman, for they have been changed, they have been interfered with. Infection exploits the interface between the biological and the technological, and between bodies of different species. The Rage virus of *28 Days Later* and *28*

Weeks Later is born of a concentration of violent televisual images that are effectively 'downloaded' by the chimpanzees who are forced to view them. Viral digital information enters and transforms the genetic structure of the animals, who subsequently transfer it into humans. In *I Am Legend*, the infection originates in the genetically engineered Krippen virus, a biomedical marvel intended to cure cancer. Dr Alice Krippen, the accidental progenitor of the zombie hordes, comments of her invention that 'the premise is quite simple. Take something designed by nature and reprogram it to make it work for the body rather than against it.' Here the human body is conceived as a faulty computer, a biological machine controlled by programs with design flaws. The Infected are shown to be posthuman in the sense that their form is the result of a medical transgression of the border between biology and technology.

The Infected zombie can be understood to enact a form of posthuman dualism in the context of living death. Marina Warner describes a zombie as 'someone whose soul has been stolen, whose body has not exactly died, but passed into the power of a magician or owner who uses it for his (rarely her) purposes' (357). Unlike the vampire, who must die to rise again, the zombie need not be a living corpse but 'a body which has been hollowed out, emptied of selfhood' (357). The living death of the zombie thus relates to a forced separation of the mind from the body; the individual self 'dies' while their body lives on as a mindless puppet. Operated from a distance, these 'empty' vessels are driven mechanically towards their living victims. Unlike earlier filmic depictions of the zombie as an animated cadaver, the Infected reproduce this notion of mind/body separation in the context of diseased living bodies. Infected people are 'dead' in the sense that critical brain functioning and social identity have been lost, leaving only an insatiable corporeality. In Western societies dominated by posthuman and biomedical discourses, this zombie can be seen to present an intriguing model of biotechnologized flesh abandoned by intellect. Martin Rogers recently endorsed this perspective, arguing that the term 'infected' in *28 Days Later* 'modifies the traditional concern of the horror film over human bodies … into a concern over disembodiment and the transference of virulent reprogramming via the human information stream' (120). For Rogers, the concerns of Boyle's film coincide with Hayles' discussion of the posthuman condition. Both Infected and uninfected bodies, he argues, are represented as units of data moving within a networked system of information. The 'information stream' in this instance is blood, and the true horror of the Rage virus is its communicability through the network: 'its ability to quickly replicate and travel – to reproduce' (127). Rogers concludes that *28 Days Later* is 'a horror film for computers', a way for 'technological intelligence' to manage 'its anxiety over human bodies, their tenacity, and their persistent, bloody corporeality' (130). The zombified flesh, discarded by the mind, is understood as the inevitable by-product of the posthuman condition.

The posthuman notion of the body as a non-essential component of human being has been countered by those who emphasize the fundamental materiality of human existence. Bodies, as Donna Haraway famously noted, 'are not born: they are made' (208). The body is a social construct, inextricably bound up with the formation of the human self as a social actor. Elizabeth Grosz argues that biomedical science presents a passive notion of the body that fails to account for its true agency: 'bodies are not inert; they function interactively and productively. They act and react. They generate what is new, surprising, unpredictable' (xi). This perspective is useful to remember in relation to the Infected, for while the filmic gaze produces the contemporary zombie through a biomedical lens, these bodies enact an embodied state of infection which draws upon Gothic monstrosity, as well as Gothic notions of science, in both familiar and unfamiliar ways.

Infection

In both the *28* films and *I Am Legend*, zombies are born from attempts to address social malignancy at a genetic level. The Rage virus is created by medical scientists trying to locate the gene for human violence, the special ingredient that causes hate, murder and war. 'In order to cure, you must first understand', argues the doctor in *28 Days Later*, as explanation for the horrors they have unleashed. One must create the death beast, in order to discover its secret and appropriate its power over life. For all its contemporary trappings, this project draws clear inspiration from Frankenstein's utopian mission to transcend the limits of life and death, those 'ideal bounds, which I should first break through, and pour a torrent of light into our dark world' (Shelley 49). Dr Krippen understands her work as supplanting something dangerous and wilful (biology) with something safe (biotechnology): 'you can imagine your body as a highway and you picture the virus as a very fast car being driven by a very bad man ... if you replace that man with a cop, the picture changes'. A posthuman perspective on regulating, maintaining and extending life is here explicitly related to state-sanctioned policing and the elimination of deviant social elements. This conflation of biological and institutional bodies recalls Foucault's discussion of biopower, the mechanism by which 'life' overtook 'death' as the focus of disciplinary organization (*History of Sexuality* 135–145). Biopower is 'essentially a right of seizure: of things, time, bodies, and ultimately life itself'; 'a power bent on generating forces, making them grow, and ordering them' (136). The flesh does not submit easily to this seizure, however, and these films depict biopolitical structures overcome by a liminal corporeality they cannot contain. Selena, an uninfected survivor, explains to Jim how it began in *28 Days Later*:

> 'It was in the street outside. It was coming in through your windows. It was a virus. An infection. You didn't need a doctor to tell you that. It was the blood. It was something in the blood. By the time they tried to evacuate the cities it was already too late. Army blockades were overrun.'

Bearing out the promise of 'your body as a highway' the Infected simultaneously fill streets and veins with death, overflowing the physical and ontological boundaries that hold civilization in place. Death, as Foucault comments, marks biopower's limit, 'the moment that escapes it' and the Infected represent a form of living death that eludes the regulatory structures that corral the living (*Sexuality* 138). The Infected do not escape entirely, however, as will be shown further down.

While the Infected in these films are framed by similar biomedical discourses, they embody and perform different states of disease. In the *28* films, the Infected are red-eyed, gore-smeared and explosive, vomiting black blood into the faces of their victims while tearing through their skin. This horrifying exchange works to infect the victim in a way similar to how Gothic vampires are understood to 'turn' their human prey. Infection is via transfusion of bodily fluids, and blood takes on a central physical and symbolic role, both as the vehicle that carries a contagious substance and as the contagious substance itself: 'it was the blood'. The uninfected can be turned by a single drop entering their body. Unlike many earlier zombie films, in which flesh eating is a primary feature, the Infected 'life' cycle here appears to depend upon consuming the blood of the living. While these zombies are not shown eating people, they are always biting. Their mouths are smeared with old and fresh blood, and they aim for the jugular whenever possible. Survivors are aware of this propensity. 'If he is still breathing … it won't be the pasta he's interested in. It'll be your fucking neck', a young woman is told when saving food for her lost boyfriend in *28 Weeks Later*. The only way to stop the virus spreading is to quarantine the British mainland and wait for the Infected to starve to death. The physical death of the Infected is inevitable once the blood of the living is no longer available. In this way the Infected resemble the vampire, who must ingest human blood in order to maintain its state of posthumous life. Vampires, as James Twitchell puts it, engage in '[a] ghastly process of energy transfer in which one partner gains vitality at the expense of another' (3). The infected reproduce this interchange between the living and the dead, simultaneously 'turning' and consuming the life force of the victim through their blood. Just as the blood of the Infected carries a terrible mystery, death, which passes into the living, the blood of the living carries and transfers life into the undead.

The Krippen virus of *I Am Legend* creates a different form of zombie, but reproduces the notion of monstrously transformed and diseased bodies that consume the living. These Infected are grey skinned and hairless, human shaped but terrifyingly changed. Their mouths are full of razor-sharp teeth and their bodies are muscular and enlarged. They feed on those immune to the virus, as they are the only living still available, and their hunger forms a global pandemic. Protagonist Robert explains to another survivor: 'KV had a ninety percent kill rate. That's 5.4 billion people dead. Less than one percent immunity. That left twelve million healthy people.' The other 588 million became Infected: 'then they got hungry. And they killed and fed on everybody.' While these Infected resemble the traditional zombie in their consumption of human flesh, they also evoke the Gothic vampire in important ways. They cannot go out in daylight, for their skin burns at the touch of ultraviolet light. They are also obsessed with human blood. When Robert wants to catch one, he breaks a test tube of blood and waits for them to smell it. This film is based on the 1954 vampire novel of the same name (Matheson). Yet the Infected, for all their vampiric qualities, are still framed as single-minded flesh eaters in the zombie tradition. It is worth noting that nowhere in this film is the word 'vampire' mentioned. Similarly the word 'zombie' does not appear in the *28* films. This omission is not unusual in the context of zombie narratives. As many have noted, the term 'zombie' does not appear in George Romero's *Night of the Living Dead*, which is regarded as the seminal zombie film. It is less usual in the context of vampire narratives, and such categorical slippage conveys the sense that the Infected transgress not only human ontology, but taxonomies of monstrosity as well.

These two representations of the Infected have in common the idea that human flesh and blood holds a residue of life that can somehow be incorporated by the dead through the act of consumption. Living flesh and blood take on a synecdochic role, understood to posses a remnant of life that the dead can access and drain to their satiation. Gothic anxieties about the status of living and dead bodies, and the boundaries that separate them, are played out through the Infected as a model of Gothic pathology. The life stolen by the diseased Infected is certainly a potent recipe. Unlike earlier depictions of the zombie as a grudgingly mobile corpse, the Infected in all three films are hyperactive. They exert themselves strenuously in the pursuit of the living, always lunging and running, arms pumping furiously, after their prey. Becoming Infected results in a state of super-animation, a form of living death that manifests in bodily excitement. These altered individuals are infected with life, as much as with death. This energy signals, for some, their disqualification from the category of undead zombie. Romero himself has commented that 'people called *28 Days* and *28 Weeks* zombie movies, and they're not! It's some sort of virus; they're not dead' (Murray). Yet, as Warner points out, one need not be physically dead to be a zombie.

The Infected represent a contemporary form of zombieism that is as consumed with life as it is with death. In this way they reflect a biopolitical preoccupation with the idea of life: its manifestations, maintenance and regulation. Eugene Thacker argues that 'modern biological thought always makes two demands of "life itself": that it be essentially information (or pattern) and that it also be essentially matter (or presence)' (xviii). Human life is imagined simultaneously as codified and legible, a posthuman system, and as an intangible 'something' that inhabits the flesh. The parameters and substance of 'life itself' thus retain a sense of mystery that biomedical discourse works to simultaneously unravel and maintain. Alternatively, Gothic fictions are understood to be consumed with the mystery of death. As Carol Ann Howells comments, these texts 'are death-haunted, full of violent deaths and fears of death and fantasies about death' (207). But death, in Gothic, is not the end but the beginning. Its limits are there to be pushed and probed, and its boundaries are transgressed in ways that express acute cultural anxieties related to the terminality of human life. Life and death cannot be separated, however. Frankenstein discovers the secret of life while 'examining and analysing all the minutiae of causation, as exemplified in the change from life to death, and death to life' (Shelley 47). The pathologized zombie registers biomedical concerns through a re-formulation of Gothic monstrosity that pushes the question of 'life itself' to the forefront of living death.

Surveillance

Representations of living death as a pathological condition are intricately bound with the politics of medical and military surveillance. After the Infected outbreak of the previous film, *28 Weeks Later* depicts mainland Britain being repatriated by American-led NATO forces. From security cameras to intrusive rooftop snipers, returning Londoners are kept under constant watch within a guarded compound. Army personnel track their arrival in a room full of closed-circuit monitors. 'What's on TV tonight?' comments Doyle, a sharp shooter, as he trains his rifle's telescopic lens into civilians' windows. The horrors of infection are patrolled using an integrated medico-military gaze which produces the human as a benign form that, like a tumour, might easily transform into malignancy. This quarantine scenario fits well into Foucault's description of the plague town as a disciplinary model: 'this enclosed, segmented space, observed at every point, in which the individuals are inserted in a fixed place, in which the slightest movements are supervised, in which all events are recorded' (*Discipline and Punish* 197). The disciplining gaze, informed by the clinical, constitutes uninfected bodies as always potentially dangerous, requiring constant observation and constraint. The act of looking and the eye itself are here represented through a posthuman convergence of biological and technological optics. In one of Doyle's first scenes he looks towards the camera with an eye to the scope of his rifle. Magnified, the eye appears greatly enlarged. The camera later shows what this enormous eye sees: the interior of the civilians' rooms. The organic eye and the filmic lens merge into the telescopic gaze. In this way viewers are invited to observe the convergence of means by which uninfected bodies are produced both as visual spectacles in a filmic sense ('on TV') and as potential social deviants and targets. This scene and numerous others depicting military eyes set to rifle scopes are paralleled by those in which a doctor's eyes gaze through medical lenses at deviant blood. Scarlet, the army's aptly named chief medical officer, is shown in a laboratory staring into the eyepiece of a microscope. The camera then cuts to what she sees: the highly active, mutating cells of the virus. Scarlet and Doyle, representing two halves of the medico-military system, are equally implicated in the process of identifying and disciplining both 'normal' and monstrous bodies.

Eyes are of central importance here, as both the organs that survey and those that are surveyed. The returning British inhabitants of *28 Weeks Later* must undergo ophthalmological tests, supervised by armed soldiers, which survey the human eye for disease. Flashbacks in *I Am Legend* reveal army personnel using a similar technique to differentiate the uninfected from those showing early signs of infection. A small device held up to the face performs a scan of the eyes and flashes green for healthy, red for diseased. The eye operates as a window into the body which regulatory authorities may access using the penetrating 'machine vision' of biomedical technologies (Waldby 5). Tammy and Andy, the first children to enter Britain in *28 Weeks Later*, also undergo such optical scanning and Scarlet remarks on Andy's heterochromia; a rare genetic condition which results in eyes of variant colours. The camera zooms in on a screen showing a digitized image of Andy's eyes spliced together; a single eye wide open and divided down the centre, half blue, half brown. While the narrative significance of this anomaly is yet to be revealed, its state embodies a foreboding doubling reminiscent of the Infected/uninfected dichotomy. Ostensibly a medical image, this staring eye resembles what Carol Clover calls 'the opening eye of horror' (166). For Clover, the act of looking, and the imaging of the eye itself, is crucial to horror film: 'horror privileges eyes because, more crucially than any other kind of cinema, it is about eyes. More particularly, it is about eyes watching horror' (167). Here the eye becomes a locus of medicalized horror, for Andy's eyes are both innocent witnesses to infection and embodiments of its liminal threat. His heterochromia makes him a carrier, one who can become Infected without being fully transformed by the virus. His infection, when it inevitably occurs, is silent. The only sign is redness in his brown eye. His blue eye remains clear, and he is judged safe by those who escort him back into the bosom of the uninfected population.

For all the scanning through binoculars, video cameras and rifle scopes, military surveillance is unable to preserve the borders it is tasked with patrolling. As Foucault explains, 'against the plague, which is a mixture, discipline brings into play its power, which is one of analysis' (*Discipline and Punish* 197). Against the living dead, however, the architectures of discipline find themselves unable to locate anything other than mixture. The character of Andy exemplifies the impossibility of observing the boundary between living and undead, healthy and diseased. He is an innocent living child, yet he carries within his blood that which is death to others. In addition to death, he also contains the key to life, a genetic immunity which allows him to survive the virus without becoming Infected. The blurring line between Infected and uninfected collapses completely when an outbreak occurs in the 'secure' compound. The disciplinary gaze cannot penetrate the body's surface without the assistance of biomedical machinery. Unable to tell the difference between zombies and humans as they rush together into the street, Doyle and his fellow snipers are ordered to target everyone. When in doubt, all bodies are classed as dangerous and must be eliminated. The mechanisms of biopower clearly fail in their stewardship of human life as the technologies upon which control depends come apart, and they are unable to correctly identify the dichotomies they are intended to enforce. The eye scanner in *I Am Legend* falsely classifies Robert's wife as Infected, only to confirm moments later that she is uninfected. Human optics are just as flawed. 'I won't take my eyes off them', promises the officer tasked with taking Robert's wife and child to safety. They are dead soon after.

Cure

While military surveillance clearly fails to control the Infected, biomedicine rises from the ashes to offer hope. Moreover, it is within the laboratory, the very site where the Infected were born, that the promise of a cure resides. All is made clear under the microscope. Here the zombie is to be recovered, in the sense both of a recovery from illness and of a retrieval of the deviant liminal body from its transgressive state. In each film it is the promise of a cure for infection that motivates the protagonists and ultimately moves the narrative forward. The survivors of *28 Days Later* travel miles through zombie-infested Britain in search of it. Scarlet and Doyle dedicate themselves, and eventually give their lives, to protect Tammy and Andy, the siblings whose blood might hold the secret of immunity. *I Am Legend*'s Robert is himself immune to infection. He is also, usefully, a military virologist and devotes his remaining life to constructing a cure. 'I can still fix this', is Robert's mantra, which he repeats throughout the film.

When he is not working his way through New York City, street by street, looking for food, Robert is performing an equally methodical exploration of infection, body by body, looking for a cure. His basement laboratory is a sanitary haven amidst the post-apocalyptic landscape, a quiet dimly lit world full of shining surgical instruments, computers and sterilizing handwash. In the first scene set in the basement, Robert puts on a pristine white lab coat and examines a series of glass cages in which Infected rats thrash wildly, reminiscent of the chimpanzees in the opening of *28 Days Later*. As he views them, he also records their movements as streaming video which appears on a nearby computer screen. 'Compound six appears to be showing decreased aggression response. Partial pigmentation return. Slight pupil constriction. GA series, serum 391, Compound six, next candidate for human trials.' Human trials are tests on the Infected, whom Robert traps and sedates. The second scene in the laboratory shows an Infected strapped down on an operating table, attached to beeping, flashing monitors. Here the zombie is entirely encompassed within a medical framework. 'Subject is female. Likely eighteen to twenty years of age. Dilaudid push only sedates effectively at six times human dose. Core temperature, 106 Fahrenheit. Pulse, 200 bpm. Respiration elevated.' Despite the obvious nature of zombieism, physical details are itemized and categorized until an objective diagnosis is achieved: 'Symptoms and tissue samples confirm subject is infected with KV.' Robert is also his own test subject, regulating and observing his own continuing life at an objective molecular level. After a close call with the Infected, he returns home to check his blood under a microscope. 'Blood tests confirm that I remain immune to both the airborne and contact strains', he notes in his video diary. Subjective assessments, even of one's own biology, are inadequate compared to the medical gaze, whose microscopic lens reveals that which is hidden.

Robert's power to diagnose is augmented by a power over life and death. The compound fails to cure and the Infected woman dies on the table with an horrific scream, her heart monitor flat-lining. Her doctor shakes his head in disappointment before casually injecting her with a stimulant that restarts her heart. A close shot shows the Infected woman's gasp as she comes back to life. Robert holds the power of life and death over his Infected patients, and in his quest for the secret of immunity, the secret of life, Robert brings mass death. His laboratory wall is covered with hundreds of pictures of failed test subjects: dead Infected. Lonely and obsessed, Robert has become the mad Gothic doctor, surrounded by death. Like Frankenstein, who comments that 'sometimes, on the very brink of certainty, I failed; yet still I clung to the hope which the next day or the next hour might realize' (Shelley 49). The zombie genocide is worth it when Robert finally locates a cure within the very zombie he gave up on. 'You are sick and I can help you', Robert shouts at the Infected, 'I can save everybody! I can fix everything! It's working.' He has discovered the secret of life, and 'it', like the sinister 'something' that inhabits the Infected, moves within the veins: 'the cure is in her blood!'

The liminal ontology of the biotechnologized zombie offers a return to human wholeness by reformulating living death as a curable pathology. All is not lost, we can still fix this. Such resolutions are not an unusual twist in Gothic texts, in which 'transgression, by crossing the social and aesthetic limits, serves to reinforce or underline their value and necessity, restoring or defining limits' (Botting, *Gothic* 7). The borders between life and death, destroyed by the hubristic excesses of science, can be safely reconstructed once more, by those same forces, within the laboratory. Franco Moretti argues that Gothic tales 'must restore the broken equilibrium, giving the illusion of being able to stop history: because the monster expresses the anxiety that the future will be monstrous' (83–84). The scientific plausibility of the Infected zombie, 'it could happen', makes their presence in the imagined future an even greater threat (Bishop 28). Success or failure in this quest for a cure depends upon the presence of a Gothic doctor: one who perceives the integration of biomedical intricacies and speculative ontologies that characterize contemporary living death; specifically, human blood's ability to represent the 'key' or 'secret' to life and death simultaneously. In each film the meaningful yet inexplicable paraphernalia of medicine takes on the aura of what Deborah Lupton calls 'medical magic': 'the trappings of technology: the complex machinery, the flashing lights, the "blips" of the monitors, the graphs measuring the strength and regularity of the pulse' (57). The supernaturalism of the zombie narrative is not precisely lost in this context, rather it is transposed into the sphere of biomedicine. Through the power of 'medical magic' biomedicine promises a cure to the pathological horror of living death and a vaccine for fear.

The contemporary zombie can also be seen to represent a vision of a post-human race striving to recover its human origins. The Infected body speaks of fears relating to a loss of ontological wholeness within the context of merging biological and technological realms. Posthuman 'life' is represented not only as a form of living death, however, but as a state from which one can return. The Gothic doctor devises a way for the mind to merge once more with its material body. Thus these films offer the fantasy that, from the midst of a frightening posthuman condition, the borders of 'normal' human ontology can be reinstated. We might make ourselves into something 'other', but any real threat is diluted by the way we can then unmake the horror. In this way the contemporary zombie's posthuman pathology leads back to an organic, materially situated definition of the human.

Generated from an amalgam of Gothic and science fiction, the Infected represent a reformulation of the zombie as a figure of monstrosity. Embedded in the horrors of the imagined future, this figure nonetheless draws upon historical narratives and tropes in ways both synergistic and transformative. Biomedical intervention supplants supernatural possession for the Infected zombie. Yet this new creature retains and revises the principle of mind/body separation embodied by previous incarnations through the frame of posthuman dualism. The Infected manifest an established Gothic pre-occupation with the borders of life and death. By placing special emphasis upon the 'living' aspect of the living death dichotomy, however, each film reflects twenty-first-century concerns regarding the technologies by which human life is monitored, augmented and extended. A fusion of vampire and zombie characteristics sees this convergence of past and future reflected in the physical body, in which different categories of historical monster merge to form a new beast. Thus the Infected embody a gestalt whose form is testimony to the ever-mutating promise of Gothic science fiction.

Works cited

28 Days Later. Dir. Danny Boyle. 2002. DVD. 20th Century Fox, 2004.
28 Weeks Later. Dir. Juan Carlos Fresnadillo. 2007. DVD. 20th Century Fox, 2007.
Bey, Hakim. 'The Information War.' *Virtual Futures: Cyberotics, Technology and Post-human Pragmatism*. Ed. Joan Broadhurst Dixon and Eric J. Cassidy. New York: Routledge, 1998. 2–10. Print.
Bishop, Kyle William. *American Zombie Gothic: The Rise and Fall (and Rise) of the Walking Dead in Popular Culture*. London: McFarland, 2010. Print.
Botting, Fred. *Gothic*. London: Routledge, 1996. Print.
—. '"Monsters of the Imagination": Gothic, Science, Fiction.' *A Companion to Science Fiction*. Ed. David Seed. Oxford: Blackwell, 2005. 111–126. Print.
Clover, Carol. *Men, Women, and Chainsaws: Gender in the Modern Horror Film*. Princeton, NJ: Princeton UP, 1992. Print.
Dinello, Daniel. *Technophobia!: Science Fiction Visions of Posthuman Technology*. Austin, TX: Texas UP, 2005. Print.
Foucault, Michel. *The Birth of the Clinic*. 3rd ed. London: Routledge, 2003. Print.
—. *Discipline and Punish: The Birth of the Prison*. 10th ed. London: Penguin, 1991. Print.
—. *The History of Sexuality, Volume 1*. London: Penguin, 2008. Print.
Grosz, Elizabeth. *Volatile Bodies: Towards a Corporeal Feminism*. St. Leonards, NSW: Allen & Unwin, 1994. Print.
Haraway, Donna J. *Simians, Cyborgs, and Women: The Reinvention of Nature*. New York: Routledge, 1991. Print.

Hayles, Katherine. *How We Became Posthuman: Virtual Bodies in Cybernetics, Literature, and Informatics*. Chicago, IL: Chicago UP, 1999. Print.

Howells, Carol Ann. 'The Gothic Way of Death in English Fiction 1790–1820.' *British Journal for Eighteenth-Century Studies* 5 (1982): 207–215. Print.

I Am Legend. Dir. Francis Lawrence. 2007. DVD. Warner Bros, 2008.

Lupton, Deborah. *Medicine as Culture: Illness, Disease and the Body in Western Societies*. 2nd ed. London: Sage, 2003. Print.

Matheson, Richard. *I Am Legend*. 6th ed. London: Orion, 2006. Print.

Moretti. Franco. *Signs Taken for Wonders: On the Sociology of Literary Forms*. London: Verso, 2005. Print.

Murray, Noel. 'Interview: George Romero.' A. V. Club. Onion, 2008. Web. 19 July 2010.

Night of the Living Dead. Dir. George Romero. 1968. DVD. Weinstein Company. 2008.

Rogers, Martin. 'Hybridity and Post-Human Anxiety in *28 Days Later.*' *Zombie Culture: Autopsies of the Living Dead*. Ed. Shawn McIntosh and Marc Leverette. Lanham, MD: Scarecrow, 2008. 119–133. Print.

Shelley, Mary Wollstonecraft. *Frankenstein; or The Modern Prometheus*. London: Chicago UP, 1982. Print.

Thacker, Eugene. *The Global Genome: Biotechnology, Politics, and Culture*. Cambridge, MA: MIT, 2005. Print.

Twitchell, James. *The Living Dead: A Study of the Vampire in Romantic Literature*. Durham, NC: Duke UP, 1981. Print.

Waldby, Catherine. *The Visible Human Project: Informatic Bodies and Posthuman Medicine*. London: Routledge, 2000. Print.

Warner, Marina. *Phantasmagoria: Spirit Visions, Metaphors, and Media into the Twenty-first Century*. Oxford: Oxford UP, 2006. Print.

7. Ruined Skin: Gothic Genetics and Human Identity in Stephen Donaldson's *Gap* Cycle

Emily Alder

Since the mid-twentieth century, science fiction has used biotechnology to probe the nature of what it means to be human. Octavia Butler's trilogy *Xenogenesis* (1987–89), for example, uses the genetic manipulative capabilities of the alien Oankali to de- and reconstruct familiar characteristics of human identity such as body shape and reproduction.[1] While Butler's project is to critique established models of race, gender and family, she does so by offering sustainable alternatives and a transformed perspective on the nature of humanity.[2] Through a Gothic lens, however, genetic engineering can be seen to perform darker work. In Stephen Donaldson's 1990s science fiction *Gap* series, genetic engineering is conceived as producing a troubling excess of biological plasticity within the human form, which ruptures bodily boundaries and destabilizes conventional constructions of human identity.[3]

Donaldson's narrative engages with a continuing debate: whether, as we advance our understanding of our biology through the study of genetics, we risk debasing human nature through its reduction to a collection of molecules and microbes, despite the medical benefits. *Gap* presents this excess of knowledge – our ability not only to understand but also to manipulate our molecular being – as damaging: 'human nature' is left in ruins, its place taken by inhuman monsters that exist solely on a molecular level. In Donaldson's novels, humanity is threatened with this fate by a race of alien geneticists, the suggestively named Amnion, whose imperialist drive leads them to assimilate other species through genetic mutation. *Gap*'s adherence to a normative human form and an ideology of free will and individuality brings liberal humanism into conflict with the posthuman identities offered by a future world irrevocably shaped by emergent biotechnologies. In *Gap*, this paper argues, the physical and ideological boundaries of human identity, represented by skin, are ruptured by an excess of biologization, in contrast to the digitization of personality suggested by texts such as

Gibson's *Neuromancer* (1984) and Powers's *Galatea 2.2* (1995) and which forms the focus of much posthuman theory.[4] Through the ruination of skin, established constructions of human identity are exposed as fundamentally unstable, imitable and emptied of meaning even as the text attempts to reaffirm them by contrast to the monstrous 'other'.

The several threads of *Gap*'s twisting plot are played out between a series of marginalized characters struggling to survive against human and alien enemies on the fringes of human-controlled space, and a group of people in positions of power who manipulate them from a central position on Earth. Morn Hyland (the heroine) and her son Davies, in uneasy alliances with their sometime enemies Nick Succorso and Angus Thermopyle, strive to save humanity from both the alien threat of the Amnion and the corruption of its own leaders, particularly Holt Fasner, CEO of the United Mining Companies and Warden Dios, Director of the UMC Police, whose corporate partnership dominates human government. Through several encounters with the Amnion and their advanced genetic practices, Morn and her companions confront significant questions about the nature of humanity and the relative value of genetic and moral being.

These questions are legible within the context of the 1990s controversy over genetic research, for example over human embryo research in the US, and during the Human Genome Project. The Project's completion in 2003, six years after the final volume of Donaldson's series was published, revealed a genome complex far beyond initial expectations of 'a single "normal" sequence ... a norm of health against which all discrepancies would be judged as morbid abnormalities' (Rose 18). Jablonka and Lamb, however, note a simplified account of the human genome, understanding genes, for example, as simple causal agents, still circulating even among (non-geneticist) scientists (6). Donaldson's presentation of 'the' human genome as a homogeneous entity allows it to play a significant role in his narrative, offered as an inviolable foundation of human nature with the capacity to place clear boundaries around the limits of normative human identity.

Nelkin and Lindee point out that the language surrounding the Human Genome Project portrayed the genome 'not only as a powerful biological entity but also as a sacred text that can explain the natural and moral order' (29). Genes garner a symbolic importance underpinning human identity that goes beyond their actual biological influence on our shape and physiology: 'DNA has taken on the social and cultural functions of the soul. It is the essential identity – the location of the true self – in the narratives of biological determinism' (41–42). The genome's perceived position as a foundation of moral as well as biological selfhood means that its alteration is seen to impact not only on our bodies but also on the more conceptual ways in which we understand ourselves as human.

What these impacts will mean, however, is still up for debate. Gregory Stock identifies potential in humanity's ability to shape its future: 'Progressive self-transformation could change our descendents into something sufficiently different from our present selves not to be human in the sense we use the word now.... *Homo sapiens* would spawn its own successors by fast-forwarding its evolution' (4). If some interpret genetic manipulation as offering limitless possibilities for human life, however, others perceive dangers. '[T]he most significant threat posed by contemporary biotechnology', claims Francis Fukuyama, 'is the possibility that it will alter human nature and thereby move us into a "posthuman" stage of history' (7). As a result of its genetic codification, Fukuyama seems to be saying, human nature becomes terminally manipulable; posthuman, rather than being evolution or reinvention of the human, is what we become when our human nature is lost.

Late modernity, argues Richard Walker, is characterized by 'its millennial anxieties, its nihilistic embracing of the possibility that the human may indeed be posthumous, and its concern for the status of the body in a post-technological culture of artificial intelligence and cyborgian subjectivity' (89). In posthuman discourse, the body risks becoming lost in the reduction of human identity to data patterns, including the representation of genes as coded information and as technologically reproducible (Graham 117–119). For N. Katherine Hayles, however, the posthuman holds the potential to reconcile informational with embodied identity: 'my dream is a version of the posthuman that embraces the possibilities opened up by information technologies without being seduced by fantasies of unlimited power and disembodied immortality ... and that understands that human life is embedded in a material world on which we depend for our continued survival' ('The Posthuman Body' 266). Hayles's dream is not necessarily something that 1990s texts like *Gap* are able unequivocally to accept or envision, however. Yet biological posthumanity, enabled, perhaps, by genetic engineering, occupies a unique position in the relationship between humans and technology, simultaneously enmeshed in flesh and mechanism, body and information.

Genetic technologies do not attempt to divorce human identity from embodiment. Instead, as Nikolas Rose points out, they work to 'reshape vitality from the inside: in the process the human becomes, not less biological but *all the more* biological' (20, emphasis original). This excessive biologization has implications for more than just our bodies. Rose goes on:

> What if our minds too become bodily, fleshly things, to be anatomized, dissected, re-engineered? Suppose we can identify and re-engineer the neural pathways and enzyme activities responsible for variations in human impulses and our capacity to control them – what then for ideas of free will and criminal responsibility? (21)

If mentality itself becomes subject to molecular re-engineering, those aspects of human nature contingent on an independent mind become subjugated to biology. Corporeality starts to exceed its established boundaries, expressed, as we will see, by ruination of skin, while, as with digital codifying at the other extreme, human nature is seen paradoxically as reduced, redefined by biological patterns and codes.

Gap's fascination with posthuman transformation, then, has more to do with an excess of corporeality than with the loss of it. For the alien Amnion, mind and behaviour are no less reshapeable at the molecular level than is body. Thus, the alternative genetics the Amnion introduce into the human sphere also entail an alternative, non-hierarchical social and behavioural model; all Amnion are impelled by a common genetically determined purpose. Their project of domination and assimilation of other species is termed 'genetic imperialism' by the text, capturing the combined biological and political destruction with which humanity is faced: through enforced transmutation into Amnion forms, humans are robbed of not only their embodied identity but also their free will and individuality. The Amnion represent a potential extreme posthuman future in which genetic biologization would exceed acceptable limits and thereby bring about a profound ruination of human nature.

Donaldson's characters resist such a future. Approaching the Amnion outpost Enablement Station, in the second book, Morn Hyland feels 'a dread so visceral that it was almost cellular; her genes themselves might have been crying out in fear.... [The Amnion] were a threat to the integrity of her membership in the human species. They had power to change the most fundamental thing she knew about herself.'[5] Here, the human genome is presented as the dominant defining characteristic of humanity. Boarding the Amnion ship *Calm Horizons*, Warden Dios similarly 'fought down terror – a blind, atavistic dismay which seemed to spring straight from his genes' (5:298). Genes are personified to justify the characters' horror of the Amnion; not only their persons but what they perceive to be the sacred building blocks of their beings as human are under threat. Mutation, thinks Davies Hyland towards the end of the final book, is 'a ruin far more complete and cruel than any kind of death' (5:603). Against this threat, this terrible, unthinkable ruin, the human characters maintain a belief in what Scott Bukatman calls 'the utopia that lies in *being human*' (16, emphasis original). The individual set of values and characteristics seen as defining 'human' is something to be clung to and cherished, even at some cost. 'Being human' is presented by the *Gap* series as both genetically and politically defined, and is encapsulated in the representation of skin.

Skin, both the physical and the symbolic perimeter of human identity, is also the site of its destabilization. Skin encloses the human body in its recognizable shape – a shape partially dictated by the human genome – and appears to define the human body as individual and self-contained. Yet as a boundary, skin is deceptively fragile. In *Gap*, it exposes the body to penetration by Amnion injections, as well as genetic possession from within, in a replay of Gothic narratives of bodysnatching and vampirism. 'To steal, simulate, or construct a body is to begin disentangling an entire network of intricate hierarchies and relationships. The monsters of gothic and science fiction, whether idealised or degraded figures, participate in a process of defending or transgressing corporeal borders', writes Botting (*Gothic Romanced* 183). In *Gap*, the monstrous bodies created by Amnion genetic transformation suggest a corporeality that breaches bodily boundaries from within. Ruination of human identity, '[t]hat which remains after decay and fall' ('Ruin'), is played out through the broken and damaged skin of Amnion and human bodies.

After she received a mutagenic injection on an Amnion ship, Morn's fear of cellular transmutation is expressed through imagined effects on her skin: 'she seemed to see the red patch on her skin swelling like an infection; it would suppurate and burst; mutagenic pus would seep from the wound, gnawing at her flesh and her DNA until she screamed' (3:150–151). Morn does not distinguish between the anticipated attack on her skin and that on her genes; the mutagens no longer operate solely at a cellular level but join fleshly secretions in a carnivorous assault. As the protecting drug Morn has taken proves effective, however, her skin reassures her of her continued membership of her species: 'the redness … was fading. Her skin was as pallid as the underlying bones – and as whole' (3:151). The 'wholeness' of Morn's skin indicates the purity of her humanity; the ruin of her skin indicates its loss.

By contrast, Amnion bodies (especially those which originated as human) display dramatically ruined skin; they are monstrously othered biologically, socially and politically. In *Gap*, human and alien identities and otherness are played across, under and through the skin. 'Skin', argues Judith Halberstam, 'houses the body, and is figured in Gothic as the ultimate boundary, the material that divides the inside from the outside.... Slowly but surely the outside becomes the inside and the hide no longer conceals and contains, it offers itself up as text, as body, as monster' (7). While Morn relies on her skin to signal her humanity, in Amnion bodies, excesses of genetic self-knowledge start to render the boundary of the skin monstrous. The connections assumed to exist between genes, skin shape and humanity are disrupted as humans become Amnion and Amnion look human. As monsters, the Amnion not only serve to mark the limits of normative humanity but prise them open with questions about the integrity of that humanity.

The stable human relationship between skin shape and genetic interiority is broken by the irrelevancy of shape to the Amnion. The physical horror of a genetic posthumanity is expressed through the transformation of human shape to something alien and other. One Amnion is described as 'a bipedal tree with luxuriant foliage and several limbs' (2:233). Instead of skin, they have 'a protective crust, as rough as rust, which made garments irrelevant' (2:219). The importance of intact skin is a human construction and skin shape means nothing to Amnion: 'Their racial identity was a function of RNA and DNA, not of species-specific genetic codes. They played with their shapes the way humans played with fashion, sometimes for utility, sometimes for adornment' (2:219). Their identity, inhumanly, has nothing to do with bodily integrity; instead, their endlessly manipulable genetic code bursts the boundaries of their form with an excess of bodiliness. The Amnion, Nick Succorso explains, 'don't recognize people by name. And they sure as hell don't recognize them by what they look like. As far as they're concerned appearance has nothing to do with identity. The only thing they recognize is genetic code' (2:200). The construction of the Amnion as a monstrous genetic and physical 'other' serves to reinforce the 'normal' human body, a fixed and individual shape, preserved in Nick and Morn by an 'immunity drug' – terminology which itself constructs Amnion genetics as invasive and diseased.

The Amnion's ability to render identity entirely molecular and corporeal enables them to sever the connection between appearance and interiority. Genetic manipulation also enables them to construct bodies in which shape ceases to mean what it should. Amnion bodies represent more than one potential biological posthumanity. They not only reveal the precariousness of the relationship between body and identity, but also show how cherished characteristics of skin shape, self-determination and individuality are emptied of meaning; skin, as we will see, is ruined precisely because it is meaningless as well as meaningful.

The ruin of human form dominates the characters' fears during interaction with the Amnion, compounded by the aliens' efforts to produce genetic Amnion with human shape and brain function. Their goal is to 'produce Amnion with access to learned human thoughts and emotions. If those Amnion are grown in human shapes, they will be undetectable to humans. Then human spaces could be seeded with hosts of Amnion, and the overthrow of Earth-bred life could be accomplished at one stroke' (4:70). The Amnion seek to advance their genetic imperialism by infiltrating human society, changing a human's genetic identity without changing his or her human appearance.

In practice, their success is incomplete: aesthetically, Milos Taverner is their nearest success, outwardly human apart from his eyes. These

> betrayed the working of the mutagens which had taken away his identity. They were an acrid yellow color, lidless, with deformed irises like slits.... Genetic transformation had altered everything about him

except his appearance: rearranged his DNA strings, restructured the fundamental, definitive encryption of his nucleotides, until only a detached and sometimes imprecise memory-pool remained of the former deputy chief. (4:59)

The Amnion fail because although they can manipulate genetic information at will, they cannot replicate or simulate the 'learned human thoughts and emotions' that constitute a convincing human person. The transformed Taverner can do no more than look the part, through the simulation of his original phenotype.

Marc Vestabule, in contrast, remembers 'more of his former humanity than any other Amnioni like him', enough to pose a considerable threat to humans, but whose underlying genes, values and motivations are entirely Amnion. Physically, however, Vestabule's half-human, half-Amnion face and its 'partially lipless maw' render him more shocking than the 'bipedal trees' of the anonymous Amnion guards, despite their alien strangeness. He has 'one human arm' and 'the skin of his shins [is] pale and ordinary', while 'his shipsuit ... had been cut away to accommodate the thick knobs of Amnion skin that had taken over his knees' (2:254). Vestabule's skin has been ruptured by his internal transformation; crusty Amnion shapes have broken through the vulnerable boundary of human skin from within. Skin, following the outline of the body, is a marker of not only human intactness but also of human ruination. Its rupture produces monstrosity: that 'other' that reveals the limits of the human. The mechanical decay of Amnion skin and speech – arms 'like a metallic tree limb gone to rust' (3:78), voice 'like flakes of oxidation' (5:629) – suggest the insignificance of their dermatological integrity; Amnion skin is poorly maintained and suggests the status of the body as tool, as machine, as prosthesis.

For humans, however, skin forms an integral part of identity. 'The frailty of human skin is conducive to fear', observes the Amnion doctor on Enablement Station. 'This is a racial defect, correctable by Amnion' (2:241). While the 'frailty' to which the Amnion refers is human dermatological vulnerability in Amnion atmosphere (the humans wear spacesuits aboard the Amnion station and ships), it is also a symbolic frailty; 'corrected' by Amnion genes, humans would no longer fear for their skin physically or conceptually, but they would no longer be human. To the Amnion, genetic engineering promises practical improvements; to humans, it here represents the loss of something that makes us human. If the Amnion's mutagenic injections threaten vampire-like transformation from within, then Vestabule's horrifying liminal appearance literally demonstrates the ruin without.

As Halberstam notes, '[s]kin is at once the most fragile of boundaries and the most stable of signifiers' (163). Taverner, his Amnion eyes hidden behind sunglasses, convincingly signals humanity to Ciro, one of the few humans to see him after his transformation, revealing the stable but empty signification of his human shape (5:513). Vestabule's appearance, however, exposes the fragility of that shape. His disrupted skin shape evokes abject reactions in the human characters: 'nausea twisted Alba's face. Vector's sweat and pallor gave him the appearance of an invalid' (2:254). The incompleteness of Vestabule's transformation, his indeterminate position between species, generates a more profound horror than the sight of wholly Amnion creatures. Hybrid and impure, Vestabule embodies a crisis of ruination, a liminal moment somewhere during the process of transformation, visually demonstrating to the human onlookers the physical mutation that awaits them, while his Amnion values reveals the completeness of his underlying genetic ruination. Instead of a seamless union of body and technology, Vestabule's body signifies fracture, conflict, discontinuity, a fundamental incompatibility or irreconcilability between the two.

Between them, Taverner and Vestabule show that skin shape and bodily integrity can be separated from genetics and therefore from essential identity. The human characters live in visceral terror of this disassociation – the outward mutation as well as the more fundamental transformation of their internal genetic identity. Amnion shapes are presented as repulsive and indeterminate, but they also reveal the irrelevance of shape to identity in a way that serves to highlight the human characters' obsession with it. While for the human characters, genes, body, individuality and free will are all inextricably linked in the make-up of identity, for the Amnion, identity is no more than genetic code, as data and programming that impel them towards genetic imperialism and the spread of their species. The Amnion embody this tension lying at the heart of posthuman theory.

The biological codifying of human identity, then, has deeper implications for what it means to be human than normative shape alone. In the terms of Jean Baudrillard, Taverner and Vestabule become simulacra (of humans): copies without originals, inauthentic shells. 'Simulation', Baudrillard writes, 'is no longer that of a territory, a referential being or a substance. It is the generation by models of a real without origin or reality: a hyperreal. The territory no longer precedes the map, nor survives it' (169). The connection between reality and copy is disengaged. The 'precession of simulacra' means that the map, the symbol, exists before the 'real,' which it produces. The new Amnion Taverner and Vestabule, for example, are copies of something for which an original does not exist.

As Jenny Wolmark puts it, discussing Baudrillard, 'the relationship between reality and illusion can no longer be maintained, since the reality on which the illusory was based no longer exists' (12). Understanding Taverner and Vestabule in these terms is to understand how completely their

connection to the human has been stripped away and how entirely disconnected their appearance now is from their new genetic, moral and cultural
make-up. Vestabule's memory of the way humans think is not evidence of
a residual humanity; like his partially human skin, it is a superficial trait, a
useful illusion with solely Amnion underpinnings: 'his uniqueness among
his people was only a tool, not a matter of identity' (3:78); Amnion bodies,
similarly, are 'tools, organic artefacts, to be shaped, used, and discarded
as necessary' (5:584), recalling Hayles's critique of a posthumanity that
discards embodiment. Like skin, behaviour is likewise reduced to a set of
signs, unrelated to 'reality': 'Vestabule made a gesture that appeared to have
no meaning. It may have been intended to placate Nick. Or it may have
been merely a neural atavism' (3:79). Since Vestabule can simulate human
behaviour and methods of thought in such a way that allows him to interact
with humans and predict how they will behave, the human characters'
behavioural and psychological traits likewise seem to emerge as simulation.

Because of simulation, Baudrillard argues, it becomes *impossible to
isolate the process of the real*, or to prove the real' (21, emphasis original).
Simulations of the human undermine the possibility of a 'real' human
identity existing; it is revealed as empty, merely construction. 'It is no
longer a question of a false representation of reality (ideology)', Baudrillard
writes of the third order of simulation, 'but of concealing the fact that
the real is no longer real' (12–13).[6] By the encounter with the biological
posthumanity represented by a distinctively alien species, the realities (of
the link between genetics and skin, of self-determining autonomy) that
had underpinned human identity have been scoured away. The alien other,
then, functions as more than a means of delineating the boundaries of
the human, of defining human 'ontological hygiene' (Graham 13): it also,
through simulation, threatens to strip the whole concept of human identity
of any meaning at all.

Ferreira shows how simulacra can be used to understand representations
of human cloning as the reduction of individuality to mass production.
Baudrillard sees '[t]he genetic code … at the basis of a revolution that will
contribute to the demoting of human beings to the level of reproducible
consumer objects', she writes, while for Walter Benjamin 'the mechanical
reproduction of an object undermines its unique aura, given that through
repetition of the same they become evened out to relative unimportance
and worthlessness' (Ferreira 25). Such reproduction substitutes 'a mass
existence for a unique existence' (Benjamin 104). 'Are clones, then', Ferreira
asks 'according to Baudrillard's argumentation, simulacra, that is, copies
without an original, since they are potentially endlessly reproducible?' (26).
Ferreira raises this question in order to challenge it; however, through the
Amnion, *Gap* raises the spectre of endlessly reproducible clones in order

to display the horror of genetic posthumanity and its division from the 'ontological hygiene' defined by both human skin and human autonomy.

To be transformed into Amnion is to join their mass ranks: 'The protein soup from which more Amnion could be grown was plentiful ... any individual could be replaced by another with the same abilities and characteristics' (5:201). This generic protein soup is the condition to which the human genome is reduced by Amnion mutagens. To be turned into Amnion is to be reduced to a copiable and reproducible object, body and mind: 'when one [body] suffered damage, grew old, or died, they simply imprinted themselves upon another' (5:584). The 'clone myth', notes Wasson, 'forces us to face the dread possibility of repetition' (142). If the Amnion represent a possible posthuman future, then this reduced and repeatable identity is one of its accompanying dangers.

As a species, the clone-like Amnion are united in their common goal by their common genetics, their drive for genetic imperialism. Like the Borg of *Star Trek*, assimilation to their species entails a loss of individual human character and agency.[7] For example, as well as all individuals deriving from the same 'protein soup', we are told that the Amnion 'had no human-like personal pronouns: they needed none' (4:476). Vestabule's name is part of his usefulness as a 'tool' for dealing with humans; he also possesses 'the essentially Amnion knowledge that he had no individual significance' (3:78). The Amnion's capacity for genetic modification extends beyond physicality to influence mind, behaviour and individual values.

In the debates around genetic research, intertwined with fear about changes to the shape of human skin is a fear about the control over behaviour that could result – the bio-power identified by Foucault as 'the mechanism by which regimes of coercion and control are mediated through the emergent human sciences' (Graham 115). *Gap* explores a paradox in which genetic manipulation is seen as threatening to a fixed human shape as biologization bursts out from within, yet at the same time this excess negates itself and is seen to turn people into soulless and non-individuated bio-mechanisms. For Hayles, as Schmeink summarizes, '[t]he autonomy of the self, the questions of agency and free will, are turning into the battlegrounds for the human–posthuman predicament'. In *Gap*'s attempt to reaffirm a liberal humanist construction of identity, its engagement with biological posthumanity exposes this construction as fundamentally destabilized; its basis, in an unaltered human biology and in the autonomous self, is ruined.

Free will and individuality are presented in *Gap* as crucial parts of being human, in a clear endorsement of liberal humanist values. Yet the liberal humanist subject, Hayles notes, is 'a concept ... deeply entwined with projects of domination and oppression' ('The Posthuman Body' 266). Angus, for example, once a criminal, is turned into a cyborg by the police and is 'welded'

126 EMILY ALDER

to the control of computer chips and rigid programming. Like Vestabule, Angus 'would be the perfect tool.... In their own way, the surgeons worked to transform him as profoundly as an Amnion mutagen' (2:286). Free will, and its oppression, is comparable in its significance to the disruption of the genome, equally fundamental to the health of the human 'soul'. Although using him, Warden Dios admits to Angus that by taking away his volition the police have 'committed a crime against [his] soul' (2:410). Renegade captain Sorus Chatelaine, by betraying her Amnion blackmailers and choosing suicide, is said by Davies Hyland to have 'saved her soul' (5:384). In *Gap*, the human 'soul' is not only defined by genetics: it is defined by self-determination. By the time of Sorus's suicide, her 'soul' is figured not only as her intact genes but also as her refusal to be controlled and dominated.

We see, however, that free will is no more truthful a signifier of human identity than is skin. Morn, Davies and Nick, unaware of Angus's cyborgian welding, take his coerced behaviour for free will. Similarly, Morn, controlling her physiology with her neural 'zone implant', tricks Nick with a 'masque' of 'false and illimitable passion' (2:194, 145). Human behaviour, like its Amnion analogue, can be reduced to a simulacrum of empty signifiers. Hayles points out that the liberal human subject is defined by mind, with body as an object to be controlled: 'Identified with the rational mind, the liberal subject *possessed* a body but was not usually represented as *being* a body' (*How We Became Posthuman* 2, emphasis original). Both Morn and Angus desire control over their own bodies; Morn by wresting control of her zone implant from Angus, and Angus, later, by mastering the technology that had once controlled him. Other cybernetic technologies, such as Dios's ocular prosthesis, are likewise pressed into the service of human will rather than enabling the production of new identities. The narrative prioritizes individual agency over attainment of harmony between body and technology (be that biological or cybernetic): to humans, that the Amnion achieve this harmony is a matter of horror and loss. Skin, defining the human body, is here ruined politically, philosophically, as the body's meaning to human identity is lost in subservience to individual will.

In *Gap*, the human characters' championing of free will and their refusal of a flexible relationship between genes and skin disadvantage their species. 'They had to become capable of what the Amnion could do', Holt Fasner reasons, or 'their ultimate victory over humankind was inevitable' (5:584–5). Fasner, the despotic villain of the series, sees his 'visionary efforts' frustrated by 'self-absorbed' subordinates who value 'empty scruples' and 'incomplete power' more than their species, and fails to acknowledge the extent to which he owes his own political power to the manipulation of such values (5:585). Morn and Angus cherish their genetic make-up and their free will to such an extent because they are ideologically conditioned to do so. 'The cops want you to be a nice little genephobe', Nick sneers at Morn, 'they wouldn't want you to understand what real genetic engineering is good for' (2:191). The practical uses of genetic engineering, on this occasion 'force-growing' Morn's foetal child into a sixteen-year-old boy, are elided by the state's need to control people by promoting their fear of the Amnion. Fasner has built his corporate empire on the construction of Amnion as genetically and politically 'other' and the prizing of genes and free will as the basis of human identity. The resultant struggles among the human characters, as individuals strive for control, render their species vulnerable to another.

When Morn declares her resolution 'not to betray [her] humanity' (2:245), she is not declaring a loyalty to her species, which she wilfully undermines by allowing the Amnion to take a sample of her blood containing the 'anti-mutagen' (or 'immunity drug') that is humanity's only defence against alien transformation, but to her individual self. This act betrays the human species, yet preserves Morn's own life and identity – an act consistent with the individualistic society of which she is a product. Manipulated, owned and directed by forces beyond her control (usually men but also technology, sickness and aliens) for most of the story up to this point, and thus fundamentally disempowered, Morn is put in a position in which she has no other option except to 'betray her humanity'. Dominated and oppressed first by the ideology of the UMC Police, and then by the abuse of Angus and Nick, her own zone implant and, finally, by the Amnion, it is perhaps not surprising that Morn reacts by asserting her own individual agency rather than submitting to another project of control. Angus too, like Morn over her damaged body, can only reconcile himself to a cyborg identity by applying the same structures of domination that brought him to that condition in the first place.

Donaldson presents a society in which subjects are compelled to assert individual power where they can because no other options remain to them. Morn's focus on preserving the individual humanity of herself and her son reveals the inability of a society based on individualism to embrace a posthuman future. In this way, the genetic, individualistic construction of human identity is revealed as flawed, impeding the species' success, and as empty, built on simulation. Although the human genome is championed and individuality prevails, the underlying concepts of human identity remain unstable, since the genome cannot be separated from the potential excesses of biologization that understanding it brings. The narrative is unable to realize fully an alternative mode of being in which this potential can be positively harnessed. Hayles's hope for a posthuman subject capable of reconciling flesh and technology continues to be, as she says, a 'dream', under constant assault from contention around the relative importance of genetics, technology, materiality and socialization in the make-up of identity.

Yet even here, the text is ambivalent, hinting at an alternative to the negative connotations of cloning, monstrous genetics and simulated humanity,
through Morn's son Davies. When the Amnion 'force-grow' Davies into a
teenager, Morn's own mind is copied and replicated into her son's brain to
take the place of the life experience he lacks: 'Of what use is a physically
mature offspring with the knowledge and perceptions of a fetus?' queries
the Amnion doctor. 'Therefore the offspring is given the mind of its parent'
(2:226). In this case, personality rather than genome is reduced to code
and recreated, but instead of being reduced to a dehumanized product,
Davies possesses an individual identity and continues to learn, grow and
change: 'In a short time, Morn realized, he would cease to think in ways she
could predict or even understand' (2:243). The capability to be individually
shaped by culture and circumstances, rather than entirely geneticized like
the Amnion, is something else that makes humans human.

Whereas Amnion sameness accords more closely to Benjamin's production line, Davies's cloned heritage is celebrated: for Warden Dios, Davies's
inheritance of Morn's memories and values is a cause for rejoicing and
allows Dios to entrust control of the 'welded' Angus to Davies's hands
(4:215). The Amnion pursue Davies doggedly for this reason, because he
represents a possible new way to build human identity that balances genetic
and individualistic being. In this way, *Gap* hints at an answer, one which
both accepts change and maintains human identity, but the narrative seems
unable to follow this through to its logical implications for the relative
significance of body shape and individual free will. Davies, installed with
Morn's mind, reinforces an epigenetic model of human formation in which
genetic code does not define everything. However, his presence does not
resolve the ambiguous potential of molecular biologization in the creation
of posthuman identity. Instead, the narrative's emphasis on his secure
humanity suggests that biologization is (for the time being) safely contained
and individualist values are upheld.

Throughout the *Gap* narrative, ruined skin signifies the darkest extremes
of the horrors produced in the human subject by genetic intervention. A
full understanding of genetic identity is portrayed as an excess of knowledge, an over-biologization of human nature that expresses itself through
the shattering of normative body shape. Ruined skin indicates the loss of
human identity from inside and out; it reveals a body disregarded, subject
to meaningless, monstrous re-forming. Human nature is cut loose from its
established foundations, as form and behaviour become codified, reproducible and copiable. As the text attempts to reconstruct human identity
around autonomy and self-determination as well as around genetic purity,
skin is emptied of meaning, mimicking a non-existent reality and raising
serious questions about the stability of human identity construction in a

narrative dreadfully and irrevocably engaged with nightmares of genetic engineering that it cannot ultimately resolve.

Notes

1. The trilogy was republished in 2000 as *Lilith's Brood.*
2. See also Haraway and Wolmark.
3. Vol. 1: *The Real Story* (1990), Vol. 2: *Forbidden Knowledge* (1991), Vol. 3: *A Dark and Hungry God Arises* (1992), Vol. 4: *Chaos and Order* (1994), Vol. 5: *This Day All Gods Die* (1996)
4. See, e.g. Hayles (*How We Became Posthuman*) and Graham.
5. Donaldson 1991, *Forbidden Knowledge,* vol. 2 of the series, p.195. Subsequent references to all five volumes will be cited in the text as, e.g., 2:195.
6. The fourth phase can be seen as the empty construction of human identity to which the characters try to cling and which has been shown not to bear scrutiny in the light of the earlier phases; 'it has no relation to any reality whatsoever: it is its own pure simulacrum' (6).
7. See, e.g., LaMothe (52), Botting ('Resistance is Futile' 270) and Graham (147).

Works cited

Baudrillard, Jean. *Simulation and Simulacra.* 1981. Trans. Sheila Faria Glaser. Ann Arbor: U of Michigan P, 1994. Print.

Benjamin, Walter. 'The Work of Art in the Age of its Technical Reproducibility.' 1936. Trans. Edmund Jephcott, Howard Eiland et al. Ed. Howard Eiland and Michael W. Jennings. London: Harvard UP, 2002. Print.

Botting, Fred. 'Resistance is Futile.' *Anglophonia* 15 (2004), 265–293. Print.

—. *Gothic Romanced.* London: Routledge, 2008. Print.

Bukatman, Scott. *Terminal Identity: The Virtual Subject in Postmodern Science Fiction.* Durham: Duke UP, 1998. Print.

Butler, Octavia. *Lilith's Brood.* New York: Grand Central Publishing, 2000. Print.

Donaldson, Stephen. *The Gap into Conflict: The Real Story.* London: HarperCollins, 1991. Print.

—. *The Gap into Madness: Chaos and Order.* London: HarperCollins, 1995. Print.

—. *The Gap into Power: A Dark and Angry God Arises.* London: HarperCollins, 1992. Print.

—. *The Gap into Ruin: This Day All Gods Die.* London: HarperCollins, 1997. Print.

—. *The Gap into Vision: Forbidden Knowledge.* London: HarperCollins, 1991. Print.

Ferreira, Maria Aline Salgueiro Seabra. *I am the Other: Literary Negotiations of Human Cloning.* Westport, CT: Praeger, 2005. Print.

Fukuyama, Francis. *Our Posthuman Future: Consequences of the Biotechnology Revolution.* London: Profile, 2002. Print

Gibson, William. *Neuromancer.* 1984. London: HarperCollins, 1995. Print.

Graham, Elaine L. *Representations of the Post/Human: Monsters, Aliens, and Others in Popular Culture.* New Brunswick, NJ: Rutgers UP, 2002. Print.

Halberstam, Judith. *Skin Shows: Gothic Horror and the Technology of Monsters.* Durham, NC: Duke UP, 1995. Print.

Haraway, Donna J. 'The Biopolitics of Postmodern Bodies: Constitutions of Self in Immune System Discourse.' 1989. *Simians, Cyborgs, and Women: The Reinvention of Nature.* London: Routledge, 1991. 203–230. Print.

130   EMILY ALDER

Hayles, N. Katherine. *How We Became Posthuman: Virtual Bodies in Cybernetics, Literature, and Informatics*. London: U of Chicago P, 1999. Print.

—. 'The Posthuman Body: Inscription and Incorporation in *Galatea 2.2* and *Snow Crash*.' *Configurations* 5.2 (1997): 241–266. Web.

Jablonka, Eva and Marion J. Lamb. *Evolution in Four Dimensions: Genetic, Epigenetic, Behavioural, and Symbolic Variations in the History of Life*. Cambridge, MA: MIT Press, 2005. Print.

LaMothe, Ryan. *Becoming Alive: Psychoanalysis and Vitality.* Hove: Routledge, 2005. Print.

Nelkin, Dorothy and M. Susan Lindee. *The DNA Mystique: The Gene as a Cultural Icon.* Ann Arbor: U of Michigan P, 2004. Print.

Powers, Richard. *Galatea 2.2*. 1995. London: Atlantic, 2010. Print.

Rose, Nikolas. *The Politics of Life Itself: Biomedicine, Power, and Subjectivity in the Twenty-first Century*. Princeton, NJ: Princeton UP, 2007.

'Ruin.' Def. 2b. *The Oxford English Dictionary*. www.oed.com. Web. 9 June 2010.

Schmeink, Lars. 'Dystopia, Alternate History and the Posthuman in *Bioshock*.' *COPAS 10 (2009): n. pag. Web. 14 March 2010.*

Stock, Gregory. *Redesigning Humans: Choosing Our Children's Genes.* London: Profile, 2002. Print.

Walker, Richard. 'Inhuman Romances.' *Inhuman Reflections: Thinking the Limits of the Human*. Ed. Scott Brewster, John J. Joughin, David Owen and Richard J. Walker. Manchester: Manchester UP, 2000. 89–96. Print.

Wasson, Sara-Patricia. 'Love in the Time of Cloning: Science Fictions of Transgressive Kinship.' *Extrapolation* 45.2 (Summer 2004): 130–145. Web.

Wise, Dennis Wilson. 'Science Fiction, Fantasy, and Social Critique: Stephen R. Donaldson's Gap into Genre.' *New Boundaries in Political Science Fiction*. Ed. Donald M. Hassler and Clyde Wilcox. Columbia, SC: U of South Carolina P, 2008. 290–298. Print.

Wolmark, Jenny. *Aliens and Others: Science fiction, Feminisim and Postmodernism*. London: Harvester Wheatsheaf, 1993. Print.

Part III
Gender and Genre

8. The Superheated, Superdense Prose of David Conway: Gender and Subjectivity beyond *The Starry Wisdom*

Mark P. Williams

David Conway's 'Metal Sushi' (1998) is a Gothic science fiction novella with significant implications for contemporary fantastic fiction in its interactions with wider culture. It takes a dual attitude to the form and traditions it draws upon, seeking to reach a higher level of insight, staging a reprisal of the historical form of Weird fiction. Produced within a specific British small press milieu, 'Metal Sushi' relates to the emergence of the 'New Weird' in contemporary fantasy. The story uses dense literary allusion to explore and ultimately subvert the tyranny of form in genre fiction; it blends inter-textual references to Jules Verne, Edgar Allan Poe, Edward Bulwer-Lytton, H. P. Lovecraft, Philip K. Dick and William Gibson, alongside films such as *Apocalypse Now* (1979) and *Forbidden Planet* (1956), embedding them within the stylistic structure of the hard-boiled detective narrative.

Grant Morrison, writing an introduction to David Conway's stories, describes them as 'superheated, superdense prose – part Lovecraft, part Manga, part post-human porn' because of the intensely contracted cultural allusion of the vocabulary (v). I argue that in 'Metal Sushi' this density of reference reflects the apocalyptic themes of the text by creating a sense of textual crisis through generic overdetermination. The novella's generic in-stability unmasks the way that even the most codified of fictional genres are always intrinsically unstable. Furthermore, this challenge to genre stability is intimately bound to challenges to *gender* stability: the hermaphroditic human of 'Metal Sushi' – Amorphibian – reflects a crisis in subjectivity caused by the shift in the boundaries of gender and sexuality in the human form. These crises in gender and genre, embroiled in the apocalyptic plot, demand revelatory renewals of thought and form.

Fiction attempting to bring a social, political or therapeutic benefit to the subject in contemporary life through aesthetic innovation clearly draws on Modernism, since this is a defining purpose of Modernism as conceived and explored by critics such as Clement Greenberg and Karl Popper, by Donald Kuspit in *The Cult of the Avant-Garde Artist* (1993) and more recently by Peter Gay in his survey *Modernism: The Lure of Heresy from Baudelaire to Beckett and Beyond* (2007). I argue that Conway's 'Metal Sushi' operates on aesthetic terms that blend decadence and Modernism, and that the specific textual repertoire and rhetorical techniques it employs are important for under-standing the emergence of the New Weird, and also for speculating on the development of genre beyond the New Weird. After considering the milieu in which Conway was writing, I will identify the elements of 'Metal Sushi' in terms of their stylistic pre-texts, particularly in the work of H. P. Lovecraft, and indicate how these unite with gendered language in the description both of the body and of role, in social and generic senses. The paper will conclude with an exposition of how the narrative challenges the reciprocal gendered and generic determinants of its prose to open up a new space.

First, it is important to examine the milieu that produced 'Metal Sushi', since it reflects a more widespread interrogation of genre and form. David Conway is a founder member of the idiosyncratic band My Bloody Valentine (see Cavanagh); leaving the band, he turned to writing, with a selection of Gothic science fiction stories for British alternative publishers Creation Books, formed in 1989. Creation Books' style is governed by the meeting of the avant-garde and the pulp, the cult and the alternative: in the Creation catalogue reprints of Arthur Machen's *Great God Pan* (1894) and Sade's *Philosophy in the Bedroom* (1795) sit alongside science fiction novels by Philip José Farmer, Surrealist texts by Antonin Artaud – *Heliogabalus* (1933) and his adaptation of M. G. Lewis's 1796 Gothic novel *The Monk* (1931) – and the post-punk avant-garde imprint Attack! Books, edited by Steven Wells. Creation has also published a variety of experimental texts by contemporary avant-garde artists and writers, including Pierre Guyotat, Bill Drummond and Mark Manning, and Jake Chapman; contemporary manifestations of Decadence, Surrealism and excess are important cultural indices for alternative fiction at this time.

Creation Books' significant Gothic output includes the anthology *Red Stains* (1991) edited by Jack Hunter, where Conway's story 'Eloise' was first published alongside work by cult poet and novelist Jeremy Reed, respected horror novelist Ramsey Campbell and musician Stephen Sennitt. It later published the Gothic science fiction anthology *The Starry Wisdom: A Tribute to H. P. Lovecraft* (1994), edited by D. M. Mitchell, consisting of reinterpretations of Lovecraft by, among others, Ramsey Campbell, J. G. Ballard, William S. Burroughs and comic book writers Alan Moore and Grant Morrison; along-side them is the story 'Black Static' by Conway, which Ramsey Campbell describes as 'an authentically Lovecraftian marriage of contemporary science and the cosmic' (Campbell 6). The stories in this collection create a unity of experimental textual technique and conceptual expression through the appropriation of forms drawn from Weird fiction.

Following on from the interests of *The Starry Wisdom*, D. M. Mitchell started independent label Oneiros Books, publishing a series of texts which merge science fiction and Gothic fantasy of a particularly Lovecraftian flavour – Oneiros Books has since become Creation Oneiros. The first publication of Oneiros Books was David Conway's *Metal Sushi*, an anthology republishing Conway's stories 'Eloise' and 'Black Static' from the Creation anthologies, alongside a selection of other unpublished short fictions, including the longer novella, 'Metal Sushi'.[1] Their second publication was a collection of Grant Morrison's prose and theatre writing entitled *Lovely Biscuits* (1998), featuring an introduction by Stewart Home; and their third was a graphic adaptation of Lovecraft stories by artist-designer John Coulthart, *The Haunter in the Dark and Other Grotesque Visions* (1999), with additional text by Alan Moore. Conway's 'Metal Sushi' is thus emblematic of a milieu that synthesizes established genre forms with avant-garde techniques to produce new innovations at both textual and conceptual levels. In 'Metal Sushi', as we will see, these generic and formal innovations also push the boundaries of established models of gender.

The story of 'Metal Sushi' takes place in a post-apocalyptic Earth in which the polar ice has melted, flooding arable land and forcing humanity to farm the seas. In this reordering of the ecology, a new human phenotype and gender identity has emerged, the Amorphibian (amphibious hermaphrodite); the Amorphibian body challenges the classification of generic human both by being amphibious and by being excessively gendered, and has become subject to oppression under the regulation of the 'Generic Stability Decrees'. Through the investigations of an Amorphibian Private Investigator sent to infiltrate an extremist-supremacist cult in one of the Amorphibian ghettos, the cult's millennialist ambitions precipitate an apocalyptic awakening.

Significantly, in 'Metal Sushi' Conway treats the unification of Gothic and science fictional impulses as a chimerical marriage with the potential to produce an unprecedented new form from the supersession of existing genre forms. This resonates clearly with the practices of New Weird writers such as Jeff VanderMeer and China Miéville. In exploring what is meant by 'New Weird', Jeff and Ann VanderMeer's anthology, *The New Weird* (2008), offers us a spectrum of descriptions from science fiction and fantasy writers and editors across Europe. The general consensus understands the 'New Weird' as the mixing of established forms within the fields of science fiction and fantasy with a literary sensibility; it embraces stylistic and conceptual innovation but, being committed to treating Weird worlds seriously as worlds rather than as textual games, makes relatively little use of postmodernist textual practices.

The European editors in the VanderMeers' anthology all agree that New Weird uses form and established formulae in a particular way, recombining elements to create space for something new and that, in general, New Weird writers develop their imaginary worlds using 'baroquely lush cityscapes and eclectic, astounding locations, filling them up with multicultural and multiethnic societies of humans, monsters, and all kinds of their hybrid forms' (Walewski, qtd. in VanderMeer and VanderMeer 359). The New Weird, then, is a *synthetic* form; words like 'alchemy' are often used both within the worlds of such fiction and in attempts to describe it, and the language of alchemy often manifests within the text. Terms such as 'baroque' and 'lush' suggest abundance expanded to superabundance or excess, a decadent style. This is unified with an attempt to create new forms and new ways of expressing significant concerns about the socio-economic forces of modernity in an aesthetic space.

Stylistically, Conway's novella presents the reader with a hybrid of Lovecraftian and cyberpunk modes, a fusion which requires some exploration. Howard Philips Lovecraft is one of the most-often imitated writers of horror-fantasy of the twentieth century; his stories of ancient alien beings existing in strange, non-Euclidian folds of space in the inaccessible places of earth, and their hidden influence over humans, particularly in isolated communities, form a distinctive current in contemporary fiction. In his essay 'The Supernatural Horror in Literature' (1925), Lovecraft suggests a particular notion of the Weird, related specifically to the writers Edgar Allan Poe, M. R. James, Arthur Machen and William Hope Hodgson, as a stylistic synthesis of the rationalism of science fiction and the irrationalism of Gothic fiction. Lovecraft's personal innovation was to create a unified cosmos of unspeakable, indescribable alien creatures which could operate in both rationalist and irrationalist ways. 'Weird fiction' in Lovecraft is a formalization of the tropes of horror, fantasy and early science fiction of the early twentieth century. Written to unsettle the reader's expectations, Weird fiction derives from the nineteenth-century Gothic fictions of Europe, Britain and America, but its social context is that of the market for pulp fiction.

Weird fiction appeared around the turn of the century, becoming popular in America in the 1920s with the advent of the pulp magazines. These magazines began as miscellanies of genre gathered under broad titles, a format taken from the two most successful publications, *The Argosy* and *The All-Story Magazine*, begun around 1905. The publishers of these magazines branched out into specialist forms dealing with Detective, Romantic and Western, an economic gamble which proved successful. In 1923, a new magazine devoted to fiction derived from the Gothic emerged: *Weird Tales* (Murray). From this populist environment Lovecraft emerges as a writer with a characteristic decadent style owing a great deal to favourite precursors, chief among them Edgar Allan Poe and M. R. James, but which engages readily in a process of cross-fertilization with the work of his contemporaries, creating fantastic stories which tested the boundaries of the magazine genres. Lovecraft organized his unified cosmos around god-like alien creatures to which he gave suggestive names such as Great Cthulhu, the Old Ones, the Deep Ones, Nyarlathanotep, Azathoth and Shub-Niggurath, to form a pantheon or 'Mythos'. This Mythos became the template for much of the stylistic imitation that we now know as Lovecraftian fiction. From its conception, Lovecraft's Mythos made space for collective contribution by his contemporaries; the style thrived on imitation and appropriation (certain Lovecraftian names were actually coined by Lovecraft's friends, fellow writers Clark Ashton Smith, Robert Bloch and Frank Bellknap Long).

Lovecraft's stories themselves are distinguished by their synthetic and decadent character and by a strong emphasis on abstract language and terms such as 'cyclopean', 'unknowable' and 'abyssal.' His most famous creation, Great Cthulhu, him/her/itself is described as beyond human comprehension: '[t]he Thing cannot be described – there is no such language for such abysms of shrieking and immemorial lunacy, such eldritch contradictions of all matter, force, and cosmic order ... a mountain walked or stumbled' ('The Call of Cthulhu' 95). This decadent style and its 'unknowable' content are the essence of the Lovecraftian; Conway employs the language of psychoanalysis, post-structuralist linguistic uncertainty and reference to quantum physics take on the same function in his fictions. However, the most pertinent Lovecraft intertexts for considering Conway's 'Metal Sushi' are those in which his most alien beings receive least mention: *At the Mountains of Madness* and 'The Shadow over Innsmouth' (both 1931).

In 'The Shadow over Innsmouth,' a man visits the mysterious and backward New England port of Innsmouth only to find that the area is home to a group of amphibious beings who worship the alien deities Father Dagon, Mother Hydra and Great Cthulhu; much of the story is a protracted chase, but at the tale's conclusion the narrator learns that he too is of the same amphibious heritage and relinquishes his former human life. The plot of *At the Mountains of Madness* concerns an Antarctic expedition – launched from Arkham, New England – by a team of academics. In crossing the pole by plane, making regular stops to bore into the ice for analysis, they discover, amidst the frozen peaks of an uncharted mountain range, a massive city of unknown origin. It transpires that this deserted city was once the home of a vast alien civilization, the Old Ones, which predates most advanced life on Earth, and, furthermore, may still exist in certain hidden places of the Earth.

Lovecraft's personal aesthetic features centrally in *At the Mountains of Madness*, because it is through their art that the archaeologists uncover the narrative of the Old Ones' civilization, its decadence and decline. Regarding art, Lovecraft expressed apparently contrary beliefs, holding that avant-garde art is degenerate, yet also stating that producing true art requires 'rejecting normality and conventionality in toto, and approaching a theme purged utterly of any usual or preconceived point of view' (*Lord of a Visible World* 121). It is aesthetically significant therefore that both 'The Shadow over Innsmouth' (1931) and *At The Mountains of Madness* (1931), as narratives of decadence, are also rare occasions in Lovecraft's work where his narrators express direct and explicit sympathy and fellow feeling with the nonhuman.

Commenting on the civilization they find, Lovecraft's narrator observes that its artistic 'technique … was mature, accomplished, and aesthetically evolved to the highest degree of civilized mastery, though utterly alien in every detail to every known art tradition of the human race' (*At the Mountains* 77). Of the Old Ones' art and culture, the chief characteristic is an 'almost universal system of mural sculpture, which tended to run in continuous horizontal bands', 'rendered with astonishing vividness', which have their 'closest analogue in certain grotesque conceptions of the most daring futurists' (78).

Lovecraft's attitude to art is perhaps akin to that of Wyndham Lewis, that much artistic experimentation constitutes '[i]nfantile extremist sensationalism' (Lewis 184); Lewis asserts that certain trends in art are symptomatic of 'civilised life, plunging over the side of the precipice – the exhibitionist extremist promoter driving the whole bag of tricks into a nihilistic nothingness or zero' (184). This is how the alien art of the Old Ones is presented, as part of an atavistic decline, the degeneration of a once-great culture; but it is presented ambivalently: 'Radiates, vegetables, monstrosities, star spawn – whatever they had been, they were men' (*At the Mountains* 126). Conway's story adopts this starting-point: that the definition of the human within the Lovecraftian subgenre is ultimately elastic, extending even to the alien.

In *The Gothic Body: Sexuality, Materialism and Degeneration at the Fin de Siècle* (2004), Kelly Hurley borrows William Hope Hodgson's term 'abhuman' to refer to the presence of a concept of non-human subjectivity in Weird fiction. Hurley writes that 'the abhuman subject is a not-quite-human subject, characterized by its morphic variability, continually in danger of becoming not-itself, becoming other' (3). This is precisely the characteristic that defines the position of the amphibians in 'The Shadow over Innsmouth' and the Amorphibians in 'Metal Sushi'. For Lovecraft, becoming-other is a status that his narrator in 'The Shadow over Innsmouth' grows to accept and embrace. Conway's narrative, however, offers becoming-other as the only truly liberating possibility open to humanity; in 'Metal Sushi' it denotes an escape from abjection towards a more advanced and desirable 'posthuman' state. This new identity is an escape from socially determining forces such as gender roles; in this way, the story also points towards the conceptions of posthuman subjectivity found in the New Weird. This is partly derived from the superheroic texts of modern comic books which fill the popular imaginary with ideas of super-humanity, such as Grant Morrison's *New X-Men* (2001–4), and Warren Ellis's *The Authority* (1999), in which 'posthuman' suggests beings which are recognizably human but with vastly increased powers and abilities.

'Abhuman', in Hurley's conception, takes on the tense, uncertain position of the abject as a state between subject and object but invested with the possibility of cognitively overturning those categories. The position of Amorphibian in Conway's text as socially abject and physically abhuman points towards a similar overturning, specifically related to the generic patterns invoked by the narrative. Abhuman and posthuman can be used interchangeably in respect to 'Metal Sushi' because the multiplicity of allusion already present in the story refers simultaneously to the history of fantastic fiction of the late nineteenth and early twentieth centuries and also looks forward to the end of the twentieth century. Through this double frame of reference we can consider the posthuman as a return to the abhuman at a higher level of insight; extending this, we can see the New Weird as a historical return to the Weird fiction of what we might term the Lovecraftian moment, reappropriated for future uses that no longer view the abhuman as necessarily synonymous with 'horror'.

The New Weird holds a Janus-like attitude; it contains the elements of an early twentieth-century aesthetic, but pointing towards that of an emergent twenty-first century. By emphasizing this double-time present in the allusion by 'Metal Sushi', I wish to demonstrate that it, like the texts of the so-called New Weird, operates nomadically on and across a particular borderland. This borderland is stylistic; it consciously melds pre-existing terms that act antagonistically upon one another, reflecting the stylistic and generic tensions of combining the Gothic and science fictional modes.

'Metal Sushi' begins with a dream which is also a flashback-cum-hallucination:

> The corridors contract insanely, assuming the twisted perspectives of an Expressionist nightmare, the stilted asymmetry of an ancient UFA studios fantasy, hand coloured by autistic children, slate grey, indigo, violet and black; the funereal hues of a sombre, fauvist lithograph contrast with the sensual vulnerability of my own luminous flesh – ivory infused with icy turquoise – the stark lividity of an exquisite corpse....
>
> The gun in my hand is a dull weight, its static charge of death suggesting lethal potentialities. I move through a fluctuating matrix of warped angles and mismatched planes: an abstracted kaleidoscope of unfolding space, inverted time. (86)

The coruscating imagery is clearly intended to provoke: with its movement between 'Expressionist' and 'fauvist', its cultural reference to a specific studio style of fantasy film-making, and its introduction of 'autistic children' to an 'Expressionist nightmare', this hallucination emphasizes both 'vulnerability' of the body and the unification of bodily presence with subjective experience. The paragraph also intensifies the feminization of the body as an 'exquisite corpse', which can only be understood as a passive presence; the references to the 'lethal potentialities' of the gun and its phallic presence masculinize the following paragraph, where it is described sensuously as containing a 'cold cache of ballistic kisses' (87), foreshadowing gender ambiguity. As we shall see, this has a particular effect on the story as a whole, but it can only be understood when related to the parts of the story individually, to reveal how plot, character and setting reinforce each other's tensions.

From the above dream-sequence we awaken with our narrator, Satori Thule, into a moment of introspection which makes plain the importance of gender to the narrative. In this opening of the story proper, we are presented with an instance of doubling: Thule, awake, contemplates the sleeping body of hir sexual partner, Kyoko, another Amorphibian. Kyoko is described as 'a mystery ... despite the fact that Krell's Variation has rendered us so much alike' (88), so that Thule's meditation on 'hir naked body barely covered by the crumpled sheets' is also a meditation on Thule's own body by proxy; under hir gaze, Kyoko mirrors Satori Thule (87). Shortly thereafter, Thule enters the bathroom, to bathe and to access hir hidden cache of weapons, there s/he pauses to perform a 'frank appraisal of [hir] naked body' in the mirror (96), focusing on hir own sexuality:

> The *slint* – a fully-functional, hermaphroditic sex-organ – symbolizes all the repulsion, fear, contempt and fascination with which we *squids* are regarded by so-called *normals*. Our aberrant sexuality has inspired such a climate of atavistic terror that the Cadre's Strategic executive felt compelled to force through the punitive Generic Stability Decrees, prohibiting us from the professions, academia, the judiciary and law enforcement. Aside from the introduction of compulsory sterilisation ... [t]hey've fallen shy of the last resort of *mass liquidation*. (97)

The normals' view of Amorphibians as Other is exemplified in the narrator's brief description of hir lover Kyoko's burlesque act; Kyoko, we are told, used to be one half of the Nagasaki Dragon Babies. Hir act involved performing a representation of a Japanese woodcut illustration 'Dream of the Fisherwife' with hir pet 'cephalopod simulacra', performing 'a tableau of anthropomorphic sensuality in which s/he is playfully ravished by the cephalopods' (92). Hir burlesque act is thus the performance of the exoticized (Occidental) image of the highly sexualized Oriental for the titillation of a gazing audience; s/he is acting out, or simulating, a sexual fantasy scenario, 'the living recreation of various *shunga*, the erotic prints of ancient Japan' (92), originally drawn from a non-realistic treatment of the subject of sexuality. Levels of reality in this briefly evoked description play with the presentation of image-as-reality as at once a trope of Orientalism and of lesbian/gay campness.

Conway's Amorphibians exist in a kind of apartheid, a position closely reflecting the worst examples of twentieth-century abuses; although the authorities have 'fallen shy of the last resort of *mass-liquidation*', they have imposed a programme of 'compulsory sterilisation' (Conway 97, emphasis original). It is worth remembering that in Lovecraft's 'The Shadow over Innsmouth' the amphibious members of the Innsmouth population are ultimately consigned to concentration camps by the FBI. The sense of horror in 'Metal Sushi' comes not from the presumed reader's response to the abject but from the kind of bigotry and ignorance which are the real cause of the social 'problem' of aliens in society: social intolerance. After the Second World War, phrases such as 'Generic Stability Decrees', and later, 'neugenics', explicitly invoke the spectre of fascism. It is further, and more problematically, accentuated by the name 'Satori Thule', which alludes simultaneously to Zen meditation and to an occult concept taken up by the Nazis in the 1930s (Nagl).

Borrowing from Lyotard's *Heidegger and 'the jews'* ('the jews' is written lower-case and within inverted commas in his text to emphasize its separation from real people), we can see the Amorphibian as subject to an immemorial oppression – neither remembered (represented to conscious-ness) nor forgotten (consigned to oblivion) – since their status is so utterly unacknowledgeable to the society they inhabit. Amorphibians are not steril-ized as human, but as 'Squid'; since they constitute a crossing of the line in the definitions of wo/man, their sexuality is completely denied and effaced in law. 'Squid' is the prejudicial, derogatory reduction of sex and race into signifiers for a 'lower' life form: 'For it is not as men, women, and children that [people] are exterminated but as the name of what is evil … that the Occident has given to the unconscious anxiety', the unconscious anxiety of boundary definition (Lyotard 27).

These details about the world of 'Metal Sushi' are all revealed in the scene of musing self-appraisal in the private space of the bathroom. Satori Thule considers the social position of the Amorphibian while examin-ing hir amphibious hermaphroditic body in a mirror; the thoughts on hir social being are a response to hir mirror self where s/he can return 'the uninhibited scrutiny of [hir] reflected gaze' (Conway 95). The separation of the sexualized, gazed-upon body is then completed by producing hir favoured handgun: 'Before leaving I walk back to the mirror again. I try a few practice draws with the gun ... blasting imaginary holes in my own reflection' (99). Thus we are introduced to the cognitive novelty of the story, the Amorphibian body, and also to the gender-ambivalent pronouns 's/he' and 'hir' which define the Amorphibians' subjectivity as a split-self as well as a synthesis of generic and gendered traits. Similarly, we find out here that it is fetishization of firearms that gives the story its title: 'Metal Sushi' is the name of Satori Thule's favourite type of bullets and a nickname s/he has acquired as a consequence of their use. In terms of narrative form, we might view the above mirror scene as a separating of the principles of masculinity and femininity between the gazing Thule, with hir phallic gun, and hir gazed-upon reflection in its nakedness; subjectivity, at this stage of the narrative, remains split in discourse and socialization even though the textual tropes suggest synthesis in the Amorphibian body; this is an important aspect of the Weird in 'Metal Sushi'.

Darja Malcolm-Clarke suggests that there is a specific unification of setting and character in New Weird texts that invites 'a particular reading of the texts' events, characters or socio-political backdrop' whereby 'two elements – bodies and cities – play a dominant [role] in the stories' symbolic or visual vocabulary' (qtd. in VanderMeer 337). The correlation of urban space and physiognomy as a means of expressing the fundamental concerns of identity under modernity might be categorized as a defining interest of New Weird: the representation of social being through its internal and external characterization. These, directly recalling Modernism, are attempts to create fictional worlds expressing the sensations, effects and crises of contemporary modernity. Whether this can be separated from postmodernism depends to what extent the ludic play of postmodernism is understood as an attempt to compensate the individual for the perceived losses of agency under late capitalism (Jameson). What is clear is that many New Weird texts have an epistemological relationship with representation; they refuse to break with the 'seriousness' of their secondary world or their characters. Characters and plans remain 'real' within the text, regardless of how unreliable or convoluted the narrative strategies become, as in Steph Swainston's *The Year of Our War* (2004), *No Present Like Time* (2005) and *The Modern World* (2007), while texts such as VanderMeer's *City of Saints and Madmen* (2002) and *Shriek: An Afterword* (2006) play on their textuality while maintaining the integrity of the fictional world. By emphasizing the physicality of text-as-document relating to an external reality the immersive fantasy world remains concrete. The baroque stylization of environment and grotesque physiognomies in the texts termed New Weird seems to mark a deliberate attempt to return to the mode of defamiliarization – the making unfamiliar of familiar language – described in Shklovsky's 'Art as Technique' (15–21) *within* the already cognitively estranged environment that, following Suvin, we identify with science fiction (Suvin, *Metamorphoses*). This can be seen at work in 'Metal Sushi'.

The earth, having been flooded, is now sustained by '*vrill*' [*sic*], 'the thriving marine protein transplanted from the ocean worlds of the Sirius system', feeding the world with 'the rich yields of its quarterly harvests' (Conway 90–91). In naming his 'miracle-food' after the people of Bulwer-Lytton's *The Coming Race* (1871), the Vril-ya, Conway suggests a direct link between the environment and the emergence of the new human gender. The term Krell's Variation, which also describes the Amorphibian, is borrowed from the name of the alien race in *Forbidden Planet*, whose machines summon the powers of the unconscious mind, further foreshadowing the narrative direction of the story.

Thule and Kyoko inhabit the 'Silver Quay ghetto' in the 'grim, undisciplined sprawl of Harbourtown' (Conway 89). Harbourtown is a place of excess and of uncertain boundaries, both horizontally where it sprawls and vertically, downward into the waters: 'the entire waterfront district of Harbourtown seems to have simply congealed around the water's edge … I can imagine it simply oozing up through some fissure in the earth's crust' (90). In situating the city in the sea in this way, as an oozing up of primordial forces, Conway plays on the Jungian concept of the ocean as a representation of collective unconscious. This is particularly apparent in Thule's description of the 'sunken cities of the submerged Western seaboard' (90), which suggest that America, a paradigmatically (post)modern culture, has become a lost civilization:

> Colonies of mutant coral cultures encrust the skeletal remains of drowned stratoscrapers, a labyrinthine jungle of fossil reefs, the baroque majesty of its cavernous vaults and galleries evoking the cyclopean geometry of lost Atlantis. Most *normals* consider the sight of this submarine Eden, abandoned to the primal tranquillity of the emerald sea, to be an ominous, depressing sight.... Personally I've always found its serene topography of silent vistas and haunted grottoes both surreal and deeply poignant: a numinous vision that resonates equally with the power of phylogenic memory and the vague intimations of precognition. (90)

It is significant that these lost cities are both 'Atlantis' and 'Eden', metaphorical lands that unify all opposing principles: what the story seeks is synthesis. The compositional parts of the novella return obsessively to binary divisions at the point of crisis; forms and structures are on the cusp of being unified or collapsing into one another through the conflict of power relations between them. These elements of contradiction are echoed in the plot, which draws upon known and clichéd plot devices, collapsing their expectations.

In *The Doomed Detective: The Contribution of the Detective Novel to Postmodern American and Italian Fiction*, Stefano Tani writes that the essence of detective fiction is its ritualized mode and that the postmodern collapsing of the opposing narrative principles is, in important respects, already implied by the form from Poe onwards. Tani picks out two fundamentals:

> First, that the detective genre should be stylized, 'lifeless,' ritual-ized, essentially a rational exorcism of irrationality, a conflict between logic and multiform, mysterious reality; and second, that the two fundamental terms of the conflict, the criminal and the detective, 'the creative and the resolvant sides of the double Dupin,' should function as doubles, each a negation of the other. (15)

Tani's study goes on to explore postmodernist instances of anti-detective fiction which collapse the dualism of criminal/detective, such as William Hjortsberg's *Falling Angel* (1978) and Italo Calvino's *If on a Winter's Night a Traveller* (1979), texts which dissect and recombine these roles to some other purpose. Tani's study poses a theory of several movements – formulation, codification, collapse and reformulation – between detective and post-modernist fiction, as an exemplar of a cycle of popular cultural development in which the end result is a return at a higher level of insight. In its drastic-ally contracted form, we can see Conway's 'Metal Sushi' working through a similar conceptual process, but centring on gender.

'Metal Sushi' presents the elements of a narrative of detection (a mission and a mystery) but begins almost at the point of revelation, filling in the missing pieces in flashback while the narrator is bathing and getting dressed, or while s/he is unconscious. We recognize Thule as a postmodernist 'doomed detective' in a shorthand form by hir opening nightmare-cum-flashback, and by intertextual references. Satori Thule has been assigned by Under-Dictator Venturis to infiltrate a racial supremacist cult in the Silver Quay ghetto of Harbourtown, a city of the far future somewhere on the Eastern seaboard of the former USA. Through Thule's overdetermined body as amphibious hermaphrodite, the story critically foregrounds the blending and bending of both genre and gender in setting up this scenario. As an Investigator, Thule's work in 'confidential enquiry' is a heavily gendered role (Conway 102); the Under-Dictator refers to Thule as a 'Private Slint', after the gender-ambivalent Amorphibian sex organ (102). Thule's presence as Amorphibian in the private rooms of official society, the 'shameless luxury' of the 'ultra-privileged ... totalitarian elite of the Cadre's upper echelons', is conditional upon having a social role as 'underling or hired help of some description[;] Domestic, Whore, Investigator' (105).

The narrative brings to consciousness the gender-typing of specific prose techniques and conventions as it employs them. In this world, the 'authentic' masculinity of the 'Private Dick' is replaced by the much more ambiguous subject position of the hermaphrodite, whose physiognomy suggests the roles of both Private Investigator and femme fatale. The hard-boiled detective narrative as a mode of pulp writing is here extended to an archetype, exemplifying binary gender roles; simply reading the pronouns 's/he' and 'hir' throughout the story presents the reader with a persistent reminder of the determining effect of gendered language on subjectivity. Gender is thus an integral part of the textual novum.

Thule's role as a detective appears mainly as memory, or after s/he has been drugged and kidnapped by the *Heilige Kraken* cult s/he was infiltrating; the active or masculine role as hard-boiled detective is thus framed by the passive or feminizing function of sacrificial victim to the cult. The pressure of the plot ultimately forces Thule to transcend this internal split in hir identity: the sacrifice is never completed by the fascist, millennialist cult (and Thule hirself kills Xavier Malthusian), but it is completed accidentally by the mindless warrior-drones of the regime Thule was working for, the Sieglanders.

The 'Sieglanders', creatures that are 'relics of the Azrael Project, one of the many neugenics programmes hatched at the height of the Commodities War' (Conway 139), are safely exploitable because they do not threaten the status quo; they are not seen to think for themselves and have no gender, a significant contrast with the excessive gender of the Amorphibian. Further, because the Sieglanders are cyborgs who accidentally complete a mystic ritual, their function within the narrative is conflicted; they form a science fiction trope which completes an overdetermined fantastic trope of prophecy – they are another manifestation of contrariness.

The plot is both fulfilled and denied: Thule reaches a bodiless apotheosis, folding time and space around hirself, but the *Heilige Kraken* cult and its ambitions to use Thule as their path to godhead are destroyed by the military forces of law and order. Somewhere in between these forces of narrative determination, Thule's subjectivity survives. The collapse of the overdetermining gendered language and the gender roles combines with the collapse of the generic expectations signalled by the dense intertextual references to produce apocalyptic patterns in both narrative and language. Satori Thule's first-person narration becomes an omniscient narration and sets about removing the other named characters from the story in gory fashion. S/he erases both of the antagonistic forces that had previously determined hir roles within the plot: Hayden Venturis, who used hir as a hard-boiled detective to destroy the millennialist cult, and Xavier Malthusian, who used hir as a sacrificial victim.

The story concludes with Thule as a vengeful godhead travelling out into the universe; surviving the narrative of hir demise as a postmodernist 'doomed detective', s/he begins a new narrative of excess and new subjectivities. Through this battle between reactionary oppositions, Satori Thule has managed to progress beyond the determinations of socially (gendered) and politically (generically) coded forms as a constantly exceeding, constantly unfolding being in the same way that the narrative itself has exceeded the determining generic markers which characterized it.

'Metal Sushi' produces a conceptual collage of narrative innovation with narrative cliché, forcing the two together to a point where they form new metaphors for the disruptive meeting of modernity and postmodernity as allegories for our encounter with our own histories and cultures. As in the New Weird, the story's textual surface joins up and grammatically compares tropes and concepts taken from the specific (sub)cultural contexts of science fiction and Gothic fantasy in a way that reveals its own double motion as subject to the determining forces of genres as market categories. The narrative of 'Metal Sushi' reveals the irreducibility of subjectivity in the face of the determinants of language and social pressure. The unification of Gothic and science fictional modes charts a narrative of liberation here, as in the New Weird, producing a whole which is greater than the sum of its parts, and indicating analogously how its defamiliarization and its textual novum reflect critically on social relationships in the world.

Notes

1. The titular novella of Oneiros Books' first publication will be the subject of this article; to avoid confusion, all further reference will only be to 'Metal Sushi', the novella.

Works cited

Apocalypse Now. Dir. Francis Ford Coppola. United Artists, 1979. Film.
Artaud, Antonin. *Heliogabalus; Or, The Anarchist Crowned*. 1933. Trans. Alexis Lykiard. London: Creation Books, 2003. Print.
—. and Lewis, M. G. *The Monk*. 1931. Trans. John Philips. London: Creation Books, 2003. Print.
Bould, Mark. 'The Dreadful Credibility of Absurd Things: A Tendency in Fantasy Theory.' *Historical Materialism* 10.4 (2002): 51–88. Print.
—. and China Miéville (eds). *Red Planets: Marxism and Science Fiction*. London: Pluto Press, 2009. Print.
Bulwer-Lytton, Edward. *The Coming Race*. Edinburgh: Blackwood, 1873. Print.
Calvino, Italo. *If on a Winter's Night a Traveller*. 1980. Trans. William Weaver. London: Vintage, 1998. Print.
Campbell, Ramsey. 'Introduction.' *The Starry Wisdom: A Tribute to H. P. Lovecraft*. Ed. D. M. Mitchell. London: Creation, 1994. Print.
Cavanagh, David. *The Creation Records Story: My Magpie Eyes Are Hungry for the Prize*. London: Virgin Books, 2000. Print.

Conway, David. *Metal Sushi*. Swansea: Oneiros, 1998. Print.

Coulthart, John, with H. P. Lovecraft and Alan Moore. *The Haunter of the Dark and Other Grotesque Visions*. Swansea: Oneiros, 1999. Print.

Dick, Philip K. *The Three Stigmata of Palmer Eldrich*. 1964. London: Gollancz, 2003. Print.

Ellis, Warren. illus. by various. *The Authority*. La Jolla: Wildstorm, 1999. Print.

Forbidden Planet. Dir. Fred M. Wilcox. MGM, 1956. Film.

Freedman, Carl. 'Towards a Theory of Paranoia: The Science Fiction of Philip K. Dick.' *Science Fiction Studies* 32, 11.1 (1984): 15–25. Print.

Gay, Peter. *Modernism: The Lure of Heresy from Baudelaire to Beckett and Beyond*. London: Vintage, 2009. Print.

Haraway, Donna. *Simians, Cyborgs, and Women: The Reinvention of Nature*. London: Routledge, 1991. Print.

Hills, Matt. 'Counter Fictions in the Work of Kim Newman: Rewriting Gothic SF as "Alternate-Story Stories".' *Science Fiction Studies* 30.3 (2003): 436–455. Print.

Hjortsberg, William. *Falling Angel*. 1978. London: Arrow Books, 1987. Print.

Hodgson, William Hope. *The Night Land*. 1912. *The House on the Borderland and Other Novels*. Introd. China Miéville. London: Gollancz, 2003. Print.

Hunter, Jack, ed. *Red Stains*. London: Creation, 1991. Print.

Hurley, Kelly. *The Gothic Body: Sexuality, Materialism and Degeneration at the Fin de Siècle*. Cambridge: Cambridge UP, 2004. Print.

Jameson, Frederic. *Postmodernism: Or, The Cultural Logic of Late Capitalism*. London: Verso, 1991. Print.

Kuspit, Donald. *The Cult of the Avant-Garde Artist*. Cambridge: Cambridge UP, 1993. Print.

Lewis, Wyndham. *The Essential Wyndham Lewis*. Ed. Julian Symons. London: Vintage, 1989. Print.

Lindsay, David. *A Voyage to Arcturus*. 1920. Manchester: Savoy, 2002. Print.

Lovecraft, H[oward] P[hillips]. *At the Mountains of Madness*. 1931. *The H. P. Lovecraft Omnibus 1: At the Mountains of Madness*. London: HarperCollins, 1994. Print.

—. 'The Call of Cthulhu.' 1926. *The Best of H. P. Lovecraft: Bloodcurdling Tales of Horror and the Macabre*. Introd. Robert Bloch. New York: Ballantine, 1982. Print.

—. *Lord of a Visible World: An Autobiography in Letters*. Ed. S. T. Joshi and David E. Schultz. Athens: Ohio UP, 2000. Print.

—. 'The Shadow over Innsmouth.' 1931. *The H. P. Lovecraft Omnibus 3: The Haunter of the Dark and Other Tales*. London: HarperCollins, 1994. Print.

—. 'Supernatural Horror in Literature.' 1925. *The H. P. Lovecraft Omnibus 2: Dagon and Other Macabre Tales*. London: HarperCollins, 1994. Print.

Lyotard, Jean-François. *Heidegger and 'the jews'*. Trans. Andreas Michel and Mark Roberts. Minneapolis: U of Minnesota P, 1990. Print.

Machen, Arthur. *The Great God Pan*. 1894. London: Creation Books, 1993. Print.

Mendlesohn, Farah. *Rhetorics of Fantasy*. Middletown: Wesleyan UP, 2008. Print.

—. and Edward James. *A Short History of Fantasy*. London: Middlesex University, 2009. Print.

Mitchell, David M., ed. *The Starry Wisdom: A Tribute to H. P. Lovecraft*. London: Creation Books, 1994. Print.

Morrison, Grant. 'Introduction.' *Metal Sushi*. By David Conway. Swansea: Oneiros, 1998. Print

—. *Lovely Biscuits*. Swansea: Oneiros Books, 1998. Print.

—. *New X-Men: E is for Extinction*. Illus. Frank Quitely, Leninil Francis Yu and Ethan Van Sciver et al. New York: Marvel Comics, [2001] 2005. Print.

—. *New X-Men: Here Comes Tomorrow*. Illus. Marc Silvestri et al. New York: Marvel, 2004. Print.

Murray, Will. 'Lovecraft and the Pulp Magazine Tradition.' *An Epicure in the Terrible: A Centennial Anthology of Essays in Honor of H. P. Lovecraft*. Ed. David E. Schultz and S. T. Joshi. London: Farleigh Dickenson University, 1991. 101–31. Print.

Nagl, Manfred. 'SF, Occult Sciences, and Nazi Myths.' *Science Fiction Studies* 1.3 (1974): n. pag. Web. 11 October 2010.

Sade, D.A.F., The Marquis de. *Philsophy in the Bedroom*. 1795. Trans. Meredith Bodroghy. London: Creation Books, 2000. Print.

Shklovsky, Viktor. 'Art as Technique.' 1916. *Literary Theory: An Anthology*. Ed. Julile Rivkin and Michael Ryan. 2nd ed. Oxford: Blackwell, 2004. 15–21. Print.

Suvin, Darko. *Metamorphoses of Science Fiction*. New Haven, CT: Yale UP, 1974. Print.

—. *Positions and Presuppositions in Science Fiction*. Kent: Kent State UP, 1988. Print.

Swainston, Steph. *The Modern World*. London: Gollancz, 2007. Print.

—. *No Present Like Time*. London: Gollancz, 2005. Print.

—. *The Year of Our War*. London: Gollancz, 2004. Print.

Tabbi, Joseph. *Postmodern Sublime: Technology and American Writing from Mailer to Cyberpunk*. Ithaca, NY: Cornell University Press, 1995. Print.

Tani, Stefano. *The Doomed Detective: The Contribution of the Detective Novel to Postmodern American and Italian Fiction*. Carbondale: Southern Illinois UP, 1984. Print.

VanderMeer, Jeff. *City of Saints and Madmen*. London: Tor/Pan Macmillan, 2004. Print.

—. *Shriek: An Afterword*. London: Pan Macmillan, 2006. Print.

VanderMeer, Jeff and Ann VanderMeer. *The New Weird*. San Francisco: Tachyon, 2008. Print.

Wells, Steven. *Tits-Out Teenage Terror Totty*. London: Attack! Books, an imprint of Creation Books, 1999. Print.

9. Spatialized Ontologies: Toni Morrison's Science Fiction Traces in Gothic Spaces

Jerrilyn McGregory

The Gothic elements of African American writer Toni Morrison's work are widely acknowledged. Early in her writing career, literary critic Bernard Bell identified Morrison's countertexts as 'gothic fables', and Kari Winter surmises: 'I know of no work that reconstructs and illuminates both the female Gothic and the slave narrative traditions better than *Beloved*' (13). Situating Morrison as 'Gothic science fiction' is, however, more controversial, given that, with her Nobel-laureate standing, Morrison's capital is not generally consumed as science fiction.[1] Yet if we recognize science fiction as social texts offering depictions of race, gender, and the environment, enabling recognition of difference, then Morrison's speculative fictions can be recognized as part of the genre: as Brian Aldiss argues, science fiction can 'venture where the solid realistic social novel could not go' (16).

Morrison constructs some of literature's most memorable Gothic science fiction spaces, each edifice and structure serving as a spatialized ontology in the sense that it embodies social processes as lived by African Americans. Significantly, Ed Soja theorized postmodern geographies and how they delineate a material framework to establish 'the spatiality of social life' (119). Similarly, Minrose Gwin suggests how metaphorically 'social relations are concretized and embedded in space' (15). Morrison's Gothic science fiction architectronics convey these same intricacies, shaped by Other times, Other beings, Other minds, and Other worlds.[2] Dani Cavallaro notes that the Gothic characteristically features 'dark places', each a 'locus of torment, punishment, mystery, corruption and insanity – the place in which, as in Matthew Lewis's *The Monk* [1796], defenceless victims are trapped, often in the unwelcome company of dismal apparitions and abject creatures' (27). Morrison uses such sites to 'endarken' the socio-spatial realities experienced by African Americans.

Coined by Cynthia Dillard, the term 'endarkened' is a play on 'enlightened', conveying 'a distinguishable difference in cultural standpoint, located in the intersection/overlap of the culturally constructed socializations of race, gender, and other identities, and the historical and contemporary contexts of oppressions and resistance' (3). By endarkening her prose narratives, Morrison inverts the Western ideation system. Inversion is Morrison's *modus operandi*; lacking the sentimentality of the Western *Märchen*, her tales are not dependent on the formulaic 'living happily ever after' leitmotif but engage important survival imperatives.

In science fiction parlance, Morrison's representation of the othering process articulates African American life, history, and culture, within her own variation of Suvin's 'cognitive estrangement' ('On the Poetics' 372): enchantment. In an interview with Christina Davis, Morrison states: 'My own use of enchantment simply comes because that's the way the world was for me and for the black people that I knew' (Davis 414). Early anthropologist Robin George Collingwood, in *The Philosophy of Enchantment*, defines enchantment as 'a magic sensibility that modern humanity has almost forgotten among the urgencies of self-definition in a world of increasingly utilitarian values and national striving' (lxii). Morrison differentiates the epistemic status of African Americans from Western knowledge systems. Her deft treatment recentres cognitive estrangement. Morrison uses enchantment dialectically, employing textual effects of estrangement and the uncanny to serve as political allegory.

While acknowledging Carl Freedman's significant theoretical discourse, I veer from simply accepting his proposition that 'all fiction is, in a sense, science fiction' (16). Nor do I choose to disregard Darko Suvin's definition of science fiction as cognitive estrangement. Yet Suvin's definition here is famously exclusionist, especially toward fantasy and the fairy-tale. While enchantment is a construct largely privileged in fantasy by way of fairy-tales, Morrison's enchantment-driven novels often depend on cultural specificity, in which natural and supernatural worlds inhabit the same plane of reality. Moreover, she syncretizes her imagination within the Gothic literary tradition. In *A Companion to Science Fiction*, Marleen Barr concurs with Robert Scholes' positioning of '"structural fabulation" as constituting a realm separate from ordinary reality yet related to it' (142). This commentary invites slippage on the grounds that Morrison situates Western notions of the fantastic as 'a way of not talking about the politics' (Davis 414). The fantastic or fabulation constructs affirm a Eurocentric realist point of view. These modalities fail to communicate a consensual reality that comprises the everyday among many non-Westerners.

In addition, Patricia Melzer argues that 'alien constructions' function as metaphoric 'testing grounds for feminist critical thought' (11). However, while Melzer explores chiefly a feminist agenda, Morrison's creative agenda is far more expansive. Morrison attacks a racial and gendered Othering, complicated by an alien world-view, fuelled by scientific racism. In an interview with Eugene Redmond, Morrison elaborates:

> Racism is a scientific, scholarly pursuit. Beginning with Malthus, it's a specific, examined, learned, recorded body of study. Whether it's I.Q. testing or the size of one's brain, it's all a systematized study. Racists always try to make you think they are the majority, but they never are. It's always the minority against all of the poor, all of the women, or all of the blacks. (Redmond 31)[3]

As Melzer says of Octavia Butler's fiction, Morrison's 'discussions of gender always imply the construction of race and vice versa' (80). The science in Morrison's fiction privileges the modern academic practices that focused on eugenics to investigate differences and to justify political inequality.

I position *A Mercy* (2008), Morrison's latest publication, as a crucial new text relative to this interrogation. In *A Mercy*, Morrison queries 'what if' the founding of America were not predicated on models of racial oppression and a bourgeois ideology.[4] Morrison actively pinpoints a defining moment when a harsh natural environment could have enabled an equalitarian American society to develop, instead of succumbing to racial systems of oppression and proto-capitalism. In these Other times, too, religion came to inform the means to rationalize slavery's perpetuity. In this manner, spatially, Morrison articulates her own version of Suvin's novum (*Positions and Presuppositions* 72), in an open-ended exposé of the past and present amnesia surrounding American history.

The historical space Morrison presents invokes the seventeenth-century colonizing of the New World based on indentured servitude and the turn to race slavery, notably, up North. The long history of northern slavery in the US and the region's enslavement of Native peoples escape general knowledge. Joanna Russ notes: 'Like much "post-modern" literature (Nabokov, Borges), science fiction deals commonly, typically, and often insistently, with epistemology' (11). Epistemology concerns what we know and how we know it. Take, for example, Native American Lina's prose narrative about the (white) hunter's unwarranted attack upon an eagle's nest, which futuristically presages the destructive rise of capitalism and colonialism: 'The traveler laughs at the beauty saying, "This is perfect. This is mine." And the word swells, booming like thunder into valleys, over acres of primrose and mallow. Creatures come out of caves wondering what it means. Mine. Mine. Mine' (Morrison, *A Mercy* 62–63). Lina's narrative is etiological, explaining the arrival of an overarching ideology of power in its formative stages. John Reider notes that Darko Suvin and Mark Bould 'agree not only that science fiction's impossible "facts" must be pieces of a coherently imagined world that differs significantly from one agreed upon by contemporaries as the real, but also that the organizational principle behind this coherent divergence from reality is absolutely crucial' (63). Going on to cite the 'riddle of the landscape', Reider establishes grounds for reading Morrison's participatory literary style as a framing device upholding 'a self-conscious generic feature' (63). Morrison's Other worlds are chiefly inspired by US contexts, as Morrison outlines in her essay collection *The House that Race Built*. In one essay therein, 'Home,' Morrison confirms that the 'racial house has troubled my work' (5).[5] In this statement, Morrison crisply encapsulates the way that the spatial trope of the built edifice carries significant social force in her work.

In *A Mercy*, Anglo-Dutch John Vaark personifies the rise of a masculinist dominator culture. His northern farm nears utopia, harboring difference, multiplicity, heterogeneity, diversity, and plurality. Yet, he revokes Lina's epistemological privilege, instilling himself as the patriarchal head of household, sealing the fate of his motley crew:

> But it was she who taught him how to dry the fish they caught; to anticipate spawning and how to protect a crop from night creatures.... He ignored her warning of using alewives as fertilizer only to see his plots of tender vegetable torn up by foragers attracted by the smell. Nor would he plant squash among the corn. Though he allowed that the vines kept weeds away, he did not like the look of disorder. (50)

In keeping with the idea of science fiction as a projection of the American future, Morrison's text ends ambiguously and without the disingenuous friendship that orthodoxy usually manufactures to satisfy racially diverse audiences.[6] Vaark is known as Sir; his sudden demise exposes the vulnerability of the women (who had functioned as if a sisterhood – despite race, gender, and class). They splinter on account of his wife's betrayal of the others. They conflate into 'no one except servants' (99), while she 'laundered nothing, planted nothing, weeded never. She cooked and mended' (145). When faced with her own death and powerlessness, she succumbs to her neighbour's bourgeois Christian values upon which the New Republic will depend.

Like the Gothic, science fiction can arguably be read as a matter of traces rather than a formal genre: as Reider says, it can be defined as 'a group of objects that bear a "family resemblance"' (16). It is on this basis that I situate Morrison's science fiction traces. *A Mercy* functions as the prequel to *Beloved*, her first raced text (relative to major white opponents). One must read between the historical spaces to recognize these two novels' movement from utopia to dystopia, within two hundred years. To quote Valerie

Smith: 'Set in Cincinnati in 1873, eight years after the end of the Civil War, *Beloved* is nevertheless a novel about slavery. The characters have been so profoundly affected by the experience of slavery that time cannot separate them from its horrors or undo its effects' (345). Instead of proffering fully fledged utopian or dystopian societies, here Morrison invokes the spirit of critical near-utopia and near-dystopia. Temporally and spatially, her texts occur on the cusps of utopic and dystopic societies.[7] After all, *A Mercy* and *Beloved* are creative productions that resist a north/south binary to fill gaps, disclosing alternative realities and values relative to pre-chattel slavery, the antebellum and the post-bellum periods. They allegorically suggest the perennial lingering ghosts of slavery.

Throughout Morrison's work, she uses terror to explicate the intangibles of oppression. Bernard Bell identifies significant Gothic markers in Morrison's novels: 'magic, mystery, and terror' (174). Her oeuvre consistently invokes these Gothic qualities. Gwin records Morrison's own comments at a reading of *Beloved*: 'Both she and the reader, she said, needed to do what the slaves had done: "enter that space helplessly"' (27). Morrison's penchant is to dramatize psychologically aberrant behaviour in lived sites of earthly horror. Most notably, *Beloved* opens with the synecdoche: '124 WAS SPITEFUL. Full of baby's venom. The women in the house knew it and so did the children' (3). Morrison's fiction repeatedly constructs habitats unfit for humanity. Her assortment of terrifying edifices corresponds directly to the lives of their occupants. As a prelude to *Beloved*'s Sweet Home plantation and the brutal chattel slavery to come, Vaark designs 'a profane monument to himself' (*A Mercy* 44). The haunted house, at 124 Bluestone Road, centres on a chamber of horror, or the 'shattered world [Morrison] built' ('Unspeakable Things' 22).[8] In essence, 124 seethes with undulating currents that produce physical fear among most: thus, 'its claim to local fame' (37). For any ardent reader of Gothic literature, no further recuperative explanation need stand: 'Ghosts return to haunt the living out of a desire for revenge conducive to often extreme acts of violence and brutality that may include the victimization of the innocent' (Cavallaro 63). Cloaked with an endarkened representation of motherhood made spectacular through infanticide, *Beloved* signifies how past racial and gender politics continue to erode the psychological spaces inhabited by African American women and men.

In *Song of Solomon*, Morrison's representations of Gothic science fiction are more subtle and subversive. Here, she offers a spatialized critique of capitalism. Macon Dead, Sr. acts as one of the proprietary sources of post-Second World War ghettoization: 'He knew as a Negro he wasn't going to get a big slice of the pie. But there were properties nobody wanted yet, or little edges of property somebody didn't want Jews to have, or Catholics to have, or properties nobody knew were of any value yet' (63). He operates in

counterbalance to the societal norms of Gothic fiction that Keeling identifies: 'Whatever is perceived as "alien" here – whatever seems to intrude
into the otherwise stable and usually bourgeois world – is always perceived
as "evil" as well' (113). With alterity, Macon Dead's strivings alienate him
from the community that capital exploits and the cultural domains that it
spawns. The latter is important in the configuring of how shifting to another
political economy (capitalism) produced 'another culture of time and space'
(Soja 60). For African Americans the shift to capitalism does not trigger
progress, but further community rupture.

In an interview, Morrison argues: 'Art is a route into developing a
language in order to talk about all sorts of things that are unspeakable'
(Hostetler 202). With consistency and cultural specificity, Morrison captures
resulting monstrous behavior. For people of African descent, who eschew
endogamous relationships with blood kin, *Song of Solomon*'s cousins Hagar
and Milkman breach a profound sexual taboo (Gutman 82–93). Even
without full knowledge of this cultural code, readers generally react with
shock. In this way, the text relates to Suvin's 'parables of de-alienation':
Suvin argues that science fiction's ultimate aim is 'the shock of estrangement reorienting the reader's perception –in modern times, making her
recognize the alienated world she lives in' (*Positions and Presuppositions* 142).
The stark horror of their incestuous tryst is exacerbated by the fact that it
is initially Hagar's grandmother who introduces them: 'This here's your
brother, Milkman' (43). The tryst between the pair commences when Hagar
is seventeen and Milkman is twelve, lasting for years: 'In fact her maturity
and blood kinship converted her passion to fever, so it was more affliction
than affection' (127).

Hagar's primary vice, however, is not violating a sexual taboo. Even more
gravely, she clings in a monstrous attachment to bourgeois capitalism and
'commodity consumption [which] mutilates black personhood' (Willis 178).
Therefore, Morrison again inverts Keeling's dictum of evil in Gothic fiction
as relates to the 'stable and usually bourgeois world', by signifying this
world as alien (113).[9] I concur with Mayberry's assessment: 'What keeps
these characters off kilter is the intrusion of sterile, white, middle-class
notions of property, propriety, and competition; their struggle for selfhood
involves not only gender differences but conflicts or race, class, and age'
(73). Readers should not take the indictment lightly for, allegorically speaking, in African American literature, the quest for freedom and literacy is
dependent on the protagonists' conscious awareness of their historical,
political, and cultural past (Harris).

One common architectural feature endarkens each spatial unit described
over the course of five pages of action related to Hagar's stalking of Milkman:
the porch. For instance, giving expression to her unrequited love, Hagar

'moved around the house, onto the porch, down the streets, to the fruit stalls and the butchershop [sic], like a restless ghost, finding peace nowhere and in nothing' (127). Later, proving herself 'to be the world's most inept killer', she gains access to Milkman's room via the porch (129). Learning of Hagar's murderous intent, his mother, Ruth, storms home: 'She climbed the porch steps and went into the kitchen. Without knowing what her foot was planning to do, she kicked the cabinet door with the worn lock under the sink' (133). The porch is a regular element in African American literature and abounds in connotations of a space rooted in shared knowledge and conviviality. Yet, even given their ubiquity, these cultural spaces go unacknowledged by Hagar as well as by Ruth, as they travel across them in agitation.

Additionally, *Song of Solomon* is rife with the kinds of Other beings long associated with science fiction, such as the immortal Circe, midwife to Pilate, who '[b]orned herself' and is without a navel (246). Within the text, the ontological journey of young Macon 'Milkman' Dead, Jr. actualizes Istvan Csicsery-Ronay's 'science-fictional sublime', 'a response to a shock of imaginative expansion, a complex recoil and recuperation of self-consciousness coping with phenomena suddenly perceived to be too great to be comprehended' (146). In essence, in the novel's dénouement, Milkman either dies or flies. Drawing on the mythic legend of African people who could fly, Morrison positions Milkman's heredity as empirical fact among the enslaved who (in discovery of the trauma yet to come) soared home to Africa: 'For he knew what Shalimar knew: If you surrendered to the air, you could ride it' (341). The leap is toward freedom as desired by every generation of enslaved African and their consciously aware descendants. In this way, culturally speaking, Morrison demands that readers reclaim and traverse a distinctive ideological space.

Gender experience is at the heart of Morrison's play with both Gothic and science fiction forms. Morrison's *Sula* can be read as exemplifying feminist science fiction, in that the title character represents the outlaw adventuress within an apocalyptic context. While it would simplify my task to merely locate Morrison within the field of feminist science fiction, it would be disingenuous to do so. Morrison defies ideological labelling beyond her own African American identity politics. Morrison's stance adheres most closely to Alice Walker's womanist theory. In the introduction to *In Search of our Mothers' Gardens*, Walker defines womanism as being more radical than feminism in that it is not oppositional to men, seeking the survival and unity with men as well as women (xi). Toni Morrison, too, demands a more nuanced reading.

Placing *Sula* in perspective, Maxine Lavon Montgomery argues that '... to be Black in America, the novel implies, is to experience calamity as an ever-present reality, to live on the brink of apocalypse' (127). Sula's stronghold has Gothic proportions. The following description portrays the spatiality associated with Sula:

> Sula Peace lived in a house of many rooms that had been built over a period of five years to the specifications of its owner, who kept on adding things: more stairways – there were three sets to the second floor – more rooms, doors and stoops. There were rooms that had three doors, others that opened out on the porch only and were inaccessible from any other part of the house; others that you could get to only by going through somebody's bedroom. (30)

The house depicts a radical alteration of the bourgeois family model. The 'creator and sovereign of this enormous house', Eva Peace, epitomizes a macabre sentient being: an amputee, enthroned in a wagon and emotionally governed by 'a concentration of manlove' (42). In essence, 'those Peace women loved all men. It was manlove that Eva bequeathed to her daughters' (41). Still, her son, a First World War drug-addicted veteran 'to whom she hoped to bequeath everything', instead provokes excessive maternal love (45). This time, Morrison endarkens the text via filicide: '[Eva] rolled a bit of newspaper into a tight stick about six inches long, lit it and threw it onto the bed where the kerosene-soaked Plum lay in snug delight' (47). The stairways, psychological spaces of Eva's creation, enable her destructive path to restore his manhood through a fiery death.

Although ostensibly an inheritor of this encompassing 'manlove', Sula alienates her community, outlawed by virtue of undertaking an adventure-some 'experimental life' (118). In keeping with the endarkened paradigm shift, in her essay 'Unspeakable Things Unspoken', Morrison acquaints us with Sula's 'outlaw quality' as 'new world black and new world woman ex-tracting choice from choicelessness, responding inventively to found things. Improvizational. Daring, disruptive, imaginative, modern, out-of-the-house, outlawed, unpolicing, uncontained and uncontainable. And dangerously female' (25). In an interview in 1985, Morrison again characterizes Sula as the 'outlaw and the adventuress' (Denard 26). Similarly, Karla Holloway describes Sula 'as the ideal of feminine imagination set free' (79). The adjec-tives used could apply to many science fiction heroines. With her lineage, Sula's powers escalate beyond the allowed community-based boundaries and extend to her dethroning her grandmother and occupying her space. According to Soja, 'As a social product, spatiality is simultaneously the medium and outcome, presupposition and embodiment, of social action and relationship' (129). By the chapter entitled '1939', Sula's Bottom com-munity designates her as its pariah. *Sula* documents the coming of age of this 'new world woman', who in feminist science fiction comprises a strong, self-reliant woman, 'motivated to survive' (Roberts 102).

Ironically, Sula does not survive to participate in the brewing apocalypse. To the dismay of readers and some of the other characters alike, she physically succumbs three chapters before the dénouement. Sula is also oddly absent from the opening chapters: Morrison opens the novel by introducing the character Shadrack and National Suicide Day, delaying the titled character's appearance. Shadrack is a First World War shell shock survivor and National Suicide Day is his brainchild. Twenty-two years after the first celebration, Sula's death triggers a false sense of optimism: 'Never before had they laughed. Always they had shut their doors, pulled down the shades and called their children out of the road. It frightened him, this glee, but he stuck to his habit – singing his song, ringing his bell and holding fast to his rope' (159). En route, deemed as rescuing African American people from racial discrimination by offering death instead, Shadrack leads many into oblivion. Such catastrophic fiction, like most science fiction writing, is imbued with a political subtext. Roger Luckhurst links apocalypse to historical moments of 'political and economic instability' (230), and Morrison's *Sula* exemplifies this link. In *Sula*, Morrison objectifies an attack on 'the tunnel they were forbidden to build' (161), resulting in a climatic cataclysm.[10] The construction of the tunnel, materially, makes concrete their subjugation.

Morrison's fiction perennially faces male bashing-charges (e.g. Crouch; Johnson; Reed). Many of her African American male characters epitomize Gothic conceits, object lessons in masculine sadism and demagoguery. For instance, *Bluest Eye*'s Soaphead Church is a sociocultural monstrosity – a rank paedophile who 'palm[ed] himself off as a minister' (135). Corrupt clergy are a regular trope of the Gothic, and Morrison's Caribbean Elihue Micah Whitcomb, nicknamed Soaphead, is a particularly menacing incarnation of the trope on account of his appropriation of the African American Hoodoo system of belief: 'His business was dread. People came to him in dread, whispered in dread, wept and pleaded in dread. And dread was what he counseled' (136). His metamorphosis into such a monster is worsened by the way he has internalized the ideas of the colonizer: even among African Americans, he garners cultural capital on account of the prestigious Anglophone English he speaks. His cruelty and scorn for others can be seen in the callous way he shapes his living space to his own whims, cruelly killing a cherished animal. 'The lodgings were ideal in every way but one. Bertha Reese had an old dog, Bob, who, although as deaf and quiet as she, was not as clean' (135). Contemptuous of decay and disorder, Soaphead articulates this expression of theodicy: 'He, God, had made a sloven and unforgivable error in judgment: designing an imperfect universe' (136). To him, the child Pecola embodies this imperfection, leading Elihue Micah (meaning who is like God) to 'cause a miracle' – 'I gave her the blue, blue, two blue eyes' (143) – as a selfish and egotistical act to have Pecola poison the dog.

Thematically, to go inside the Other mind of the beleaguered child Pecola
Breedlove is to engage one of Gothic's most abhorrent internal psychological
spaces. She embodies the consequences of institutionalized racism and
internalized oppression. While her state of mind should constitute a mere
aberration, it actually exposes the ubiquitous norm. Standardized norms
of beauty assail the psyche of African American ingénue girls who, unlike
Pecola's nemesis, Maureen Peal, fail to 'enchant the entire school' (*Bluest Eye*
53). Those without the defensive armament of sisters Frieda and Claudia are
predisposed to suffering. Instead, the sisters 'looked hard for flaws to restore
our equilibrium, but had to be content at first with uglying up her name,
changing Maureen Peal to Meringue Pie' (53). Pecola lacks such resourceful-
ness, damaged as she is by her father's incestuous assault. Gwin captures
the horror: 'In the Breedlove kitchen of Morrison's novel ... the father's
violence – Cholly Breedlove's rape of his daughter – is enacted against the
backdrop of what in another house might have been a nurturing domestic
space for eating and talking' (75). By the novel's conclusion, traumatized,
Pecola's mind splits in two: 'A little black girl yearns for the blue eyes of a
little white girl, and the horror at the heart of her yearning is exceeded only
by the evil of fulfillment' (*Bluest Eye* 158). The quest theme, often typical
of science fiction, now extends to Pecola's attaining 'the bluest eyes.' She
illuminates the endarkened psyche of the oppressed, while attacking reified
notions of beauty with the intent to enlighten.

Morrison's *Love*, too, performs spatially. The endarkened spirit of the
space cohabited by Christine and Heed is infused with patriarchy, a site
where Bill Cosey's 'portrait loomed' (25). The narrator, L, uncovers and
bears witness to his paedophiliac bent that resulted in his marriage to
Heed, age eleven and best friends with his twelve-year-old granddaughter,
Christine. His house at One Monarch Street is said to be '[b]ig as a church'
or 'a jailhouse' (14). Additionally, Morrison writes:

> the house was graceful, imposing, and its peaked third-story roof
> did suggest a church. The steps to the porch, slanted and shiny with
> ice, encouraged caution, for there was no railing. But the girl clicked
> along the walk and up the steps without hesitation. Seeing no bell, she
> started to knock, hesitating when she noticed a shaft of light below, to
> the right of the porch. She went back down the sloping steps, followed
> the curve marked by half-buried slate, and descended a flight of iron
> stairs lit by a window. Beyond the window, a door. No wind buffeted
> her there. The area had the look of what was called a garden apartment
> by some – by others, a basement one. (19)

This description exemplifies Cavallaro's description of Gothic 'dark places'
as 'locus of torment, punishment, mystery, corruption and insanity' (27).

All the inhabitants, even Bill Cosey, the phantom patriarch (whose father was nicknamed Dark), are tormented by what can be called 'adultism': oppression of younger people by adults, leading to youth internalizing oppressive structures in the same way as occurs in racism or sexism. In this text, characters' minds are dominated by projections of negative relationships with father figures. Cosey's resort empire and most of his actions operate as attempts to compensate for 'having grown up the son of a stooge' (104). L notes: '*Whenever I see his righteous face correcting Heed, his extinguished eyes gazing at Christine, I think Dark won out*' (200, italics in original). Cavallaro describes 'dark psyches' in Gothic literature: 'Narratives of Darkness [*sic*] evoke a universe of taboos in which the non-things which culture represses are brought to the foreground' (48). Paedophilia is one of the 'non-things' repressed within many African American families and communities.

Morrison's novel *Love* continues Morrison's genre play. A plot-driven and intricate text, *Love*, generically speaking, embraces not only Gothic science fiction, but mystery writing as well. The novel's plotting emulates what is known as 'cozy' mysteries, befitting the surname of the murder victim, Bill Cosey. A cozy is a woman-centred mystery, usually with a female sleuth ('Cozy Mysteries List'). As another recurrent Morrison motif, a Bible verse deconstructs the text's narrator, simply called L: '*If your name is the subject of First Corinthians, chapter 13, it's natural to make [love] your business*' (199, italics in original). Lacking a Western metaphysical dualistic way of thinking, and possessing a name not dependent on the King James Version of the Bible – as such, an apparition herself – L's primal confession privileges the language of charity and the seven heavenly virtues. She identifies being an oppressor and internalizing oppression as both learned responses. No one suspects L to be Cosey's charitable murderer of an '*ordinary man ripped, like the rest of us, by wrath and love*' (200, italics in original).

Cozy mysteries are most dependent on characterization. Morrison's tendency is to allegorize so that her characters personify abstract qualities. For instance, in conjunction with the mnemonic device known as PEG'S LAW, each character is entrusted with a moral dilemma as relates to pride, envy, gluttony, lust, avarice, and wrath. Perhaps the most intriguing representation is that of the young female Junior, the only outsider. Her complicated personal history gifts her with fused toes and her behaviour likens her to the sloth: 'Not just the messy hair and tacky clothes; there was some bold laziness in her manner' (*Love* 24–25). These creatures are most noted for fornicating and eating, and Junior does not disappoint.

It is an old employee, Vida, who broaches Cosey's mysterious death: 'Vida had seen the water cloud before [Cosey] drank it and his reach not to his chest, where the heart exploded, but to his stomach' (37). The village setting is of relevance to the novel's dynamic spatiality: 'The small size of the setting makes it believable that all the suspects know each other' (Cozy-mystery.com). *Love* provides a basic treatise and virtually a contemporary morality play denoting what occurs when the oppressed become oppressors themselves; the complicity of women in creating targets that enforce their own victimization; and how love should extend to include charity. Cozies are considered 'gentle' books, sex, violence, and profanity are minimal. Of course, a hybrid text like *Love* subverts all of these specifications. It transforms a black resort with the motto: 'The best good time this side of the law' (33) into a nonfelicitous space (Gwin 78–79).

Finally, Morrison's creative imagination reinscribes Other worlds, as native to science fiction writing but endarkened by the African American ontological journey away from more traditional regional and cultural domiciles. Science fiction, as a genre of the beyond, opens up new constellations of possibilities for African Americans in the US and within the African diaspora. In three of her novels, Morrison deploys geopolitical spaces outside of her usual repertoire of places: *Jazz*, *Tarbaby*, and *Paradise*. Of these, New York City is the primary context for *Jazz*. Cavallaro notes, regarding the Gothic theme of 'Dark Places', that '[t]he city may be the source, not merely the setting, of dislocating and distressing experiences' (34). The kernel of the narrative highlights the arbitrary violence long associated with this Gotham City. Wedded to Violet, Joe murders youthful Dorcas in cold blood. He admits his obsession: 'For when Joe tries to remember the way it was when he and Violet were young, when they got married, decided to leave Vesper County and move up North to the City almost nothing comes to mind' (*Jazz* 29). The City comes to represent a geographical space that is a world apart for former agrarians: 'The City is smart at this: smelling good and looking raunchy; sending secret messages disguised as public signs: this way, open here, danger to let colored only single men on sale woman wanted private room stop dog on premises absolutely no money down fresh chicken free delivery fast. And good at opening locks, dimming stairways. Covering your moans with its own' (64). Migratory subjects of the 1920s Jazz Age encounter an alien space, delineating what happens when two worlds collide.

The conceptualization of 'The City' in *Jazz* resembles certain science fictional conceptions of outer space: 'as a cold, black, empty nothingness ... a deadly place' (Gunn 185). In an essay, Morrison expressed the following insights about this historical moment: 'A modernity which overturns pre-war definitions, ushers in the Jazz Age (an age defined by Afro-American Art and culture), and requires new kinds of intelligences to define oneself' ('Unspeakable Things' 26). If written to cement the growth of new alternative epistemologies for women, *Jazz* enshrines also their rarity: 'Read carefully the news accounts revealed that most of these women, subdued and broken, had not been defenseless. Or, like Dorcas, easy prey. All over the country, black women were armed. That, thought Alice, that, at least, they had learned' (74). 'They were armed' becomes a refrain signifying the Jazz Age as a defining moment when women developed self-defensive mechanisms. While not using the science fiction tropes of superhuman power or artificial intelligence, Morrison details the gradual accessing of an intelligence that constitutes the mainstay of science fiction's contemporary heroines. Outside of the Jazz Age and the cosmopolitanism of the City, Morrison's women chiefly reconfigure Gothic's damsels in distress by presenting them with options.

Furthermore, in *Tarbaby*, Morrison enlarges her usual setting to encompass the African diaspora. As Susan Mayberry puts it, '[Morrison] set loose the nigger in the woodpile by removing her Americans from homeland culture to relocate them in the French Caribbean and allow them the isolation and detachment required for self-discovery' (118). The context decentres the author's usual ploys. On the fictional Isle des Chevaliers, the estate L'Arbe de la Croix, while not without its architectural quirks, is more idyllic, lacking the usually overt Gothicity:

> It was a wonderful house. Wide, breezy and full of light. Built in the days when plaster was taken for granted and with sun and the airstream in mind, it needed no air conditioning. Graceful landscaping kept the house just under a surfeit of beauty. Every effort had been made to keep it from looking 'designed.' Almost nothing was askew and the few things that were had charm: the little island touches here and there (a washhouse, a kitchen garden, for example) were practical. (8–9)

Along with her aunt and uncle, African American Jadine occupies this colonized space belonging to a white US candy magnate named Valerian Street.

Yet, despite its tribute to a near-Edenic setting, because of Jadine's social positioning within this Other world, *Tarbaby* fits within science fiction's tradition of the entropic novel. Once the stowaway, Son, endarkens the estate, suitably hiding out in Valerian's wife's closet, Jadine faces personal chaos. For the first time, she feels unhomed, whether on the island, in New York, or especially with Son in the southern United States. Son has been homeless for some eight years and like a host of other 'undocumented men': 'Anarchic, wandering, they read about their hometowns in the pages of out-of-town newspapers' (*Tarbaby* 143). On the other hand, orphaned by the age of twelve, fashion model Jadine 'never lived with [her surviving relatives] except summers at Valerian's house when she was very young. Less and then never, after college' (41). However, it is while in Paris that Jadine initially experiences a form of entropy when a dark-skinned woman in yellow, Afrocentric garb spits at her, causing Jade to feel '[l]onely and inauthentic' (40). This gesticulation propels Jadine back to the Isle des Chevaliers, out of season.

The stuff of science fiction's Other worlds, the Isle is the habitat for a constituency of wondrous mythic beings. Mayberry describes these:

> In addition to the river and tree matrons, a cornucopia of lesser airs, sprites, and creatures populate the island, all of which Morrison depicts as traditionally black and female. These include a pushy waterlady, prophesying fish, testifying clouds, alert moon, oppressively affection-ate maiden aunt fog, complacent bees, gossipy angel trumpets, nosy emperor butterflies, seductive teenaged avocado tree, arrogant swamp women, and workaholic soldier ants, plenty of sisters to fill the church pews. (120–121)

Nonetheless, it is the representation of the male, legendary Four Horsemen of the Apocalypse figures which trumps all. They, ultimately, signal Jadine's entropic decline, for 'She has forgotten her ancient properties' (*Tarbaby* 263); whereas Son is emboldened by them: 'They are waiting in the hills for [him]' (263). With typical complexity, Morrison decolonizes his mind and this island paradise.

Geographically, *Paradise* is set in the Far West in the US. The state of Oklahoma geography grants an unorthodox landscape of power relative to African Americans' usual geographical context in literature. Located west of the Mississippi River – beyond Morrison's typical southern and urban stages – nowhere else did so many African Americans construct, occupy, and govern their own communities. From 1865 to 1920, African Americans founded more than fifty towns there. Once again, addressing science fiction as a genre of beyond, defamiliarization hinges on the alien world of histori-cizing an African American presence within a 'western' context.[11] Originally, Morrison entitled this novel *War*. Advised against it, she later noted: 'the novel wasn't about war as we know it, with armies, navies, and so on' (Marcus). Like the space opera trope, the text is eponymous, delineating the warring spirit of ten generations of African Americans: 8-rock families, a unique species of chosen people. They comprise 'a contingent of families who had lived with or near each other since before Bunker Hill', during the American Revolution (*Paradise* 192). They honour their deeply black pigmentation as a sign of a racial purity/superiority. Pioneering historian of African Americans in Oklahoma, Arthur Tolson, indicates the extent to which many turned to Booker T. Washington's 'ideologies of economic advancement, self-help, and racial solidarity' (O'Dell). However, *Paradise* complicates such bootstrap politics by showing a society that also reeks with discrimination and abuse, especially against women. In accordance with

Morrison's themes, excessive Godly love propels the 8-rock men's extreme act of militarism against a coterie of defenceless women.

Morrison notes of the book's final title, *Paradise*, that 'a sort of question mark is implied behind it' (Mellard 350). For her, the question is why paradise necessitates exclusion. The assailants target a convent-turned-Catholic mission school – Christ the King School for Native Girls –now, by the time of the 1976 American Bicentennial, a makeshift women's shelter. The material geography of this site teems with centuries of oppression directed toward women in the name of religion and colonization. Specifically, the Gothic machinery of the built edifice cannot be denied; the convent was originally converted for the pacification and assimilation of Cheyenne/Arapaho girls. Yet Morrison's women, far from being imprisoned, as the Gothic norm, use the space differently: they defiantly create their own disjointed community of female 'misfits' who are deemed 'a coven' by the men seeking to conceal their own wanton nature and disunity.

The vast frontier land of the US permits space for the erection of a mystery play with a family resemblance to a space opera. Morrison turns to a Brazilian urban legend of a convent run by black nuns who took in abandoned children and practised Catholicism on one floor and Condomble in the basement; the nuns are murdered by a posse of local men. *Paradise* features men who were themselves disallowed from an Oklahoma town by privileged, fair-complexioned African Americans. Thereafter, the townsmen celebrate and traditionalize the most heinous aspects of their family and personal history, generational military training, and (of course) devotion to the Bible. Within the novel, Morrison sanctifies the martyred women by spiritual resurrection, linking these brave women to the Christian narrative of ascension. Jack Morgan notes that Morrison's endorsement of a macabre aesthetic within the Christian tradition of religious terror is 'another significant bearer of morbid motifs prefiguring later gothic ones: *memento mori* underscoring the ignoble end of our bodily careers, exotic postmortem punishment scenarios, and so forth' (48). Ultimately, in an appearance reminiscent of Christ's resurrection, one of the women, Seneca, displays her stigmata (bloodied hands), which is signifier enough that these women are now divine as they prepare to '[shoulder] the endless work they were created to do down here in Paradise' (*Paradise* 316–318). Geographically, *this* world will be their spiritual home.

In conclusion, the critical discussion presented here is not intended to be exhaustive. As I position the scope of Morrison's science fiction traces – Other times, minds, beings, and worlds – they conceivably can apply multivocally to her entire opus. Since most taxonomies and genres blur, I suggest a few possible historical, cultural, psychological, and geographical spaces to highlight Morrison's connection to Gothic science fiction. As horrific sites of female disempowerment, her spatialized ontologies are rich in social commentary. Whether a store front converted into living quarters for the Breedlove family or a palatial convent offering sanctuary to society's female rejects, Morrison's framing of recurrent Gothic motifs (within atypical dwelling places) becomes quite apparent. I seek a space for the acceptance of a science fiction connection as well. At the very least, Morrison's texts subsume numerous literary forms. Intertextually, they conjoin with one another as well as span a complicated universe of intellectual history to advance her enchanted novum: 'creating a memorial through art for those who have no memorial' (Denard 49).

Notes

1. I speculate that Toni Morrison might subscribe to the same 'pathological, knee-jerk science fiction aversion' that Marleen Barr recognizes in Margaret Atwood (Barr 429). Yet this chapter suggests the genre category is nonetheless still useful for approaching Morrison, on the grounds that science fiction is actually a genre that engages richly with socio-political complexity. As Joanna Russ says, 'The technology-obsessed – including those who read, write, and study SF – must cultivate a similar little voice: "Eat a little economics. Eat a little political analysis. You'll think better"' (39). Aptly, Morrison's participatory style advocates for this kind of affective and cognitive thinking. For further discussion of the potential for speculative fiction in engaging with the experience of Black women, see McGregory.
2. I capitalize 'Other' in each instance to signify Morrison's re-theorizing the scope of the textual and cultural space of the so-called Other.
3. While Meltzer and others who give definition to feminist science fiction strictly gender their encoding of women as the alien Other, instead, Morrison relies on allegory to represent African American life, history, and culture in ways that deconstruct excessive universalism, regarding race, gender, and class. As a result, her science fiction traces are more expansive.
4. 'What if' is a query that can apply to all fiction, but, as Carol Pearson notes, 'Feminist Utopian Fiction implicitly or explicitly criticizes the patriarchy while it emphasizes society's habit of restricting and alienating women' (63). Morrison actively pinpoints defining moments when a harsh reality could imbue a sexually and racially equalitarian American society instead of succumbing to economic and racial systems of oppression.
5. Compare also Patricia McKee's discussion of the interlocking relationship between home and freedom, spatializing geographies within larger American history.
6. Additionally, Carol Franko suggests how, on the one hand, 'the love interest is used to affirm the value of the utopian society' and, on the other hand, dystopian fiction uses 'thwarted romantic love to symbolize the individuality and freedom denied by the totalitarian state' (93). Morrison merges the two motifs; and thereby the death of Vaark and the breach in Floren's relationship with the freeman serve as harbingers of perpetual, race-based slavery (cf. Crawford).
7. Tom Moylan offers a critique of utopia literature beyond its 'Western origins'.
8. Unfortunately, Carl Malmgren engages this text only from a Eurocentric perspective, as a mere 'ghost story' (96). As I show here, Morrison's text demands attention to its African American context.

9. Anna Sonser examines how Morrison, among others, subverts and redefines the American Gothic. However, in making her pointed comparisons, she neglects the role of consumption in the *Song of Solomon*.

10. See Maxine Montgomery's discussion of apocalypse as a trope in African American literature.

11. By casting *Paradise* in the Far West, Morrison defies most assessments even by those who attempt to disrupt north/south binaries (e.g. Sonser, 7–8).

Works cited

Aldiss, Brian W., and David Wingrove. *Trillion Year Spree: The History of Science Fiction*. London: Gollancz, 1986. Print.

Barr, Marleen. 'Feminist Fabulation.' *A Companion to Science Fiction*. Ed. David Seed. Malden: Blackwell, 2005: 142–55. Print.

—. 'Introduction: Textism – An Emancipation Proclamation,' *PMLA* 119 (2004): 429–41. Print.

Bell, Bernard. *The Contemporary African American Novel: Its Folk Roots and Modern Literary Branches*. Amherst: U of Massachusetts P, 2004. Print.

Cavallaro, Dani. *The Gothic Vision: Three Centuries of Horror, Terror and Fear*. London: Continuum, 2002. Print.

Collingwood, R. G. et al. *The Philosophy of Enchantment: Studies in Folktale, Cultural Criticism, and Anthropology*. Oxford: Clarendon Press, 2005. Print.

'Cozy Mystery List.' *Cozy-mystery.com*. Web. 12 October 2010.

Crouch, Stanley. 'Aunt Medea.' Review of *Beloved. New Republic* 19 October 1987: 38–43. Print.

Csicsery-Ronay, Istvan. 'Alternative History.' *The Seven Beauties of Science Fiction*. Middleton: Wesleyan UP, 2008. Print.

Davis, Christina. 'Interview with Toni Morrison.' *Toni Morrison: Critical Perspectives Past and Present*. Ed. Henry Louis Gates and K. A. Appiah. New York: Amistad, 1993. Print.

Denard, Carolyn. *Toni Morrison: Conversations*. Jackson: UP of Mississippi, 2008. Print.

Dillard, Cynthia. *On Spiritual Strivings: Transforming an African American Woman's Academic Life*. Albany: SUNY, 2006. Print.

Franko, Carol. 'The I–We Dilemma and a "Utopian Unconscious."' *Political Science Fiction*. Ed. Donald Hassler and Clyde Wilcox. Columbia: U of South Carolina P, 1996. Print.

Freedman, Carl. *Critical Theory and Science Fiction*. Middletown: Wesleyan UP, 2000. Print.

Gunn, James. *Inside Science Fiction*. Lanham: Scarecrow, 2006. Print.

Gutman, Herbert. *The Black Family in Slavery and Freedom, 1750–1925*. New York: Vintage, 1976. Print.

Gwin, Minrose. *The Woman in the Red Dress: Gender, Space, and Reading*. Urbana: U of Illinois P, 2002. Print.

Harris, Norman. *Connecting Times: The Sixties in Afro-American Fiction*. Jackson: UP of Mississippi, 1988. Print.

Heiland, Donna. *Gothic and Gender: An Introduction*. Malden: Blackwell, 2004. Print.

Holloway, Karla and Stephanie Demetrakopoulos. *New Dimensions of Spirituality: A Biracial and Bicultural Reading of the Novels of Toni Morrison*. New York: Greenwood, 1987. Print.

Hostetler, Ann. 'Interview with Morrison: "The Art of Teaching."' Denard 196–205.

Johnson, Charles R. *Being and Race: Black Writing Since 1970*. Bloomington: Indiana UP, 1988. Print.

Keeling, Thomas. 'Science Fiction and the Gothic.' *Bridges to Science Fiction*. Ed. George Slusser et al. Carbondale: Southern Illinois UP, 1980.

Kneale, James. 'Lost in Space: Exploring Impossible Geographies.' *Impossibility Fiction: Alternativity, Extrapolation, Speculation*. Ed. Derek Littlewood and Peter Stockwell. Amsterdam: Rodopi, 1996. 147–162. Print.

Luckhurst, Roger. *Science Fiction*. Cambridge,: Polity, 2005. Print.

Malmgren, Carl. 'Mixed Genres and the Logic of Slavery in Toni Morrison's *Beloved*.' *Critique* 36 (1995): 96–106. Print.

Marcus, James. 'Interview with Toni Morrison: This Side of Paradise.' Amazon.com. Web. 25 October 2010.

Mayberry, Susan Neal. *Can't I Love What I Criticize? The Masculine and Morrison*. Athens: U of Georgia P, 2007. Print.

McGregory, Jerrilyn. 'Nalo Hopkinson's Approach to Speculative Fiction.' *FEMSPEC* 6 (2005): 3–17. Print.

McKee, Patricia. 'Geographies of *Paradise*.' *CR: The New Centennial Review* 3 (2003): 197–223. Print.

Mellard, James. 'The Jews of Ruby, Oklahoma: Politics, Parallax, and Ideological Fantasy in Toni Morrison's *Paradise*.' *Modern Fiction Studies* 56 (2010): 349–377. Print.

Melzer, Patricia. *Alien Constructions: Science Fiction and Feminist Thought*. Austin: U of Texas P, 2006. Print.

Mohanty, Satya. 'The Epistemic Status of Cultural Identity: On Beloved and the Postcolonial Condition.' *Cultural Critique* (Spring 1993): 41–78. Print.

Montgomery, Maxine. 'A Pilgrimage to the Origins: The Apocalypse as Structure and Theme in Toni Morrison's *Sula*.' *Black American Literature Forum* 23 (1989): 127–137. Print.

Morgan, Jack. *The Biology of Horror: Gothic Literature and Film*. Carbondale: Southern Illinois UP, 2002. Print.

Morrison, Toni. *A Mercy*. New York: Knopf, 2008. Print.

—. *Beloved*. New York: Plume, 1987. Print.

—. *The Bluest Eye*. New York: Washington Square, 1970. Print.

—. *Jazz*. New York: Plume, 1992. Print

—. *Love*. New York: Knopf, 2003. Print.

—. *Paradise*. New York: Knopf, 1998. Print.

—. *Song of Solomon*. New York: Signet. 1977. Print.

—. *Sula*. New York: Plume, 1973. Print.

—. *Tarbaby*. New York: Signet, 1981. Print.

—. 'Home.' *The House that Race Built: Black Americans, U.S. Terrain*. Ed. Wahneema H. Lubiano. New York: Pantheon, 1997. 3–12. Print.

—. 'Unspeakable Things Unspoken: The Afro-American Presence in American Literature.' *Michigan Quarterly Review* (1989): 1–34. Print.

Moylan, Tom. 'Utopia, Postcolonial, and the Postmodern.' *Science Fiction Studies* 29 (July 2002). Web. 1 August 2011.

O'Dell, Larry. 'All-Black Towns.' Encyclopedia of Oklahoma History and Culture. Web. 25 October 2010.

Pearson, Carol. 'Coming Home: Four Feminist Utopias and Patriarchal Experience.' *Future Females, A Critical Anthology*. Ed. Marleen Barr. Bowling Green: Bowling Green University Popular Press, 1981. Print.

Redmond, Eugene. 'Interview with Toni Morrison.' Denard, 29–31. Print.

Reed, Ishmael. *Reckless Eyeballing*. New York: St. Martin's Press, 1986. Print.

Reider, John. *Colonialism and the Emergence of Science Fiction*. Middleton: Wesleyan UP, 2008. Print.

Roberts, Adam. *Science Fiction*. London: Routledge, 2000. Print.

Rushdy, Ashraf H. A. 'Daughters Signifyin(g) History: The Example of Toni Morrison's *Beloved*.' *American Literature* 64 (1992): 567–597. Print.

Russ, Joanna. *To Write Like a Woman: Essays in Feminism and Science Fiction*. Bloomington: Indiana UP, 1995. Print.

Shockley, Evelyn. Review of *Paradise*. *African American Review* 33 (1999): 718–719. Print.

Smith, Valerie. "'Circling the Subject": History and Narrative in Beloved.' Eds. Henry Louis Gates and K. A. Appiah. *Toni Morrison: Critical Perspectives, Past and Present*. New York: Amistad, 1993: 342–355. Print.

Soja, Edward. *Postmodern Geographies: The Reassertion of Space in Critical Social Theory*. London: Verso, 1989. Print.

Sonser, Anna. *A Passion for Consumption: The Gothic Novel in America* (Bowling Green, OH: Bowling Green University Popular Press, 2001. Print.

Suvin, Darko. 'On the Poetics of the Science Fiction Genre.' *College English* 34 (1972): 372–382. Print.

—. *Positions and Presuppositions in Science Fiction*. Kent, OH: Kent State UP, 1988. Print.

Walker, Alice. *In Search of Our Mothers' Gardens: Womanist Prose*. San Diego, CA: Harcourt Brace Jovanovich, 1983. Print.

Weldes, Jutta, ed. 'Popular Culture, Science Fiction, and World Politics: Exploring Relations.' *To Seek Out New Worlds: Exploring Links between Science Fiction and World Politics*. New York: Palgrave, 2003. Print.

Willis, Susan. 'I Shop Therefore I Am: Is There a Place for African-American Culture in Commodity Culture?' *Changing Our Own Words: Essays on Critcism, Theory, and Writing by Black Women*. Ed. Cheryl Wall. New Brunswick, NJ: Rutgers UP, 1989. Print.

Winter, Kari. *Subject of Slavery, Agents of Change: Women and Power in Gothic Novels and Slave Narratives, 1790–1865*. Athens: U of Georgia P, 1992. Print.

10. The Gothic Punk Milieu in Popular Narrative Fictions

Nickianne Moody

The Gothic punk milieu (GPM) is a narrative environment which is aligned with a particular cultural climate that is defined by responses to technological and social transition during the twentieth century. This chapter explores the popular dimension of science fiction and the Gothic tradition which has provided an imaginative locus for heterogeneous audiences, and which still resonates for the speculative imagination of an uncanny future. The distinct style of the Gothic punk milieu as a narrative diegesis has been appropriated by film, television, print fiction and digital game both as a pastiche and by more creative engagement. The examples considered here are drawn from commercial narrative media: *Metropolis* (1926), dating from the formation of science fiction as an iconic genre, and the post-industrial landscape depicted both in *Blade Runner* (1982) and in the less canonical imagery which forms the diegesis for the trading card game *Heresy Kingdom Come*™ (1995).

In his consideration of *Metropolis* as a contentious contribution to Fritz Lang's oeuvre, Tom Gunning observes '[i]nsufficient attention has been paid to the role of the clash between Gothic and modernity in this film, which often displaces the more manifest conflict between classes' (64). His analysis explores the significance of technology portrayed as 'modern magic.' The Los Angeles created for *Blade Runner* (1992) draws very much on the legacy of the modernist city which comprises *Metropolis*, but Sean Redmond argues at the beginning of his analysis that the narrative premise 'is a powerful story of social class that few writers have so far acknowledged' (213). Both writers find cogent oedipal narratives forming significant character trajectories and prevailing concerns about the power of technocracy. Both films depict class warfare in the urban disintegration of the near future.

During the time *Metropolis* was in production, science fiction became a popular and commercial genre through the publication of Hugo Gernsback's *Amazing Stories* in 1926. It was the first of a plethora of science fiction and fantasy magazines which promoted their content through the iconic, bright and shiny modernist accounts of the future on their covers. The design and outlook influenced far more than their immediate readers. However, like the undercity of *Metropolis*, the GPM rejects the visualization of such a functional and hermetic future, focusing instead on the tensions and angst of those living in the near future. A particular articulation of this rejection was given prominence in the opening to Frederic Jameson's critique of lived experience under late twentieth-century capitalism. Jameson refers to the recognizable trope of 'inverted millenarianism in which premonitions of the future, catastrophic or redemptive, have been replaced by sense of the end of this or that ...' (219). This inverted millenarianism is evident not just in the landscape of fiction but the representation of human experience. Jameson's article sets out the nature of postmodernism and the culture that it produces to support the continuation of capitalism as a global, ideological, political and economic system – a perspective which was already being used to critique the change evident in the way the science fiction film imagined the future. Guiliana Bruno located the architectural dominance of *Blade Runner's mise-en-scène* as the point at which the connection of postmodernism to postindustrialism is made visible (62). The narrative environment 'creates an aesthetic of decay, exposing the dark side of technology, the process of disintegration' (63). *Blade Runner* does not need the catacombs of *Metropolis* in order to challenge the confidence of modernism. The narrative environment of the GPM is specifically employed to pursue a popular account of the uncanny and prospective posthuman existence.

In all three examples – *Metropolis*, *Blade Runner* and the *Heresy* trading card game – this experience of the posthuman is rendered in a way that leads to characters increasing their knowledge and insight but may not necessarily have any impact on the unfolding of narrative events. This is very much the case in the states of being, archetypes and narrative engagements illustrated on the cards for *Heresy Kingdom Come*™. The diegesis presented by the cards was created by multiple artists. They combine the spiritual, physical and digital locales which make up the gameworld of Forsaken Earth. Veronica Hollinger characterizes cyberpunk as 'a "movement" in 1980s SF that produced a wide range of fictions exploring the technological ramifications of experience within late capitalist, postindustrial, media-saturated Western society' (204). Cyberpunk solidified from short stories under the editorship of Bruce Sterling and in the critical recognition given to William Gibson's first novel, *Neuromancer*, published in 1984, the diegesis for which Hollinger describes as 'a near-future trash culture ruled by multinational corporations and kept going by black-market economies, all frenetically dedicated to the circulation of computerized data' (206) – a similar fetish to that displayed in Fredersen's New Tower of Babel in *Metropolis*.

Hollinger finds cyberpunk interesting for its anti-humanism and exploration of the deconstruction of the subject. She argues that '[w]hile SF frequently problematizes the oppositions between the natural and the artificial, the human and the machine, it generally sustains them in such a way that the human remains securely ensconced in its privileged place at the centre of things. Cyberpunk, however, is about the breakdown of these oppositions' (204–5). Moreover, she notes that one of its important defining characteristics is the 'valorization of the socially marginalized, that is, its 'punk' sensibility' (205). The Gothic aspect of this narrative location lies not just in subterranean terrain, architecture and recognizably Gothic conventions but also in the anxiety about the relation of individuality to new social formations (particularly those that are gendered, or cultural change predicated on new technology), as well as fantasies of encountering the divine or supernatural and the ability to discern between reality and illusion. The uncanny future dwells on the transitions, change and augmentation to mind and body that will be required in order to survive the demands of a new labour market.

Metropolis (1926)

Although the film version of the *Metropolis* narrative was a financial and creative disaster, Thea von Harbou's novel sold with the properties of a best seller. It was first serialized, six months before the film premiered, in *Das illustrierte Blatt* (1926). The version that I am going to use to look at crucial aspects of the diegesis excised from the film was published by the Readers Library Publishing Company Ltd., London, which sold cheap versions of nineteenth-century and film-related popular texts for outlets such as Woolworths. The Readers Library edition went through five editions in 1927, printing three hundred thousand copies over the year. The editor situates the text within the preoccupation of '[t]he machine and its relation to man' which has occupied 'several writers of genius' and refers to Samuel Butler, Karel Capek and H. G. Wells (Preface). The novel is recommended to lovers of literature 'for their own pleasure, their own appreciation – and judgement' (Preface).

Thea von Harbou's novelization of her script for *Metropolis* captured the popular imagination through affordable cheap editions and its direct relationship to the resonance of Lang's cinematic imagery. There are certain aspects of the film which have become cultural referents, such as the transformation sequence where the consciousness and appearance of the Gothic heroine, Maria, is appropriated by Rotwang's android. However, due to its unpopularity, contravention of European censorship codes and narrative complexity it is the stills from the film and von Harbou's narrative that best articulate contemporary concerns. Oral histories of cinema-going in the interwar period remind us that ordinary cinema-goers were more likely to recall the social interactions and physicality of the cinema than the films they went to see.[1] They had little control over the choice of film and very few opportunities to see it, as silent film in particular was ephemeral popular entertainment.

The incongruous positioning in the film of Gothic catacombs below the functional urban elevation is a clear foreshadowing of the later Gothic punk milieu. However, it is the structural preoccupations of the two visual styles that are significant. Several major aspects of the novel – such as the group of Gothics who oppose Fredersen as master of Metropolis and the drug use which enables participants to share experience – were quickly removed from the film.[2] The original narrative emphasized the tenets of the Gothic punk exchange, which were either removed to avoid contravening censorship codes or unrealized by Lang's greater interest in modernist sensibility. The horror that von Harbou's protagonist discovers about the ten-hour working day is not stylized manual labour but the interfacing between brain and machine that powers the city:

> He felt – and saw, too – how, from out of the swathes of vapour, the long soft elephant's trunk of the god Ganesha loosened itself from the head, sunken on his chest, and gently, with unerring finger, felt for his, Freder's forehead. He felt the touch of this sucker, almost cool, not in the least painful, but horrible. Just in the centre, over the bridge of the nose, the ghostly trunk sucked itself fast; it was hardly a pain, yet it bored, a fine, dead-sure gimlet, towards the centre of the brain. As though fastened to the clock of an infernal machine the heart began to thump. Pater-noster ... Pater-noster ... Pater-noster ... The sucker of the elephant's trunk of the god Ganesha glided down to the occupied unsubdued brain which reflected, analyzed and sought. The head now tamed, sank back again onto the chest. Obediently, eagerly, worked the little machine which drove the Pater-noster of the New Tower of Babel. (46–47)

The *mise-en-scène* of von Harbou's future city lacks the debris which we associate with cyberpunk but shares other concerns that roused the censors when the film sought exhibition licences within and outside Germany (sexual explicitness in the US and representation of class conflict in the UK). The novel portrays not only a near future of alienated labour but also hedonism predicated on recreational drug use. Its hero seeks diversion from a vibrant but nihilistic youth culture when he sets out to explore the occluded Gothic locations of his father's city. The film and the novel clearly juxtapose the enclave that Freder inhabits with the subterranean social housing for the workers so as to represent the polarities of lived experience in the stratified city. Movement between the two leads directly to popular protest and the implicit criticism of corporate capitalism which coexists with striking Gothic imagery, integral to the narrative.

Central to von Harbou's conception of the city is the medieval house of the technomage Rotwang, whose processes and technologies have created the system that Fredersen oversees. The film strikingly depicts Fredersen's panoptic surveillance of the city and its workers from the telescreen in his skyscraper control centre. Nevertheless, he is unaware that Rotwang's home and laboratory lead to the catacombs. Within the catacombs, '[e]very year which passed over the city seemed to creep when dying, into this house, so that, at last it was a cemetery – a coffin, filled with dead tens of years' (von Harbou 55). Both the film and the book place great emphasis on Maria's retelling of biblical stories which inspire the workers to improve their lives, and the catacombs are the location for this activity. Social uprising is not inevitable, but this collectivity can be harnessed by the demonic machinery, which Rotwang manifests in the mechanical labour he has invented at Fredersen's behest to replace the workers' inefficiency and discontent. Gunning argues that there are three centres of figuration in the film which have distinct imagery and which intersect to form 'emblematic tableaux' (64) at key moments. These clusters of imagery are, first of all, the various images of the machine, modernity and rationality which he refers to as the science fiction elements of the film (63). The second cluster comprises images associated with the past and the Gothic, such as the struggle between Maria and Rotwang, as heroine and villain, epitomized by the chase through the catacombs and then across the rooftop of the cathedral. Gunning further notes this polarity as the contrast between 'the religion of love preached by Maria and the black magic of demonic technology mastered by Rotwang' (64). In between these two centres is the Gothic hero, ineffective and in this narrative made explicitly vulnerable by oedipal fantasies. Technology in *Metropolis*, then, is essentially a form of magic which is difficult to harness and control. The creation of a female robot brings to the surface *fin de siècle* concerns about the femininity of technology, which Gunning sees realized in *Metropolis* as 'a return to the repressed and forbidden energies of the past – this constitutes one of *Metropolis's* allegories of modernity (65). It is not the Gothic heroine who seeks to find out the truth of her mother's past but the hero, and he acquires this knowledge through hallucination, dream and the ability to see through others' eyes.

In a similar manner to many drugs found in the GPM, the drug Mahoee enables its users to 'feel the intoxication of others' (von Harbou 89). Its consumption is ritualized and it allows its consumer to connect directly with the minds of others and the commodified sharing of experience. Freder manages to evade his father's surveillance in his ignoble pursuit of Maria and nobler concern to find out more about the plight of the workers. He exchanges clothes with a worker who uses their cachet and the money he has been given to enter Yoshiwara. In contrast to the 'House of Sons' where we first meet Freder, Yoshiwara is one of the locations which escapes Fredersen's technological surveillance, and he has to send a representative into the nightclub in order to investigate the absence of his son. Rutsky proposes that:

> they are also secretive spaces, hidden from Fredersen's patriarchal view. They seem, in fact, to hide a power that has been repressed in Fredersen's modern, technological city: an ancient power – for these structures are all more ancient than the city that surrounds them – that lies in the connection of these spaces to the spiritual, the religious and the magical. (Rutsky 189)

The GPM is concerned with the interstices in which the celestial and the magical can be encountered but it also remains grounded in the material effects of technological systems which hold social governance. In other words, the supernatural of the GPM is very much connected to a political system sustained by surveillance and a digital economy.

The proprietor of Yoshiwara is a hybrid of all human races, earning a living in Metropolis's shadow economy. Mahoee is described as an experience of '[p]ower, desire and madness' (von Harbou 91) actively felt by one, who suffers this intoxication, but conveyed to others:

> Sir in this house there is a round room. You shall see it. It has not its like. It is built like a winding seashell, like a mammoth shell, in the windings of which thunders the surf of seven oceans; in these windings people crouch, so densely crowded that their faces appear as one face. No one knows the other, yet they are all friends. They all fever. They are all pale with expectation. They all have clasped hands. ... And suddenly a man is standing in the middle of the shell, in the gleaming circle, on the milk-white disc. But it is no man. It is the embodied conception of the intoxication of them all. He is not conscious of himself.... A slight froth stands on his mouth. His eyes are stark and bursting and are yet like rushing meteors which leave waving tracks of fire behind them on the route from heaven to earth.... He stands and lives his intoxication. He is what his intoxication is. From the thousands of eyes which have cast anchor into his soul the power of intoxication streams into him. (90–91)

The significance of this account of collective drug-induced hallucination and sharing of interior experience is the way in which von Harbou uses it to break up the introduction of the android. Fredersen's first acknowledgement of Rotwang's creation is the sensation of coldness which he feels while trying to read the strange symbols on the map of the labyrinth circulated by the workers who follow Maria. The coldness emanates from a being shaped and clothed as a woman:

> Cold streamed from the glazen skin which did not contain a drop of blood. The being held its beautiful hands pressed against its breast, which was motionless, with a gesture of determination almost of defiance.
>
> But the being had no face. The beautiful curve of the neck bore a lump of carelessly shaped mass. The skull was bald, nose, lips, temples merely traced. Eyes, as though painted on closed lids, stared unseeingly, with an expression of calm madness, at the man – who did not breathe. (61)

In this sequence she is described as having a skeletal hand, transparent skin and being fleshless. She is uncanny, taking the semblance of a human woman with a 'voice full of horrible tenderness' (61). Rotwang refers to her by many different names, and the one that is most picked out to distinguish between the virginal Maria and the highly sexualized robot Maria is 'Futura', but the scientist tends to refer to her more often as 'Parody', and that is the name that I will adopt for the android.

The most memorable and reproduced sequence from the film is the transference of Maria's identity to Parody. Gunning describes this as 'the ultimate sequence of Gothic modernism', which 'remains mysterious: imagistic and metaphoric rather than technological' (67). The importance of what Rotwang has done is ontological rather than the technological achievement of the robot. We have already seen the dehumanization of workers by the machine; now we see the android invested with the semblance of a soul which gives it limited but destructive agency. The sequence is absent in the book, where instead Freder is confronted with an aural discrepancy between the two versions of Maria, while Rotwang transfers the features of the original to Parody. Freder knows that there is something wrong with the voice that he hears calling him and that it threatens his reason:

> 'Look for me!' said the sweetly alluring, the deadly wicked voice, laughing softly.
>
> But through the laughter there sounded another voice – being *also* Maria's voice, sick with fear and horror. (von Harbou 113)

Freder is unable to withstand the experience of 'the doubling, dividing and interchanging of self' (234) engendered by the technological uncanny. Where von Harbou intimates the anxiety of being able to trust your senses in the recognition of the human, using aural experience, the film's visual rendition of the same experience, indicative of supernatural transformation, is just as effective.

Lotte Eisner comments on how Lang's mastery of screen lighting allows him to use light 'to create the impression of sound: the scream of the factory whistle is represented by a shriek of light from four spotlights' (233). Light has to be the major component of the creation of the robot indistinguishable from human in the silent film. Eisner describes the scene as a *'féerie de laboratoire'* where 'chemical retorts fill with a fluorescent light, coils of glass piping suddenly start to glow, zigzag flashes and sparks explode, rings of fire rise in the air. Lighting and superimpositions make the swirling mass of machines and ghostly elongated sky-scrapers sweep Frölich-Freder into a feverish nightmare, and he loses consciousness' (235). The technological import of Rotwang's power and will has impact on the individual long before Parody uses her new visage and physical dexterity to incite the workers to luddism.

For von Harbou the central concern of *Metropolis* is a family secret, the choice made by the Gothic hero's mother in her youth and the impact that her marriage had on the society (and the actions of the scientist) that her son now seeks to understand. Moreover, the novel relishes the power of Parody, the machine gifted with the soul of a woman which, rather than enslaving her, allows her full access to the urban environment that the other characters struggle to locate, enter and comprehend. Such is the thrill of this participation in social change that Parody laughs as she is dragged to her execution and the crowds see her transform back into the uncanny metal Doppelgänger. Under the order of routine, surveillance and mass society created by the Rotwang-Process, and despite von Harbou's anaphoric homilies, the labyrinth of the under-city sustains human agency through the subversive potential of irrational knowledge, the formation of insurgency (directed towards technology), and by producing culturally resonant villainy (the capitalist, a version of the mad scientist, and the destructive android) – all of which are narrative conventions and components which were later appropriated and renegotiated in the popular imagination of the GPM.

Blade Runner (1982)

Blade Runner is not a film which references magic and its generic hybridity is located in the way that the iconography of science fiction film is combined with the narrative devices and visual motifs of film noir. As already mentioned, the *mise-en-scène* of the film constantly references refuse and decay as an indexical signifier of the working and recycling of the postindustrial city. Redmond identifies the 'mesmerising cityscape' (213) as part of the film's ability to make a profound impact on its viewers. Moreover, he argues that it is the 'expansive shots of the Gothic/patchwork city as it belches flames, chokes on its own smog, and produces the discernible sense of an omnipresent decay that eats into the very fabric of the (lower) buildings' (219) which has led to the film's dominance as a cultural referent of the near future. This is the GPM where human and machine hybrids have to sell not just their labour but particular skills and knowledge in order to survive. Desser is emphatic that *Blade Runner* does more than just reference the imagery of *Metropolis*. Instead, it reworks that narrative 'in significant and deliberate ways, especially by highlighting the linked issues of race, space and class and by utilizing its production design for symbolic as well as for spectacular purposes' (93). The reasons that this can be done lie in the way that *Metropolis* is a work of popular fiction that is 'contradictory, conflicted and ambiguous' (81) which has sustained its cultural fascination for late twentieth-century audiences.

Claudia Springer asserts that science fiction film has 'been instrumental in visualizing and narrativizing the qualities associated with postmodernism: disorientation, powerlessness, fragmentation, disintegration, loss of boundaries and hybridization' (205) especially in the way that it has depicted the cyborg. Science fiction film continues to explore the thematic concerns of the GPM found in print fiction and disseminated more broadly by television and the graphic novel during the 1980s and 1990s. Moreover, science fiction cannot eradicate its inclusion of the supernatural in favour of the scientific, and however much critics may wish to purify the genre, as Sobchack observes, it retains the 'transcendentalism of magic and religion, in an attempt to reconcile man with the unknown' (63). The blurring of distinctions between the organic and the artificial, which is the nature of scientific enquiry in *Blade Runner*, returns us to the Gothic horror of *Metropolis*. The posthuman existence that interests Hollinger in cyberpunk reproduces what we have seen in Rotwang's laboratory: 'the subjectivities of humans whose "personalities" have been downloaded into computer memory and human bodies are routinely cloned' (Hollinger 207), which now become artificial intelligence, sought and encountered in the mutable Gothic spaces of cyberspace. Sterling, whom Hollinger credits with developing cyberpunk as a creative and literary movement, outlines the recurrent themes of this fiction 'body invasion: prosthetic limbs, implanted circuitry, cosmetic surgery, genetic alteration. The even more powerful theme of mind invasion: brain-computer interfaces, artificial intelligence, neurochemistry – techniques radically redefining the nature of humanity, the nature of the self' (Sterling xiii). All of which are challenges to the workforce in the popular account of the GPM.

The replicants which inhabit the diegesis of *Blade Runner* are the slave labour that Fredersen envisages and commissions from Rotwang. Redmond describes them as being worn out by their ephemeral, 'alienated and impoverished lives', and the narrative takes place because they have joined together 'to resist the oppression they face' (227). Bruno is also interested in the visual spectacle that is made of the replicants' execution (67). The religious iconography inherent in *Metropolis* provides an important tenor for the conclusion to the replicants' narrative of resistance. Their leader 'dies an implicitly religious death: half-dressed as if in a loincloth, he "saves" Deckard from an early/earthly death, puts a nail through his palm, and at the moment of his own death releases a white dove into the heavens' (Redmond 228). This leaves one replicant left, who is cast as a femme fatale but is not part of the workers' conspiracy. Unlike the other replicants, she does not know that she is not human. Yet, Rachael suspects that her human status is in doubt and she seeks to lay claim to her identity whilst learning that her memories cannot be relied upon. The ultimate horror faced by heroines in eighteenth-century Gothic is the loss of their social position and their entry into public space, which will be denied to Rachael once her status has become resolved and she learns the truth about her origins.

Claudia Springer further outlines the narrative environments of 1990s science fiction film which feature in the various media forms of the GPM '[a] combination of environmental destruction, late capitalist corruption, drug resistant diseases and increasingly sophisticated electronic technology (not to mention alien invaders) threatens human existence' (203). Her example – *Johnny Mnemonic* (1995), based on a Gibson short story from the previous decade – was made in the same year that the trading card game *Heresy Kingdom Come*™ was released, and this narrative of a data courier returns us to the market driven economy of *Metropolis*. We first meet Fredersen when he is being observed by his son overseeing human management of the machine:

> The brain-pan of the New Tower of Babel was peopled with numbers.
>   From an invisible source the numbers dropped rhythmically down through the cooled air of the room being collected, as in a water-basin, at the table at which the great brain of Metropolis worked, becoming objective under the pencils of his secretaries. (von Harbou 28)

One of these secretaries makes a mistake and is immediately dismissed '[a] thin, concise penal-line crossed out a name' (von Harbou 28). Fredersen explains to his son that the worker is obsolete and cannot compete with the machine. In fact there is no need at all to have people actually checking the machine. After Freder's eyes are opened, on his meeting Maria, he realizes that unemployment condemns humans to irredeemable redundancy. The fear of obsolescence and competition with the machine compels the human workforce to augment their bodies and minds with increasingly sophisti- cated technology. Incorporation of such technology often results in threats to personal ontology or the requirement of managing unstable subjectivity. The security of mechanical upgrades is often fleeting, despite the immense financial and mental demands needed to achieve it. Like the replicants in *Blade Runner*, the life expectancy of this technology and the competitive edge that it affords have built-in obsolescence, which becomes part of the risk of the work environment which may, just like *Metropolis*, promote luddism as a narrative response.

Staiger characterizes these science fiction narratives as 'future noir' (96) where it is the narrative logic of lived social relations in these films which comes to define them, rather than the *mise-en-scène*. The inhabitants 'fear the pervasiveness of information systems that overwhelm human senses' (Staiger 100). The specific dystopian city architecture serves to comment on anxiety about new technology, more than on any cultural desire for it (100). These cities are 'entropic, characterized by debris, decay and abandonment' (100), the waste observed by many critics and evident in the inverted millennialism of the late twentieth-century science fiction film. The waste consists not only of outmoded technology, but also of obsolescent workers, suddenly denied not just their social identity provided by employment but by their ability to consume.

Play

> Play is an occasion of pure waste: waste of time, energy, ingenuity, skill and often of money ... (Caillois 5)

The GPM is popular rather than literary and exists across a number of narrative forms. It can be considered as an imaginative construct which is employed by many different authors, readers and media forms, all negotiat- ing the anxieties of cultural change, dislocation from the family and disquiet about contemporary norms and mores. One way to consider the milieu is as a recognizable narrative environment which connects texts, enabling the reader to generate their own story-telling and re-engage with wider Gothic punk imagery, emotional responses, ideas, characters and uncompleted fictional trajectories:

> The only way that a genre model or genre rules can be said to exist is as ... a *memorial metatext* and on that level alone. It is because viewers/readers operate with sets of expectations and levels of predict- ability that is possible to perceive instances of variation, repetition,

rectification and modification. In this way genre can be considered as one single continuous text. (Leutrat 35–36)

Cyberpunk, the contemporary science fiction film and the technological thriller may influence or draw upon the Gothic punk milieu, but its narrative environment is defined by the way that both Gothic and science fiction interrogate human experience under extreme circumstances. As generic narratives, their social function is to identify sites of cultural tension and negotiate them, frequently dwelling on a speculative account of the taboo and using their conclusions to posit the assimilation of change in alignment with prevailing beliefs or values (Cawelti 36–7). The GPM is an environment for story-telling and play as important to the contract between the reader and the author of the Gothic as it is to the creative engagement required by the participant in media narratives in the late twentieth century.

Caillois's 1958 work on play builds on Huizinger's 1944 conception of play as an activity which takes place within a 'sacred' area which is separate from ordinary life. In his typology of play proposed in order to study its diversification, which he feels Huizinger does not fully acknowledge, Caillois identifies two concepts which manage the creative nature of games. *Paidia* is defined in various ways by his translator, Meyer Barash, as 'active, tumultuous, exuberant and spontaneous' (Caillois vii). *Ludus*, which disciplines and enriches *paidia* (29), is, in contrast, 'calculation, contrivance and the subordination to rules' (vii). Caillois's interest in the social consequences of play examines how games express and reflect a culture. Ultimately, Caillois feels that games are unproductive, 'creating neither goods, nor wealth, nor new elements of any kind; and, except for the exchange of property among the players, ending in a situation identical to that prevailing at the beginning of the game' (11). If we consider play as a form of popular fiction as well as culture, we can adopt Cawelti's hypothesis to replace Caillois's reductive analysis of play. Therefore, we can propose that the purpose of the GPM is to provide a speculative space for contemplating the near future and the types of change necessitated by new social formations, especially in relation to economic and political systems, the non-human or paranormal, environmental crisis and familial institutions, as well as technological innovation. The narratives are not necessarily resolved; instead they are likely to be revived in different episodes and forms and require the repeated re-engagement of the player, viewer, or reader.

Narrative in the GPM negotiates the rift between the magical and secular world-view in the face of encountering the unknown. Jesse Molesworth's study of eighteenth-century literature, including the Gothic novel, examines the metaphors and imagery of card playing, chance and the lottery which feature in these earlier Gothic texts, and he proposes that readers began to activate the fantasies associated with the repetition of such scenes. Such a consideration of the phenomenology of reading posits fluidity in the relationship between character and reader, a relationship of appropriation rather than straightforward identification. Christine Gallagher argues that readers do not emulate the behaviour of characters but appropriate their fictional experience as an 'emotional resource' (qtd. in Molesworth 29). Molesworth's examination of the context for the representation of gambling and speculation in the eighteenth century sees 'the mania for specula- tion was precisely that – a mania built not only on credit and chattel but also on fantasy, paranoia and narcissism' (59), a mania nurtured by the response to narrative fantasy. Narrative thinking and narrative rules are still enshrined in the novel, despite the rise of scientific and secular thought in eighteenth-century popular culture. Reading and the engagement with fiction is, for Molesworth, 'an avocation, or form of play' (134), one which has consequences for a cultural as well as individual world-view and deci- sion making regarding risk.

When it comes to examining the Gothic novel, Molesworth wants to do so in conjunction with a second contemporaneous cultural institu- tion: tarot cartomancy. Like games of chance, he sees tarot cartomancy, too, as interrogating 'the uncanniness of coincidence and the doubting of chance' (209). Molesworth identifies that tarot as an entertainment practice originates from 1785, through the best selling *Ettelier's Guide*, which offered 'the magical fascination of the past with the psychological realism of the present' (213).[3] The major arcana cards of the tarot are pictorial images accompanied by names which form the speculative symbolism for interpretation. An arcanum is, from its Latin derivation, a tightly shut treasure chest holding a secret (Semetsky 106) – the essence of Gothic narrative. Although the meanings of the cards are codified, the *ludus* exerts control over the *paidia*: the stages of the narrative have to be interpreted and therefore elide any absolute fixity of signification. The narrative can therefore oscillate between rational and irrational explanations of events. Ettellier presented tarot cartomancy as story-telling rather than divination; his text 'offered endless narrative pleasure in the form of wonder that could be re-experienced over and over again' (Molesworth 218). It is the narrative potential of these cards as a game rather than an oracle which is empha- sized: 'the thrill of tarot, that is, lies in its conception of human experience as a series of hinge points, or plot nodes – the necessary insistence that numerous cards impinge on the reading of the story' (222). Molesworth argues that eighteenth-century Gothic fiction adopts a mode of story-telling which is like Etellier's account of the tarot, 'ever in transition, ever seeking to contradict its own causal logic, ever seeking to imbue coincidence with the fateful atmosphere of the uncanny' (230). Like tarot, Gothic fiction is open to interpretation, rearrangement, refashioning of the author's ellipsis or elision according to the reader's interests or preoccupations. Molesworth views the social purpose of the Gothic novel as a means to make the strange familiar and counteract a source of anxiety in the experience of modernity in an age of disintegrating traditional familiar networks (242). By contrast, the later GPM overturns this consensual device, making the familiar, even the self, become strange and disquieting, to such an extent that paranoia becomes a legitimate survival strategy.

Inna Semetsky's Jungian reading of the imagery and cultural practice of tarot finds that the cards 'represent multiple points of human experience and habitual behaviours accompanied by the spectrum of feelings, emotions, desires, beliefs and other psychodynamic processes and related affective and mental states' (106). An understanding of the tarot from this perspective needs to register that speculative alternatives are a vital part of reading the text formed by the cards in play. Reading play offers a journey of individuation, which, as Molesworth observes, is present in any narrativization of a card game, but in this instance one which takes on abstract ideas from the names of major arcana cards, such as justice and the nature of governance and authority, as well as more Jungian concepts such as the shadow. The symbolism of the Jungian concept of the collective unconscious and the way that it is embedded in different forms of story-telling is conducive for personal development and therefore future possibilities rather than revelations about the past. The archetype of the shadow weaves in and out of the imagery of the major arcana. Semetsky discusses the ways in which the practice of tarot can support the integration of the shadow into positive personal transformation: 'the concept of the shadow describes a cluster of impulses, complexes, shameful and unacknowledged desires, self-indulgences and being a slave to one's own primitive instincts' (110). The shadow encompasses those desires outside of social norms and established order which cause us to reflect upon its nature and creativity in the playing out of the game. Parody's expression of *paidia* throughout *Metropolis* is set into motion by the *ludus* of Fredersen's calculation and desire for control.

Eve Kosofsky Sedgwick alerts us to an influential family of Gothic conventions which relate to spatial metaphors of interiority and surface. She is interested in the recurrence of the veil as 'the locus of the substitution of one person for another, in the service of an indiscriminate metonymic contagion of its own attributes' (258–59) and '[w]riting in blood, writing in flesh – even when the formulas are figurative, they represent a special access of the authoritative, inalienable and immediate; the writing of blood and flesh never lies' (260). Brigitte Helm, the actress who portrays Maria and Parody in *Metropolis*, contrasts the calm, rational and purposeful actions of the woman even when subject to terror in the catacombs with the sinuous, tumultuous exuberance of the machine as she dances and incites her audience. Sedgwick argues that 'although these Gothic conventions about writing give primacy to surfaces, they by no means exclude depth but admit it in certain slippages' (260). Since Parody is not destroyed by the witch burning, how does she continue in the rebuilding of Metropolis and how much of Maria's repressed being enables Parody to embrace *paidia*? The face of Parody, which Sedgwick finds so important in the Gothic novel (262–63), dominates the stills associated with and reproduced from the film. The machine's face is impassive, waiting for trauma, dissolution and transference to make it active through excitation and the loss of control.

Heresy Kingdom Come™ (1995)

> In his choice of authors, that liberal and industrious artist was reduced to comply with the vicious taste of his readers: to gratify the nobles with treatises on heraldry, hawking and the game of chess, and to arouse the popular credulity with romances of fabulous knights and legends of more fabulous saints. (Gibbon 537)

Caxton's (1421–91) main contribution to the history of printing was his decision to publish his English translations of Continental romances as a commercial venture. The accuracy of Gibbon's description of the books that Caxton printed is contested, but its contempt is clearly evident. Nevertheless, amongst his early publications was his translation of *Recuyell of the Historyes of Troye*, a narrative still being retold for twenty-first-century audiences, and *The Game and Playe of the Chesse*, which was printed in Bruges circa 1475. The woodcut illustrations in this text undercut the instructive and scholarly purpose. Making full use of the dramatic woodcut, they represent in sensational detail the combat and field of battle for the chess pieces as we are introduced to the moves they can make and the strategies players can employ. Imagining the game as an unfolding narrative has been a crucial part of entertainment media since the beginning of popular publishing

The Gothic punk setting is acknowledged by many commercial role-playing games, digital games and fictions, but the milieu is a narrative location which speculates on the future rather than just the integration of the supernatural or the paranormal. To do so, it has a particular iconography, adapts the narrative preoccupations of cyberpunk science fiction and concerns itself with mortality and the speculative nature of posthuman existence. The discussion of *Heresy Kingdom Come™* (*Heresy*) which follows will concentrate on the diegesis rather than game play. Trading card games, which combine collecting with a competitive strategically played game, became popular in the US in the 1990s. The first was *Magic: The Gathering* (Garfield 1993), published by Wizards of the Coast, the company which bought *Heresy* from its original publisher, Last Unicorn Games. The cards are specially designed, with great attention paid to card illustration. *Heresy* used twenty-six artists, one of whom, Matthew Sturm, was part of the overall design team.

The rules for each game system are different. For *Heresy* the minimum number of cards to play for an optimum two to five players is sixty. Packs of this number are sold as starter sets, but players are expected to buy, trade and collect cards in order to build up their unique deck. This customization allows them to increase their opportunity to use particular combinations and interactions, in this instance no more than four cards of one type except for locations. The players' guide sets out the objectives, categories of the cards in the set (whether the player has yet purchased them or not) and the rules governing the protocols of play, how cards interact and the turn sequence which sets out the order in which actions take place. A common ludic structure, and one used by *Heresy*, is to consider the cards as a resource, so that the way in which cards move from a player's hand into the field of play is controlled and strategic. In order to play a card, the player must have enough resource points saved up in the other cards they hold, in this instance 'aura', which brings character cards into play, 'tau', which will enable the player to complete the final winning move of the game, and 'virtual support', which allows them to sustain the strategy that they are building. Therefore the game proceeds with players taking turns to play the cards and perform game-related actions. The central action is conflict, and in *Heresy* it is the main way in which tau is earned.

The players' guide for *Heresy* introduces it as a game of 'action, strategy and influence' through an imaginative scenario. The game's premise features angels who have fallen to a Forsaken Earth which they need to rebuild and control in order to achieve re-ascension. The cards are the resources that they have available, and the object of the game is to collect tau points in order to rebuild the computer matrix and activate a digital portal. Locations are divided between the ruined cities of Forsaken Earth and the data storage facilities for tau energy. Character cards are divided between Host and Heathen, a set of supernatural and cyberpunk archetypes inhabiting the wilds and the matrix, a division maintained by the designated areas of play on the card table. The Heathen 'are typically members of religions, gangs, corporations, secret societies, mercenary groups and mystical orders as well as digital phantoms, virtual personalities and artificial intelligences' (Moore, Seyler and Sturm 11), but the Host also manifest essential characteristics and preoccupations of inhabitants in the GPM.

Other cards introduce artefacts, celestial power, miracles and enhancement into play. The population of Forsaken Earth are further differentiated by the convictions they hold, and players need to be able to influence them, call them into play and use them as a resource to rebuild the matrix. The convictions are a series of lifestyles which are reminiscent of the competing beliefs held by different social groups and characters in Metropolis: rebellion (anti-authority), devotion (religious belief), preservation (ecology), acquisition (capitalism), tradition (law), stagnation (nihilism), evolution (science) and technology (non-sentient things). The game play, which can take between thirty minutes and two hours, is focused on the accumulation of points, collecting appropriate combinations of cards to declare an attack and the strategic placing of cards to sustain a defence. So *Heresy* is not a story-telling game per se, but it is predicated on attractive narrative elements which can be referenced during play, and also outside collective interaction. The descriptions on each of the cards are evocative and not necessarily connected to how they are specifically to be played. A good example is 'Nile Shard', one of the cards detailing a location in the game. The place is designated as being connected with technology, which is important for game play, but its description on the card goes further than this. It reads '[e]ven though the Cartels control the Shard, they don't touch the Seeker pilgrim caravans that wander its datascapes. Guess they figure it's bad karma or something.' This card notation refers to characters and activities which do not feature in actual play but which form a diegesis for speculation. The cards offer multiple ways of visualizing characters, concepts, decision making and alterity present in other instances of the GPM.

The range of concepts, representations, narrative engagements and characters drawn upon by the card illustration is immense, and further accentuated by the requirement that cards should be considered in combination.[4] The Heathen, who populate the ruined cities, have limited or prohibited access to the arrays created by the Host, and are divided into different groups: zealots, teks, mystics, fanatics and militia, all very recognizable characters from cyberpunk.[5] They are portrayed on the street. The Cacophonites demonstrate their nihilism through their shredded clothes, random tattoos, wasted flesh, nihilistic gestures and the mindless graffiti behind their figures. The Chromeopaths seem more purposeful in that they embrace technology and 'equate scientific achievement with ecstatic experience' (Moore, Seyler and Sturm 7), but they hold old-style weaponry, have a grungy appearance and wear the same glasses and skull imagery as the Cacophonites. In contrast, the Gabrielites are marked with a bleeding tattoo on the forehead, are clothed in voluminous white and are shown, hands clasped, viewing an organically shaped data screen. The Fanatics are back out on the street, with scarred muscular bodies, clutching a book and issuing a challenge to the viewer of the card. Other aspects of these groups are displayed in cards that invite particular game play, such as the

Mystics, portrayed through abstract symbols and bold colours, skeletal hands and impassive faces. Other cards illustrate actions such as demon invocation, neuroplug sockets embedded in a Heathen forehead, or the work of recycling which takes place in the Wilds. Taken together, the cards envisage a rich, competing set of lifestyles, aspirations and work within the low technological and data access of the ruined cities on Forsaken Earth.

In a similar fashion to the evocative figures and moments of change found on tarot cards, those for *Heresy* are interspersed with recognizable terms: affirmation, subterfuge, prophecy, invocation, repair, temperance, banish, rapture, charity and imprisonment, all of which lend themselves to further narrative speculation even if the ludic structures governing the game limit these narrative trajectories during play. Artefacts, such as The Clavicule, which modify play are given images which portray particular concepts such as the ancient book, which becomes digitally accessible. The card titled 'Ghost in the Machine' is an enhancement where 'the boundaries between dream and death, virtual and real have been blurred' (Moore, Seyler and Sturm 8) but the most creative elements of this version of the GPM are the Host, Celestial and Infernal, all categories which have come to dominate twenty-first-century Urban Fantasy. These categories are manifested as characters which are also named and assigned to groups. Middle-aged Verchiel stands against a neon graffiti wall holding a vast number of artists' brushes and a customized spray can in his hands. Tartaruchi is a tortuously augmented cyborg whose arms have become cannons. Sithriel, who prefers to inhabit the matrix, is depicted as vampiric, with red eyes and a face reminiscent of the android Parody. Other Host draw on sado-maschochistic imagery. Mansemat is a mercenary hired to extract information, so her backdrop is a blood-spattered wall and a few instruments of her trade. She is shaven headed, her face marked by black circles and spots contrasting with her white skin. She wears a dress cut to display her sinewy muscular arms and she is in the act of covering them with long gloves. Azrael and Arakab depict the pleasures and perils of addiction, whereas other Host mentor, enslave and succour Heathen according to their desires, predilections, or tendencies or habitual choices in engaging with technology.

The imagery and the scenario underpinning the objectives of the game draw upon the coalescence of cyberpunk fiction in the 1980s and the visual patterning that develops within the diegesis of science fiction films that feature the cyborg: the urban decay of inverted millennialism and the feral youth of near-future postindustrial culture. However, the introduction of the Host and their desire to harness Heathen for their own ends constructs a narrative diegesis of the cultural clash between young and old that comprises the GPM. The protagonist or player navigates the social world through their increasing knowledge of origin, ability to detect illusion and judgement regarding transgression. Each location hosts a series of shifting personal and economic interrelationships which encompass encounters with technology and spirituality. The narratives that ensue are still preoccupied with conspiracy, the expansion of consciousness and occult knowledge, whether it be engagement with the supernatural or cyberspace.

The urban, wilderness, old city and technotopian enclaves of this game world cohere in response to shared cultural reference, which is indicative of why the GPM stayed current during the twentieth century. It created a space for negotiation of pragmatic rather than abstract fears, particularly for the young at the forefront of social-technological innovation, now delivered to us as entertainment and social networking rather than forms of unregulated working practice with increasing surveillance and accountability. The GPM provides a creative space for challenging the superordinate and exploring specific forms of knowledge for the evaluation of risk in social environments, predation, emotional encounters with the ephemeral and decisions that have to be made about the relevance of the past or between competing belief systems regarding the future.

Notes

1. Dadoun, writing his Freudian analysis of *Metropolis* during the 1970s, sets out a detailed summary of the film because, he argues, even those who have seen the film will only remember 'brief snatches … Fleeting images are lost forever (occasioning what has been called *le deuil cinématique*, or the mourning of the lost image)' (137).
2. Fredersen is the father of Freder Fredersen, the Gothic hero of *Metropolis* and principal investigator of the different enclaves of the city.
3. Molesworth is referring to *Etteilla, ou manière de se récréer avec le jeu de cartes nomées tarots*, published in 1773 but gaining in popularity with the second edition published in 1784 when Etteilla's guide to tarot was reprinted in a volume alongside Henri Decremps's *Le magie blanche dévoilée*.
4. I am referring to a sample from the sixty cards in my possession which were sold as a starter deck for the game in 1995. Currently there is only one existing website which provides any visual evidence of *Heresey's* card illustration and graphic design: http://www.frothersunite.couk/files/UnclEvl/Heresy/HeresyIntro.html. I was able to observe the game played twice and I have chosen cards to describe because of their relationship to the GPM.
5. In the starter pack at least, female punk heathen are not in evidence, although they are more equally distributed amongst the host.

Works cited

Blade Runner. Dir. Ridley Scott. Warner Bros, 1982. Film.
Bruno, Giuliana. 'Ramble City: Postmodernism and *Blade Runner.' October* 41 (Summer 1987): 61–74. Print.

Caillois, Roger. *Man, Play and Games.* 1958. Trans. Meyer Barash. New York: The Free Press, 1961. Print.

Cawelti, John G. *Adventure, Mystery and Romance.* Chicago: U of Chicago P, 1976. Print.

Dadoun, Roger. '*Metropolis* Mother-City-"Mittler"-Hitler.' 1974. *Camera Obscura* 15 (1986 Autumn): 137–63. Print.

Desser, David. 'Race, Space and Class: The Politics of Cityscapes in Science-Fiction Films.' *Alien Zone: The Spaces of Science Fiction Cinema.* Ed. Annette Kuhn. London: Verso, 1999. 80–96. Print.

Eisner, Lotte. *The Haunted Screen Expressionism in the German Cinema and the Influence of Max Reinhardt.* 1952. London: Secker and Warburg, 1973. Print.

Freud, Sigmund. 'The Uncanny.' 1919. *The Standard Edition of the Complete Psychological Works.* Trans J. Strachey and others. Vol. XVII. London: Hogarth Press, 1966. 217–56. Print.

Gallagher, Catherine. 'The Rise of Fictionality.' *The Novel, vol 1: History, Geography and Culture.* Ed. Franco Moretti. Princeton: Princeton UP, 2006. 336–63. Print.

Garfield, Richard. *Magic: The Gathering.* Seattle: Wizard of the Coast, 1993. Card game.

Gibbon, Edward. 'An Address &c.' 1793. *The English Essays of Edward Gibbon.* Ed. Patricia Craddock. Oxford: Oxford UP, 1972. 534–42. Print.

Gibson, William. *Neuromancer.* London: Gollancz, 1984. Print.

Grant, Barry Keith '"Sensuous Elaboration": Reason and the Visible in Science-Fiction Film.' *Alien Zone: The Spaces of Science Fiction Cinema.* Ed. Annette Kuhn. London: Verso, 1999. 16–30. Print.

Gunning, Tom. *The Films of Fritz Lang: Allegories of Vision and Modernity.* London: British Film Institute, 2000. Print.

Hollinger, Veronica. 'Cybernetic Deconstructions: Cyberpunk and Postmodernism.' *Storming the Reality Studio.* London: Duke UP, 1991. 203–18. Print.

Huizinger, Johann. *Homo Ludens: A Study of the Play Element in Culture.* 1944. London: Maurice Temple Smith, 1970. Print.

Jameson, Frederic. 'From Postmodernism or The Cultural Logic of Late Capitalism.' *Storming the Reality Studio.* Ed. Larry McCaffery. London: Duke UP, 1991. 219–28. Print.

Keiner, Reinhold. *Thea von Harbou und der deutsche Film bis 1933.* Hildesheim: Olms, 1984. Print.

Leutrat, John-Louis. *Le Western.* Paris: Armand Colin, 1973. Print.

Metropolis. Dir. Fritz Lang. Wiesbaden: Stiftung F. W. Murnau, 2010. Film.

Miller, D. A. *The Novel and Its Discontents: Problems of Closure in the Traditional Novel.* Princeton: Princeton UP, 1981. Print

Minden, Michael. 'The City in Early Cinema: *Metropolis, Berlin* and *October.*' *Unreal City: Urban Experience in Modern European Literature and Art.* Ed. Timms, Edward and Kelley, David. Manchester: Manchester UP, 1985. 193–213. Print.

Molesworth, Jesse. *Chance and the Eighteenth Century Novel: Realism, Probability and Magic.* Cambridge: Cambridge UP, 2010. Print.

Moody, Nickianne. 'Untapped Potential: The Representation of Disability/Special Ability in the Cyberpunk Future.' *Convergence* 3.3 (1997): 90–105. Print.

Moore, Christian, Owen Seyler and Matthew Strum. *Heresy Kingdom Come.* New Cumberland: Last Unicorn Games, 1995. Game.

Redmond, Sean. 'Purge! Class Pathology in *Blade Runner.*' *The Blade Runner Experience.* Ed. Will Brooks. London: Wallflower Press, 2005. 213–29. Print.

Rutsky, R. L. 'Between Modernity and Magic.' *Film Analysis.* Ed. Jeffrey Geiger and R. L. Rutsky. London: Norton, 2005. 128–95. Print.

Sedgwick, Eve Kosofsky. 'The Character in the Veil: Imagery of the Surface in the Gothic Novel.' *PMLA* 96.2 (1981): 255–70. Print.

Semetsky, Inna. 'Interpreting the Signs of the Times: Beyond Jung.' *Social Semiotics* 20.2 (2010): 103–120. Print.

Sobchack, Vivian. *Screening Space the American Science Fiction Film*. London: Rutgers UP, 1987. Print.

Springer, Claudia. 'Psycho-Cybernetics in Films of the 1990s.' *Alien Zone: The Spaces of Science Fiction Cinema*. Ed. Annette Kuhn. London: Verso, 1999. 203–20. Print.

Staiger, Janet. 'Future Noir: Contemporary Representations of Visionary Cities.' *Alien Zone: The Spaces of Science Fiction Cinema*. Ed. Annette Kuhn. London: Verso, 1999. 97–122. Print.

Sterling, Bruce, ed. Mirrorshades. New York: Warner Books, 1986. Print.

Telotte, J. P. *A Distant Technology: Science Fiction Film and the Machine Age*. London: Wesleyan UP, 1999. Print.

von Harbou, Thea. *Metropolis*. London: Readers Library, 1927. Print.

Williams, Keith. '"Seeing the Future": Visual Technology in *When the Sleeper Awakes* and Fritz Lang's *Metropolis*.' *H. G. Wells: Modernity and the Movies*. Liverpool: Liverpool UP, 2007. 73–93. Print.

11. Gothic Science Fiction in the Steampunk Graphic Novel
The League of Extraordinary Gentlemen

Laura Hilton

The League of Extraordinary Gentlemen is a series of graphic novels that adapts and appropriates earlier literary texts and cultural products, resulting in a complex, intertextual narrative structure. The novels that form a central part of the narrative in *League* include: H. Rider Haggard's Allan Quatermain novels (1885 onwards), *The Strange Case of Dr Jekyll and Mr Hyde* (1886) by Robert Louis Stevenson, *Dracula* (1897) by Bram Stoker, *Twenty Thousand Leagues Under the Seas* (1870) by Jules Verne and H. G. Wells's *The Island of Dr Moreau* (1896), *The Invisible Man* (1897) and *The War of the Worlds* (1898). The protagonists who form the League in Volumes I and II are: Mina Murray, the ex-wife of Jonathan Harker and the leader of the League; Allan Quatermain, a legendary hunter and recovering opium addict; Captain Nemo, the mysterious master of the sea who aids the League with his submarine, the *Nautilus*; Hawley Griffin, the Invisible Man who favours violence and destruction over diplomacy; and Dr Jekyll, a small and timid doctor who transforms into a monstrously large creature with astonishing strength named Mr Hyde.[1]

The *League* series currently consists of three volumes and an intermediary publication. Both Volume I (2000) and Volume II (2003) were initially published as serialized comic books before their collection into graphic novels, and Volume III, *Century*, is currently in serial production, with only the first of three parts, entitled *1910* (2009), available at present. An intermediary publication, *The Black Dossier* (2007), was printed as a complete graphic novel between Volumes II and III. Written by Alan Moore and illustrated by Kevin O"Neill, two of the leading names in the comics industry, the *League* volumes have met with widespread interest on account of their intertextual structure and overtly steampunk style. Described as 'the ultimate in crossover concepts' (Nevins, *Heroes* 175), the series draws from countless literary works, resulting in an unusually diverse readership:

'a significant number of fans of *League* are men and women who don't buy other comic books, including authors, editors, literature students and literature professors' (Nevins, *Heroes* 16).

This chapter argues that the invisibility of Griffin, from H. G. Wells's *The Invisible Man*, and the unusual appearance, size and strength of Hyde, from Robert Louis Stevenson's *The Strange Case of Dr Jekyll and Mr Hyde*, combine tropes from science fiction and the Gothic in order to challenge contemporary representations of transgression, transformation and monstrosity.[2] The analysis will be divided into three sections, opening with an overview of how the genres of science fiction and the Gothic combine in this steampunk graphic novel before moving on to a consideration of how Griffin and Hyde can be seen to function as steampunk 'superheroes'. The conclusion will discuss the representations of Griffin and Hyde during the scene depicting Griffin's death, exploring the juxtaposition between Hyde's simulation of gentlemanly behaviour and his violent actions alongside the significance of Griffin's horrific yet invisible injuries.

'Obsessed with the past': *League* and genre

The genre of the Gothic is often discussed as a direct precursor of science fiction. Brian Aldiss, for example, considers the Gothic novel to be 'the dream world ... from which science fiction springs' (8) and he argues that, in particular, science fiction embraces the Gothic custom of 'explaining' any unlikely events through the use of a distant and unfamiliar narrative setting (19). Aldiss notes, for example, that for the science fiction genre, 'other planets make ideal settings for [the Gothic tropes of] brooding landscapes, isolated castles, dismal towns and mysterious alien figures' (19). Similarly, Linda Dryden argues that H. G. Wells's Gothic 'scientific romances' provided a prototype for twentieth-century science fiction (2).

However, one might argue that critical approaches such as these attempt to over-simplify the complex relationship between science fiction and the Gothic. Most eighteenth-century Gothic novels, including Horace Walpole's *The Castle of Otranto* (1764), Ann Radcliffe's *The Mysteries of Udolpho* (1794) and Matthew G. Lewis's *The Monk* (1796), feature elements of the supernatural, but by the late nineteenth century the Gothic began a clear movement away from the supernatural and towards scientific research and experimentation. This turning-point is best illustrated in Mary Shelley's introduction to the 1831 edition of *Frankenstein*, in which Shelley notes that her novel was inspired by several evenings spent with 'volumes of ghost stories' and discussions of 'the experiments of Dr. Darwin' (361–64). By naming these twin influences, Shelley acknowledges her combination of the eighteenth-century Gothic heritage of the supernatural with scientific experimentation. Shelley's novel has been categorized as Victorian Gothic, a category notable for its mixture of science and the supernatural in addition to its movement away from 'overtly "historical" or "exotic" locations and settings' in favour of 'placing the action in the contemporary realm and the heart of the modern capital' (Mighall 26). A growing focus on scientific discovery becomes central to such late nineteenth-century Gothic texts as *The Strange Case of Dr Jekyll and Mr Hyde* and Bram Stoker's *Dracula*, and both of these novels feature significant narrative developments in the city of London. Therefore, Shelley's novel can be read as a direct influence on the future directions of both the Gothic and science fiction genres. The Gothic and science fiction have been intricately entangled ever since.

'Steampunk' is one subgenre of science fiction that exemplifies its entanglement with Gothic. Steampunk has been described as 'a kind of techno-punk set in Victorian Britain' (Seed 217), 'in which the evocation of futurity is grafted on to the rewriting of the history of classical or modern technologies' (Connor 136).[3] The subgenre originally grew out of cyberpunk (e.g. Onion 140; Seed 217), with the Victorian London of steampunk and 'its violent, polluted, *laissez-faire* anarchy' functioning as 'a precursor of the post-industrial near-future ecological wastelands of cyberpunk' (Luckhurst 213). Steampunk can be found in novels by authors such as Michael Moorcock, K. W. Jeter, Tim Powers and James Blaylock, and in a variety of cultural forms including role-playing games, music, television and, of course, graphic novels. Most steampunk fiction is situated in an environment closely resembling Victorian England where steam remains the main source of power, and any modern technological developments included in the narrative are steam-powered. Science fiction author and critic John Clute argues that steampunk was inadvertently invented by Charles Dickens, as 'his shaping presence can be felt everywhere' (64) and Cory Gross proposes that steampunk has two 'varieties': nostalgic steampunk, which generally ignores 'the more uncomfortable genuine history of the era' and resonates with the writing of Jules Verne; and melancholic steampunk, which draws attention to 'the corruption, the decadence, the imperialism, the poverty and the intrigue' of Victoriana and reflects the writing of H. G. Wells (62–63). This reference to Wells, combined with *League*'s dark and cynical narrative trajectories, suggests that Moore and O'Neill are working within the realms of melancholic steampunk in the *League* series.

Like the protagonists in their literary precursors, the central protago-nists of the *League* series are far from straightforward heroes or heroines. For example, Mina's characterization draws on her depiction as an am-biguous combination of conventional Victorian woman and New Woman in *Dracula* (Hilton). The male protagonists are equally complex in that each demonstrates identifiable antihero qualities, such as Nemo's hatred of the British Empire, Griffin and Hyde's morally ambiguous behaviour and Quatermain's connection with colonialism. This choice of ambiguous characterization complements the dark and cynical narrative trajectories of the first two volumes, which explore the racist 'yellow peril' tradition in Volume I and the fear of alien invasion, mass panic and government subterfuge in Volume II.

Since steampunk focuses on a past era, it can be classified as a more specific version of another subgenre of science fiction: alternative history. Alternative history has been succinctly defined as 'a work of fiction in which history as we know it is changed for dramatic and often ironic effect' (Duncan 209). Each central character of the *League* is based on a character from a particular late nineteenth-century novel, but significant differences are introduced which allow dramatic and sometimes ironic events to occur, in keeping with the nature of alternative history. For example, the final page of *Dracula* provides a 'Note' that records the birth of a son for Mina and Jonathan Harker (419), but no mention of this child is made in the *League* series. This alternative possibility enables Mina's characterization to move beyond the role of mother and wife in order to fully embrace the role of independent leader. Another example can be seen in relation to Griffin's death in the penultimate scene of *The Invisible Man* (Wells 180–81). The *League* series proposes an alternative explanation, that Wells's angry mob killed another invisible man and that Griffin escaped alive (I, 50, iii), thus enabling the inclusion of the original Griffin in *League*.[4] Such diversions from the original texts allow the *League* series to present an alternative Victorian London filled with fictional characters that are both immediately recognizable yet also subtly different from their original presentations.

Both steampunk and alternative history are unusual when considered within the context of science fiction as a whole because, as several critics have noted, the science fiction genre is often more concerned with speculating on the future than on the past (e.g. Roberts 25). This creates a connection with Gothic literature, since, as Fred Botting notes, 'Gothic novels seem to sustain a nostalgic relish for a lost era of romance and adventure' (5). In parallel, steampunk literature sustains a nostalgic relish for the lost era of Victoriana. Furthermore, Anne Cranny-Francis has observed that one of the 'textual strategies' used in *Frankenstein* that has 'entered into the conventions of the science fiction genre' is a more general 'displacement in time and/or space' (221). This technique is central to both steampunk in general and *League* in particular. Spatially, each member of the *League* is displaced from the context of their original novel and resituated in *League*, in an echo of the straightforward spatial displacement from European civilization to the barren Arctic in *Frankenstein*. For example, the character of Captain Nemo is displaced from his home of the mysterious island and is resituated in the League headquarters in Bloomsbury, London. He continues to maintain an ideological dislike for the British Empire but this has now expanded even further, as shown by his declaration: 'If I work with the British, it is because I no longer feel even Indian. The sea, now, is my only nation' (I, 19, ii). As a result, this example of spatial displacement and resituation creates a new ideological dimension for *League*'s adaptation of Verne's original characterization.

Displacement in time, too, is central for *League*. Volume II, in particular, can be read as an adaptation of Wells's *The War of the Worlds* set in 1898 rather than in Wells's original setting of 'early in the twentieth century' (Wells 123). This example of temporal displacement draws attention to the fact that Wells makes no concerted effort to describe any events or developments, technological or otherwise, that would emphasize that *The War of the Worlds* is set in the future. Indeed, Nevins notes that 'the story is very clearly talking about the kind of London that existed in 1898' (*Heroes* 232). Resituating Wells's narrative in the late nineteenth century is thus a smooth displacement that neither compromises nor contradicts any elements of the original narrative. The resultant displacement and resituation of characters, settings and themes combine to create an ultimately coherent steampunk narrative, blending science fiction tropes with markers of the Victorian era.

'Wonderful freaks': Griffin and Hyde

League's genre position is further complicated by its relationship to superhero narrative. Certain members of the *League* demonstrate 'powers' which are similar to those found in traditional superheroes and supervillains, and which combine tropes from science fiction and fantasy. For example, Wells explains Griffin's ability to become invisible as emerging from experimentation into optical density, ethereal vibration and drugs that decolourize the blood (Wells 109; 116; 122). At first glance it seems as though Stevenson explains Hyde's physical monstrosity in a similar fashion, briefly describing Jekyll's scientific experimentation as the cause. However, on closer examination, one notices that Stevenson's *Jekyll and Hyde* describes this experimentation only tangentially, choosing instead to focus on the tortured degeneration of Jekyll's 'spirit' and 'soul' (Stevenson 80) in a typically Gothic narrative trajectory. For example, Ambrosio, the protagonist of Matthew Lewis's *The Monk* (1796), transforms from a pious, respected monk into an incestuous rapist and murderer who eventually sells his soul to the devil and is denied final absolution, and Shelley's *Frankenstein* depicts Victor Frankenstein's soul as so tortured by the actions of both himself and his monstrous creation that he considers the situation as irresolvable by anything less than the destruction of both himself and his monster. The notion of the tortured and degenerated soul is thus a recurrent Gothic theme and is particularly relevant to the morally ambiguous and ultimately monstrous depictions of Griffin and Hyde.

Moore himself has explained that his choice of Griffin and Hyde as members of the *League* was partially due to the fact that they 'are wonderful freaks' with 'incredible visual possibilities' (Nevins, *Heroes* 220), and the discussion below will focus on how these 'visual possibilities' are fully exploited in the *League* graphic novels in order to explore the science-fictional qualities and personalities of each unique character. The inhuman appearances of both Hyde and Griffin are central to their characterization in *League*, and both characters might be argued to reflect the Gothic process that Kelly Hurley has described as the destruction of the human and the unfolding of the 'abhuman':

> The abhuman is a not-quite-human subject, characterized by its morphic variability, continually in danger of becoming not-itself, becoming other. The prefix 'ab-' signals movement away from a site or condition, and thus a loss. But a movement away is also a movement towards – towards a site or condition as yet unspecified – and thus entails both a threat and a promise. (3–4)

Hurley's description of the movement from human to abhuman is another example of the 'monstrous transformations' that appear throughout Gothic literature (Dryden 16). For Griffin, the transformation from visible to invisible results in Griffin's status as both an 'other' and an enigma, and his desire to gain power from his new-found invisibility threatens to assist the Martians in securing their dominance over London in Volume II. Furthermore, Griffin's invisibility is particularly interesting in the context of the graphic novel form because of the constant emphasis on visual, in addition to textual, narrative. This narrative style develops from Wells's original novel, where the idea of invisibility is of course solely communicated through prose rather than visual illustration. Throughout Wells's text, the character is referred to as either 'the stranger' (e.g. 7), 'the Invisible Man' (e.g. 50), 'the Voice' (e.g. 54), or finally 'Griffin' (e.g. 103), thus demonstrating how the character is, at different points in the novel, respectively depicted as an unfamiliar person, a defined Invisible Man, or a disembodied sound, before his name is finally revealed.

At first, Griffin uses bandages to conceal his invisibility, yet the villagers he meets nonetheless regard him as rather unusual. For example, he causes his host, Mrs Hall, to become 'rigid' with shock (10); Fearenside, the delivery man, thinks that: '"He's a kind of half-breed, and the colour's come off patchy instead of mixing"' (26); and Mr Cuss, the local general practitioner, declares: "'Lord! I thought, *that's* a deformity!'" (32, emphasis in original). Therefore, throughout the opening chapters, the textual description demonstrates that the villagers consider the Invisible Man to be unusual, strange and other to them.

Griffin's invisibility, however, is finally unveiled and the textual description of this physical quality is revealing. The event is described as follows: 'his face became a black cavity.... It was worse than anything ... They were prepared for scars, disfigurement, tangible horrors – but *nothing*!' (46, emphasis in original). Here, the true horror of the abhuman is invoked by Griffin's movement away from the resemblance of humanity and towards the unknowable 'nothing' of the 'black cavity'. Griffin's invisibility, therefore, is seen as utterly terrifying by those who witness its disclosure, but we learn very little about the Invisible Man himself through this description. Later, the character Mr Marvel discovers Griffin's 'muscular chest, and ... bearded face' (58–59), and later still, Griffin describes himself in the most detailed depiction provided in the narrative: 'almost an albino, six feet high, and broad, with a pink and white face and red eyes' (98). These limited and unusual descriptions of the Invisible Man result in a character the reader may well struggle to visualize. This challenge is intensified by Wells's textual descriptions, which focus predominantly on the reactions of those who interact with Griffin, rather than on the Invisible Man himself. As such, Griffin's abhumanity distressingly challenges the boundary categories perceived by the other characters in the novel, in addition to those perceived by the reader.

Since *League* is a graphic novel, however, Griffin's invisibility is conveyed through the visual as well as the textual, and conveying invisibility poses clear challenges for an illustrator. Moore notes, 'invisibility is probably the most poorly used power in comic books because ... [the artists] always draw a dotted line around [invisible characters] to tell you where they are'. '[I]t's much better if the character is completely invisible', Moore goes on to explain, because 'that's the whole point: you don't know where they are' (Nevins, *Heroes* 220). Such 'dotted line' invisibility characterizes the Invisible Woman of Stan Lee and Jack Kirby's *The Fantastic Four* (*Marvel*, 1961 onwards), as shown in the second page of the very first issue of the series (Lee and Kirby 4, ii). Such techniques risk making the power of invisibility little more than a gimmick, since the protagonist's whereabouts are never hidden from the reader in the same way that they are hidden from other characters. By contrast, Griffin's body is rendered completely invisible in *League* and no dotted lines are used. When Griffin is naked, his presence is often only indicated by the depiction of a floating, tailless speech bubble (e.g. I, 111, ix). The decision to omit any dotted lines and to instead render Griffin as completely invisible results in a much more suspense-filled experience for the reader, since they, just like the members of the League (except for Hyde, as discussed below), remain unaware of Griffin's location. As a result, Griffin's invisibility is more effective as a visual narrative device.

Most interestingly, however, Griffin's invisibility results in the reader's being unable to associate a face or any sort of facial expression with Griffin's words and actions, and in this way Griffin becomes an even more aloof and mysterious character than his original depiction in Wells's novel. Instead of 'seeing' Griffin as they see the other characters or as outlined by a dotted line, the reader is limited to viewing fragments of Griffin only on rare occasions and in somewhat unusual ways. For example, the only member of the League who can see Griffin at all is Hyde, whose ability to see body heat is depicted just twice in the narrative (I, 89, iv; II, 116, iii). These depictions provide a limited quantity of visual representation, since they are illustrated as little more than a silhouette and it is impossible to determine an accurate facial expression from these images. Another way in which Griffin is depicted is covered in bandages (e.g. II, 55, ii), but once again such a silhouette betrays no facial expressions or emotions. As such, Griffin is either invisible or presented as a mere silhouette throughout the narrative. As a result, he functions as a kind of Gothic and science fiction enigma: mysterious, indescribable and unrecognizable.

The lack of illustrated facial expressions and the resultant lack of connection between Griffin and the reader fittingly emphasize Griffin's position in the narrative as the aloof and ultimately isolated villain, especially in Volume II. However, there is one occasion in Volume I where it is necessary for Griffin to travel through London with Mina, making it necessary for him to cover his hands and face with greasepaint in order to achieve a semblance of visibility (I, 57; Figure 1). This scene presents one of the most revealing depictions of Griffin in the entire narrative, as the greasepaint allows for his facial expressions to be seen. One panel in particular (I, 57, v), placed in the centre of the page, presents Griffin with an extremely sinister expression: brow furrowed, eyes narrowed, mouth unsmiling and projecting an air of menacing calculation. This rare depiction of Griffin's facial expressions reinforces his characterization as both sinister and dangerous.

Griffin's invisibility becomes increasingly significant when considered in relation to the preoccupation of the Gothic and science fiction genres with the potentially threatening unknown and unknowable. Science fiction often extrapolates from existing scientific knowledge. An example of this would be extrapolating from rapid contemporary travel, something that the reader can experience and 'know', to time travel, something that the reader can only imagine and which consequently remains unknowable. Similarly, the

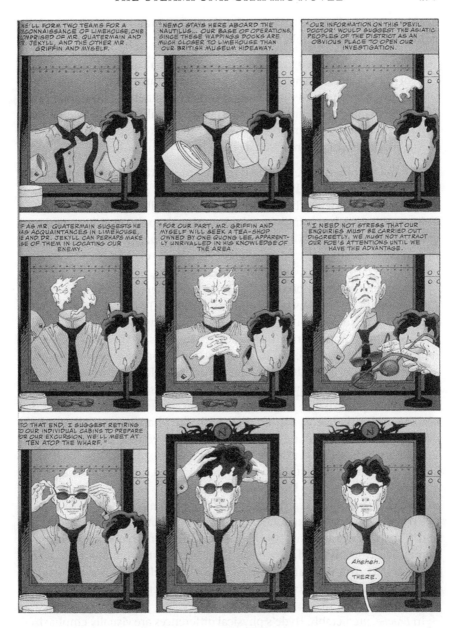

Figure 1. Alan Moore and Kevin O'Neill, *The League of Extraordinary Gentlemen: Volume I* (2000), London: Titan, page 57. © Alan Moore and Kevin O'Neill. Used with Permission of DC Comics.

Gothic genre has been described as an almost celebratory exploration of the unknown and unknowable:

> The Gothic mode emerges as a response and a counter to the impulse of the Enlightenment to repress darkness, unreason, the unknown, the Other. The locus of the Gothic is the shadowy, mysterious and unknowable space inhabited by the inhumanly unknowable Other – supernatural or human. The Gothic adventure is the journey of the normative, enlightened Self as it encounters the unknown. (Anolik 2)

The character of Griffin encapsulates both the Gothic encounter with the 'unknowable Other' and the extrapolation from scientific investigation of optical density with the result of human invisibility. By exploring the unknowable and thus bringing real uncertainty into the reading experience through the character of Griffin, *League* uses the visual elements of its narration in tandem with the context of genre in order to explore the threatening potential of Griffin as an abhuman, invisible being.

League's characterization of Hyde presents another interesting example of the abhuman: he morphs between human (Jekyll) and inhuman (Hyde), and he threatens to destroy humanity by his very existence, whilst also promising to act as humanity's salvation through his final actions. His visual representation is also integral to his characterization because his otherness and abhumanity is made immediately clear by his appearance. Hyde's monstrosity is necessarily reduced to a textual description in Stevenson's original novel and Hyde is interchangeably referred to as both an 'it' (e.g. 39; 64; 66) and a 'he' (e.g. 33; 49; 51), with the character Richard Enfield describing Hyde as a 'damned Juggernaut' (33) who is 'like Satan' (34). Enfield, an otherwise gentle and rational man, explains that he took 'a loathing to [Hyde] at first sight' (33), recalling that 'I never saw a man I so disliked, and yet I scarce know why' (35). Enfield's reaction to Hyde is not unique; another character, Gabriel John Utterson, also struggles to explain his reaction to Hyde, experiencing 'hitherto unknown disgust, loathing and fear' (41) and musing, 'God bless me, the man seems hardly human! Something troglodytic, shall we say ... or is it the mere radiance of a foul soul...?' (42). Throughout Stevenson's novel, therefore, no one can explain exactly why they despise Hyde; yet each character experiences the same reaction of hatred, disgust and fear.

In *League*, predictably, Hyde's physical differences are visually emphasized through illustration (e.g. I, 30; Figure 2): his face and teeth are animalistic; his rugged skin is dark, uneven and bristling with hair; his voice is so inhuman that, even when he is calm, Hyde's speech bubbles are angular and uneven (e.g. II, 51, i–ii); and he is consistently depicted as almost twice as tall as his companions. However, Hyde's monstrous size in *League*

Figure 2. Alan Moore and Kevin O'Neill, *The League of Extraordinary Gentlemen: Volume I* (2000), London: Titan, page 30. © Alan Moore and Kevin O'Neill. Used with Permission of DC Comics.

is particularly interesting, given that he is described in Stevenson's original novel as 'dwarfish' (41) and 'particularly small' (47) in comparison with the 'large, well-made' Jekyll (44). Stevenson's Jekyll provides an explanation for this difference in size, suggesting that the 'evil' Hyde had initially 'been much less exercised' in Jekyll's life of attempted 'virtue' and had only increased in size after he had committed a number of immoral acts (81–85). Therefore, in Stevenson's novel, Hyde's size is directly proportionate to his immoral behaviour; his physical monstrosity in *League* is a testament to his acts of abomination. This theory is confirmed by Hyde himself shortly after he murders Griffin:

> when I started out, good God, I was practically a ****ing dwarf. Jekyll, on the other hand, a great big strapping fellow. Since then, though, my growth's been unrestricted, while he's wasted away to nothing. Obvious, really. Without me, you see, Jekyll has no drives ... and without him, I have no restraints. (II, 124, vi–viii; author's ellipsis and asterisks)

In other words, here *League* is using visual images to comment on Hyde's psychology and morality.

In addition to the physical differences in relation to both size and animalistic characteristics, Hyde's other differences are also depicted through illustration. For example, as mentioned above, Hyde is able to see body heat, and this information is divulged through illustrations of how Hyde sees Griffin. In addition, Hyde has an accurate, almost animalistic, sense of smell that is depicted via a combination of text and image. In Volume I, for example, Hyde reveals that although Griffin can smell nothing, to him their location 'stinks of Chinamen and the river', and his face is illustrated as grimacing at this smell (I, 90, iv); and in Volume II, Hyde is depicted as flaring his nostrils and breathing deeply whilst creating the sound 'fnff – fnfff', indicating that he is sniffing the air (II, 113, vii). As such, the words and sounds uttered by Hyde are used in tandem with the illustrations of his actions and reactions in order to emphasize his abhuman abilities.

The transformation from the timid Jekyll to the monstrous Hyde introduces the notion of the *Doppelgänger*, a term that translates from German into 'double goer' and was first used by Jean Paul Richter (Bär 90). The *Doppelgänger* is a 'frequently noted feature of Gothic fiction' (Spooner 28) that has been defined in a number of different ways. John Herdman's definition is perhaps most helpful, explaining that the *Doppelgänger*:

> appears as a distinct and separate being apprehensible by the physical senses (or at least, by *some* of them), but exists in a dependent relation to the original. By 'dependent' we do not mean 'subordinate,' for often

the double comes to dominate, control, and usurp the functions of the subject; but rather that, *qua* double, it has its *raison d'être* in its *relation* to the original. Often, but not always, the subject and his double are physically similar, often to the point of absolute identity. (14, emphasis in original)

Here, Herdman suggests that the *Doppelgänger* is fundamentally related to the original in a deliberately ambiguous manner that involves dependence but not necessarily subordination. This reading accurately describes the dual identity of Jekyll and Hyde: Hyde is 'dependent' on Jekyll, as he could not exist without him, but he is not subordinate to Jekyll in either Stevenson's original novel or *League*; indeed, in both texts it is Hyde who eventually takes control and causes the deaths of both Jekyll and Hyde. The dominant presence of Hyde also indicates a movement towards a superhuman size and strength that is not implied in Stevenson's original novel and which relates *League*'s Hyde to the superhero tradition. As discussed in more detail below, there is some evidence to suggest that, by the end of *League*, Stevenson's Hyde has progressed to an entity more complex than a simple representation of evil, and in this respect he begins to resemble the 'most prominent modern example' of Stevenson's Jekyll/Hyde character: Bruce Banner/the Incredible Hulk (Nevins, *Heroes* 172). Indeed, despite its originality in many respects, Moore himself observes that there are 'at least superficial similarities' between *League* and 'standard superhero comics' such as *The Incredible Hulk* (Nevins, *Heroes* 281), and Griffin and Hyde in particular are the two members of the League who possess super*human*, and arguably super*hero*, powers. They are also the two members of the League who die in Volume II, a decision made by Moore early in the development of the volume because he thought 'Griffin and Hyde are essentially too unstable, psychologically, to survive for very long, realistically' (Nevins, *Blazing World* 245). Furthermore, the psychological instabilities of both Griffin and Hyde arguably result from their inherently dual identities.

Griffin embodies a dual personality, since his invisibility causes him to exist physically but not visually, to have no fixed identity and to become capable of disappearing through the removal of clothing and greasepaint. His invisibility also enables Griffin to fool other members of the League with regard to his current whereabouts. In Volume I, Griffin creates a fake 'body' for himself by wrapping a broom in clothes and bandages (I, 100, i–vii), but here Griffin's initial deceit is for an ultimately noble goal and he soon discovers that the League is being manipulated by its then employer (I, 101–2). However, when Griffin creates another fake 'body' in Volume II, the intent is to provide a distraction to enable him to secretly meet with the Martians in order to plan the destruction of the human race (II, 51, v–vi).

Griffin thus uses his invisibility to aid his leading of a politically divided, double life that works mostly for the League in Volume I and against the League in Volume II.

One of the few areas in which Griffin appears undivided is in his predilection for cruelty and violence. This characterization is consistent with Wells's original characterization of the Invisible Man, who takes pleasure in scaring and hurting people and destroying their belongings (46–50). In *League*, however, this penchant for physical abuse and petty vandalism escalates to more serious transgressions: he rapes several young schoolgirls (I, 46); he willingly places the rest of the League in danger when he tries to escape from a warship without them (I, 145, vi); he kills an innocent policeman instead of merely disarming him (I, 112–13); and he takes pleasure in physically assaulting and humiliating Mina in apparent revenge for her outsmarting, capturing and recruiting him for the League (II, 70–71). Griffin is thus a danger to both the general public and his colleagues, but he also presents one of the most terrifying threats to national security: the 'terrorist' who is invisible (Dryden 171) and, consequently, almost impossible to catch. Indeed, Wells's Griffin desires to usurp the Queen and rule the country, declaring: 'This announces the first day of the Terror ... This is day one of year one of the new epoch ... I am Invisible Man the First' (164). This announcement echoes the Terror of the French Revolution (1793–94), which attempted to establish Year One, but despite the resonance with historical atrocities this speech is nothing more than a self-inflated dream for Wells's Griffin, since he is very unlikely to gain a position of power that would result in him ruling the country. *League*'s Griffin, on the other hand, has a much better chance in his attempt, because of his increased status as a member of the League and his agreement with the Martians. Therefore, despite his being born human, Griffin's actions and choices turn him into an invisible, inhuman, abhuman villain.

Hyde is somewhat different to Griffin and instead functions as a kind of antihero in *League*. As the wicked side of Jekyll he is described as 'pure evil' in Stevenson's original novel (81), but on many occasions in *League* he is seen making positive, even heroic, choices. For example, when Mina realizes that the League can only defeat the henchmen of their enemy, James Moriarty, if Hyde, rather than Jekyll, is present, she attempts to transform the timid Jekyll into the monstrous Hyde by repeatedly slapping Jekyll's face (I, 137, ii–iv). When he appears, Hyde surprisingly restrains his desire to hurt Mina in retaliation (I, 138), and as the series develops it becomes clear that Hyde respects, and perhaps even desires, Mina. For example, in Volume II Hyde allows Mina to calm him (II, 41, ii–iii); he converses with her in a surprisingly calm and frank manner, making the astonishing admission that 'in this world, alone, I do not hate you' (II, 51, ii); he is outraged when he learns of Griffin's attack on her (II, 74); he avenges this attack by torturing, raping and eventually murdering Griffin, as discussed below (II, 116–17); and his last request before he leaves to destroy the Martians is to kiss Mina and to touch her breast (II, 140–41). He even, astonishingly, promises, 'I shall never hurt you. *Never* ... my perfect Mina' (II, 141, iii–vi, emphasis in original).

To propose that these events suggest that Hyde loves Mina may be too great an assumption, especially given Hyde's statement that he is not 'fool enough to think that what I feel for you is love' (II, 51, ii), but Hyde clearly considers Mina to be significantly different from his other acquaintances. In return, Mina seems to be the only member of the League who regards Hyde as worthy in any way. She may admit that she fears him, in the candid conversation mentioned above (II, 50, iv), but her own experiences with Dracula prevent Hyde from terrifying her to the extent that he terrifies others and this conversation thus becomes a pivotal point in the relationship between Mina and Hyde. Before this point, Mina had referred to Hyde in as derogatory a manner as the other characters in the graphic novel, calling him 'monster' (I, 32, i), 'brute' (I, 35, iii) and 'beast' (I 37, i); however, following the conversation, which Mina records in her journal as 'that extraordinary confession' (II, 59, iii), Mina changes how she refers to Hyde and thereafter addresses him as simply 'Mr Hyde' (e.g. II, 76, ii) or 'Edward' (e.g. II, 137, iv). When he is incinerated by the Martians she refers to him as 'that poor *man*' (II, 148, 2, emphasis in original), and her use of the word 'man' contrasts greatly with the derogative terms the other characters continue to use in reference to Hyde, which include 'the shit of the world' (II, 125, v) and 'spawn of a whore' (II, 139, iii). Therefore, one might suggest that for Mina, at least, who remains ignorant of how Hyde murdered Griffin, Hyde has developed from a simple representation of sin or the monstrous duality of human nature and has instead become a more complex and problematic representation of the moral complexity of the human race.

The closing events of Volume II explore this idea further. Here, Hyde dies whilst destroying the Martians and saving the world (II, 148, i), and his actions might be read in two contrasting ways: as a heroic sacrifice that relates to the superhero genre, or as a representation of Hyde's desire to kill Martians and save humans only as a consequence. Hyde's dialogue suggests that the second reading may be more accurate, as he explains his fear that his death will risk 'ending up looking rather noble, when all I really want is to slaughter something' (II, 140, iv), suggesting that Hyde self-destructs rather than self-sacrifices and is thus not necessarily acting in a heroic manner. However, Hyde's actions are nonetheless regarded as heroic by Mina (II, 148, ii), and after his death Hyde is publicly remembered by Hyde Park's becoming his alternative past namesake (II, 151, iv). Therefore, whilst the issue of Hyde's potential heroism remains unresolved, Moore's Hyde becomes more morally ambiguous than Stevenson's Hyde, who more closely resembles Stevenson's Jekyll's description of 'pure evil' (81).

Therefore, the very characteristics that make the dual identities of Hyde and Griffin superhuman, and thus potential superheroes/supervillans, are exactly what make them interesting and effective characters on both a textual and a visual level. The combination of the science fiction, Gothic, fantasy and superhero genres in the depiction of these characters, both in their original presentations and their *League* reincarnations, ensures a genre-bending representation of transgression, transformation and monstrosity. This representation is especially prevalent in one particular scene towards the end of Volume II, and a discussion of this scene will form the final section of this chapter.

'This is the life, eh, Griffin?': Griffin's death

Volume II of *League* contains a controversial scene that offers additional insight into the characters of both Griffin and Hyde: Hyde's torture, rape and murder of Griffin. A scene of just six pages in length, it is significantly placed during the abduction of Allan and Mina by the terrifying creatures who, we later learn, are Dr Moreau's animal/human hybrids. This positioning draws attention to questions surrounding the definitions and limitations of the human race, a theme frequently explored in both Gothic and science fiction literature.

The scene begins with a depiction of Hyde travelling through a dark and decaying London overflowing with drunks and looters (II, 112, i–iii). Hyde's position in a respectable horse-drawn carriage physically and hierarchically elevates him above the drunken, thieving Londoners. Upon arriving at the *League*'s base in the British Museum, Hyde walks with his trademark gentleman's cane, his huge knuckles almost dragging on the floor and emphasizing his animalistic qualities (II, 113, v). The gentlemanly cane recalls the cane that Stevenson's Hyde broke whilst beating the elderly Sir Danvers Carew to death (46), and as such ironically foreshadows the violence that follows its appearance here in *League*. Hyde enters the museum and inhales deeply, drawing specific attention to his abhuman sense of smell (II, 113, vii). Finding the room he is searching for, Hyde carefully locks the door behind him with a small brass key before stowing the key in his jacket pocket, revealing his huge hands to be unexpectedly nimble (II, 114, ii–vi). Despite his abhuman appearance, Hyde's actions in these panels are surprisingly delicate and gentlemanly in nature, contrasting with the abhuman behaviour seen in other parts of the series. Additionally, the lack of dialogue and the use of visual narration effectively juxtapose Hyde's abhuman appearance with his gentlemanly actions, suggesting that Hyde is capable of expressing, or at least simulating, a certain level of gentlemanly humanity.

The gentlemanly behaviour continues for several more panels until Hyde begins to speak. Hyde appears to be speaking to himself until he says, 'You know, this is really quite *funny*. You're thinking "If I don't make any *noise*, he won't know I'm *here*"' (II, 115, i–vi, emphasis in original). In the next panel, the shot zooms out and the reader's point of view becomes that of the person Hyde is addressing: Griffin, who has been hiding near a wall, believing that Hyde cannot see him. Hyde, however, promises Griffin that he can see him, stating: 'You have my word as a gentleman' (II, 115, ix), and it is with the word 'gentleman', ironically, that Hyde's previously gentlemanly behaviour, simulated or not, comes to an abrupt end.

In the following panels Hyde reveals that he has always been able to see Griffin's body heat, again emphasizing his abhuman attributes, and then begins to torture Griffin, proceeding to choke him, break his leg, smash his face through a window and, finally, to rape him (II, 116–17). The illustration during these panels moves from Griffin's viewpoint to Hyde's viewpoint before settling into a third-person viewpoint in order to present an omniscient narration of the unfolding events. Griffin remains invisible other than in the one panel in which his body-heat silhouette is presented, and his reactions are thus presented in a purely textual manner through shouts, screams, pleading and some final, dying pants. This narrative style marks a clear distinction from other, more gruesome scenes of violence and might even function as an ironic reversal of those occasions where Griffin has functioned as an invisible bringer of violence, such as during his attack on Mina (II, 70–71). By comparison with the blood and vomit caused by Griffin's attack, Hyde's attack on Griffin shows literally nothing: both Griffin and the injuries he sustains remain invisible.

This short scene, therefore, emphasizes and explores the abhumanity of Griffin's invisibility, in addition to the abhumanity of Hyde, who is able to smell Griffin's presence, see his body heat and break his leg with his bare hands. Furthermore, in an echo of Wells's original novel, it is only in death that Griffin regains his visibility (and, arguably, any resemblance to humanity), and this event is illustrated by the gradual appearance of Griffin's blood whilst Hyde is eating dinner with Nemo and their coach driver (II, 124–5). However, Griffin's mangled body is never revealed; the horrific extent of Griffin's injuries is suggested by both the vast quantity of blood and Nemo's outraged reaction upon discovering Griffin's remains, but they are left ultimately unspecified for the reader. This narrative technique is particularly effective, since it allows each reader to independently imagine

the horrific image and Griffin thus remains an invisible, abhuman, disturbing enigma until the very end.

The *League* series thus draws heavily on both the science fiction and
the Gothic genres in order to explore a number of mutually significant
conflicts: humanity versus abhumanity, normality versus monstrosity,
stagnation versus transformation and conservatism versus transgression.
League's depiction of Griffin and Hyde fully encapsulates these conflicts
and demonstrates that the fundamental concerns of the science fiction and
Gothic genres remain central to the steampunk graphic novel.

Notes

1. The 2003 film adaptation of *The League of Extraordinary Gentlemen* also includes the
   characters of Oscar Wilde's Dorian Gray and Mark Twain's Tom Sawyer. Both of these
   characters feature in novels published in the same period from which Moore chose
   his original texts, but as neither feature in the original graphic novels they will not be
   discussed here.
2. Since Griffin and Hyde feature only in Volumes I and II of the series, this chapter will
   focus on their representations within these publications.
3. Steampunk has only recently begun to receive critical attention; at the time of writing
   no academic monographs or collections have been published with a sole focus on
   steampunk and the subgenre has been discussed in only a small number of academic publications, such as Rebecca Onion's 2008 article 'Reclaiming the Machine:
   An Introductory Look at Steampunk in Everyday Practice'. The online publication
   Steampunk Magazine provides some worthwhile discussion alongside interviews with
   steampunk creators; and the recently published anthologies *Steampunk* (2008), edited
   by Ann and Jeff VanderMeer, and *Extraordinary Engines: The Definitive Steampunk
   Anthology* (2008), edited by Nick Gevers, aim to bring further recognition to the genre
   by showcasing short stories, discussion and recommended reading lists. Focused
   academic research into this genre, however, is currently lacking.
4. Throughout this chapter, textual references will refer to the graphic novel publications
   rather than the individual comic book issues. As the *League* graphic novels are currently
   printed without pagination, I have followed the style of Jess Nevins, author of three
   valuable encyclopaedic works on the *League* series, and have numbered the pages
   myself. To ensure accuracy, references throughout will cite volume, page and panel
   number, e.g. (I, 1, i). When no panel number is provided, the discussion refers to the
   whole page.

Works cited

Aldiss, Brian W. *Billion Year Spree: The History of Science Fiction*. London: Weidenfeld &
Nicolson, 1973. Print.

Anolik, Ruth Bienstock. 'Introduction: Diagnosing Demons: Creating and Disabling
the Discourse of Difference in the Gothic Text.' *Demons of the Body and Mind: Essays on
Disability in Gothic Literature*. Ed. Ruth Bienstock Anolik. Jefferson, NC: McFarland,
2010. 1–20. Print.

Bär, Gerald. 'Perceptions of the Self as the Other: Double-Visions in Literature and Film.' *Processes of Transposition: German Literature and Film*. Eds. Christiane Schönfeld and Hermann Rasche. Amsterdam: Rodopi, 2007. 89–118. Print.

Botting, Fred. *Gothic*. London: Routledge, 1996. Print.

Clute, John. *Look at the Evidence: Essays and Reviews*. Liverpool: Liverpool UP, 1995. Print.

Connor, Steven. *Postmodernist Culture: An Introduction to Theories of the Contemporary*. London: Blackwell, 1997. Print.

Cranny-Francis, Anne. 'Feminist Futures: A Generic Study.' *Alien Zone: Cultural Theory and Contemporary Science Fiction Cinema*. Ed. Annette Kuhn. London, New York: Verso, 1990. 219–27. Print.

Dryden, Linda. *The Modern Gothic and Literary Doubles: Stevenson, Wilde and Wells*. Hampshire: Palgrave Macmillan, 2003. Print.

Duncan, Andy. 'Alternate History.' *The Cambridge Companion to Science Fiction*. Ed. Edward James and Farah Mendlesohn. Cambridge: Cambridge UP, 2003. 209–18. Print.

Gevers, Nick, ed. *Extraordinary Engines: The Definitive Steampunk Anthology*. Nottingham: Solaris, 2008. Print.

Gross, Cory. 'Varieties of Steampunk Experience.' *SteamPunk Magazine* 1 (1 March 2007): 60–63. Print.

Haggard, H. Rider. *King Solomon's Mines*. 1885. Introd. Frank Delaney. London: Folio Society, 1995. Print.

Herdman, John. *The Double in Nineteenth-Century Fiction*. Basingstoke: Macmillan, 1990. Print.

Hilton, Laura. 'Reincarnating Mina Murray: Subverting the Gothic Heroine?' *Alan Moore and the Gothic Tradition*. Ed. Matt Green. Manchester: Manchester UP, forthcoming. Print.

Hurley, Kelly. *The Gothic Body: Sexuality, Materialism, and Degeneration at the Fin de Siècle*. Cambridge: Cambridge UP, 1996. Print.

Lee, Stan and Jack Kirby. *Marvel Masterworks*. Vol. 2. New York: Marvel, 2003. Print.

Lewis, M. G. *The Monk: A Romance*. 1796. Ed. D. L. Macdonald and Kathleen Scherf. Plymouth: Broadview, 2003. Print.

Luckhurst, Roger. *Science Fiction*. Cambridge: Polity, 2005. Print.

Mighall, Robert. *A Geography of Victorian Gothic Fiction: Mapping History's Nightmares*. Oxford: Oxford University Press, 1999. Print.

Moore, Alan and Kevin O'Neill. *The League of Extraordinary Gentlemen: Volume I*. London: Titan, 2000. Print.

—. *The League of Extraordinary Gentlemen: Volume II*. La Jolla, CA: America's Best Comics, 2003. Print.

—. *The League of Extraordinary Gentlemen: The Black Dossier*. La Jolla, CA: America's Best Comics, 2007. Print.

—. *The League of Extraordinary Gentlemen: Century: 1910*. China: Knockabout, 2009. Print.

Nevins, Jess. *A Blazing World: The Unofficial Companion to The League of Extraordinary Gentlemen Volume Two*. London: Titan Books, 2006. Print.

—. *Heroes and Monsters: The Unofficial Companion to The League of Extraordinary Gentlemen*. London: Titan Books, 2003. Print.

—. *Impossible Territories: The Unofficial Companion to The League of Extraordinary Gentlemen: The Black Dossier*. Austin, TX: MonkeyBrain Books, 2008. Print.

Onion, Rebecca. 'Reclaiming the Machine: An Introductory Look at Steampunk in Everyday Practice.' *Neo-Victorian Studies* 1.1 (2008): 138–63. Print.

Radcliffe, Ann. *The Mysteries of Udolpho*. 1794. Ed. Bonamy Dobrée. Oxford: Oxford University Press, 1998. Print.

Roberts, Adam. *Science Fiction*. London: Routledge, 2000. Print.

Sedgwick, Eve Kosofsky. *The Coherence of Gothic Conventions*. 1980. New York and London: Methuen, 1986. Print.

Seed, David. *A Companion to Science Fiction*. London: Blackwell, 2005. Print.

Shelley, Mary. *Frankenstein: or, The Modern Prometheus*. Ed. D.L. Macdonald and Kathleen Scherf. Ontario: Broadview, 1994. Print.

Spooner, Catherine. *Fashioning Gothic Bodies*. Manchester: Manchester UP, 1984. Print.

Stevenson, Robert Louis. *The Strange Case of Dr Jekyll and Mr Hyde*. 1886. Ed. Martin A. Danahay. London: Broadview, 2005. Print.

Stoker, Bram. *Dracula*. 1897. Ed. Glennis Byron. Ontario: Broadview, 1998. Print.

Twain, Mark. *The Adventures of Tom Sawyer*. 1876. Introd. John Seelye. Harmondsworth: Penguin, 1986. Print.

VanderMeer, Ann and Jeff VanderMeer (eds). *Steampunk*. San Francisco, CA: Tachyon, 2008. Print.

Verne, Jules. *The Mysterious Island*. 1874. Trans. Jordan Stump; introd. Caleb Carr. New York: Modern Library, 2001. Print.

—. *Twenty Thousand Leagues under the Seas*. 1870. Ed. William Butcher. Oxford: Oxford UP, 1998. Print.

Walpole, Horace. *The Castle of Otranto: A Gothic Story; and, The Mysterious Mother: A Tragedy*. 1764. Ed. Frederick S. Frank. Ontario: Broadview, 2003. Print.

Wells, H. G. *The Invisible Man*. 1897. Harmondsworth: Penguin, 1938. Print.

—. *The Island of Dr Moreau*. 1896. Harmondsworth: Penguin, 1946. Print.

—. *The Time Machine/The War of the Worlds*. 1895/1898. Ed. Frank D. McConnell. New York: Oxford UP, 1977. Print.

Wilde, Oscar. *The Picture of Dorian Gray*. 1890. Ed. Norman Page. Ontario: Broadview, 1998. Print.

Index